COLLABORATIVE GRANTSEEKING

COLLABORATIVE GRANTSEEKING

A Guide to Designing Projects, Leading Partners, and Persuading Sponsors

Jeremy T. Miner, Lynn E. Miner, and Jerry Griffith

GREENWOOD

AN IMPRINT OF ABC-CLIO, LLC
Santa Barbara, California • Denver, Colorado • Oxford, England

Library of Congress Cataloging-in-Publication Data

Miner, Jeremy T.
    Collaborative grantseeking : a guide to designing projects, leading partners, and persuading sponsors / Jeremy T. Miner, Lynn E. Miner, and Jerry Griffith.
        p. cm.
    Includes bibliographical references and index.
    ISBN 978-0-313-39185-9 (hbk. : alk. paper) — ISBN 978-0-313-39186-6 (ebook)
1. Proposal writing for grants—United States. 2. Endowments—United States. 3. Fund raising—Teamwork—United States. I. Miner, Lynn E. II. Griffith, Jerry, Ph.D. III. Title.
    HG177.5.U6M556 2011
    658.15'224—dc22   2010040838

ISBN: 978-0-313-39185-9
EISBN: 978-0-313-39186-6

15 14 13 12 11   1 2 3 4 5

This book is also available on the World Wide Web as an eBook.
Visit www.abc-clio.com for details.

Greenwood
An Imprint of ABC-CLIO, LLC

ABC-CLIO, LLC
130 Cremona Drive, P.O. Box 1911
Santa Barbara, California 93116-1911

This book is printed on acid-free paper ∞

Manufactured in the United States of America

CONTENTS

PREFACE

Every idea has the potential for greatness,
particularly when a community of support gets behind it.

Jud Linville

Grantseeking is extremely competitive. Particularly in this post-9/11 era sponsors must be persuaded that their funds will be used for purposeful good. More than one million assorted nonprofit groups vied for a share of the $300 billion awarded in public and private philanthropy in 2009. To get more "bang for their buck," many public and private sponsors strongly encourage, if not outright require, collaboration in grant applications.

For sponsors, collaboration reduces duplication of services and encourages project sustainability beyond the granting period. The challenge, however, is that applicants (as individuals and organizations) do not always share the same definition of "collaboration" or know how to go about collaborating. Some novice grantseekers even make grandiose promises of collaboration in their proposals, not realizing that grant reviewers are savvy and know a "phantom collaboration"—one that exists only on paper—when they see it.

In the current economic environment, collaboration may be vital to a continued existence for some nonprofits. And collaboration is not just for large organizations; the smallest of nonprofits may also find strength and success by joining hands with other like organizations. More broadly, the national and global economies tend to govern the availability of grant funds from public and private sponsors. That is, foundation funding is heavily influenced by stock market performance; corporate funding is heavily influenced by profit margins; and government funding is heavily influenced by local, state, and national economies.

To gain an edge in competitive grants, many nonprofits consult reference manuals for tips on writing proposals. But no book explains in a comprehensive and integrated fashion the nuts and bolts of successful *collaborative* grantseeking. This book aims to fill that information void.

SCOPE AND PURPOSE

As with our previous grants guidebooks—*Proposal Planning & Writing* (Greenwood) and *Models of Proposal Planning & Writing* (Praeger)—the content of this book is based on our grantseeking experiences over the past four decades in writing successful proposals, conducting grants workshops nationwide, reviewing government and foundation proposals, and critiquing application guidelines for grantmakers. We don't just talk in abstract terms about grants; we share the practical tips that have enabled us to write winning grants for years. We practice what we teach.[1]

Whereas *Proposal Planning & Writing* is an introductory guidebook to the "what" and "how" of grantseeking and *Models of Proposal Planning & Writing* is an advanced companion text that explains why specific proposal elements are persuasive to sponsors, *Collaborative Grantseeking* delves into the humanistic aspects of designing and leading successful collaborative projects. With a clearer understanding of the nature of the collaboration and a critical examination of the role of the grant leader, you will be able to write more persuasive proposals.

Collaborations are not formed without some risk. For reasons that this book addresses, well-intended grant collaborations don't always turn out as planned. But there are also many examples of outstanding sponsored collaborations that have led to new projects, new equipment, new treatment procedures, and even new organizations. *Collaborative Grantseeking* highlights key factors that influence whether grant collaborations produce painful "losses" or precious "wins."

More specifically, in this book you will learn about the different types of collaborations and characteristics that contribute to success when managing people and projects. We've pulled together under one cover the collaborative grant grist that others often don't address, questions such as the following:

1. What exactly is a collaboration?

2. Who receives collaborative grants?

3. How do sponsors call for collaborations in their RFPs (Requests for Proposals)?

4. How do I generate ideas for collaborative grant projects?

5. What steps should I take before starting up a collaboration?

6. How do I find and pick good collaborative partners?

7. What are the characteristics of an effective grant leader?

8. How do I handle the inevitable people problems that arise during a collaborative endeavor?

9. How do I assess the effectiveness of a collaboration?

10. What happens to a collaboration after the grant period is over?

11. Where can I find models of successful collaborative proposals?

12. How do I write a winning collaborative proposal?

Without a doubt, successful collaborative grant proposals have clear goals and objectives, detailed time and task charts, systematic evaluations of progress and outcomes, and precise budgets. But, more significantly, they convey confidence in the grant leadership. Effective grant collaborations are led by individuals who not only understand the benefits and barriers affecting collaborations but are skilled in managing them. As a result, collaborative proposals describe the following details of management:

- how collaborators are selected
- how progress of all collaborators is maintained
- how individuals who are not working out are re-directed
- how partners who fall behind are helped to move forward and succeed
- how outcomes are celebrated

When Gustave Flaubert uttered, "The devil is in the details," he probably wasn't thinking about writing collaborative grants—but he could have been.

TARGET AUDIENCES

Collaborative Grantseeking is intended for three categories of people: grantseekers, grantmakers (sponsors), and grant reviewers.

For **grantseekers,** this book aims to sharpen their collaborative focus and help them stay on course through systematic evaluation and communication with partners. Users represent the following disciplines:

- *Economic Development:* city planning, land use, urban revitalization, workforce development, job creation
- *Education:* day care programs, adult education, public and private schools, special education departments, colleges and universities, English as a foreign language programs, libraries
- *First Responders:* police departments, fire departments, emergency medical services
- *Government:* local, state, and federal agencies; courts, human services, parks and recreation
- *Health Care:* hospitals, nursing homes, public health organizations, Veterans Administration, international health, family health, maternal and child health
- *Philanthropy:* foundations, charitable organizations, service clubs
- *Religions:* churches, synagogues, mosques, and other houses of worship; faith-based organizations, religious education
- *Social Services:* community development, rehabilitation, mental health, welfare, senior citizens
- *Other:* fine and performing arts, senior citizens' advocates and agencies, special interest groups

Grantmakers in the public and private sectors may find our distinction of various types of collaboration useful as they issue RFPs and evaluate collaborative proposals. At the risk of insulting the alligator while crossing the swamp, many current RFPs are terribly fuzzy relative to their calls for collaborative efforts; when grantseekers and grantmakers are on a common ground of understanding, the number of creative and fitting proposals will increase. Said differently, just as grantmakers have become more particular in their requests for specific objectives, measurable outcomes, and comprehensive logic models, so too will their expectations for the level and extent of collaborative engagement. Better operational definitions will allow program officers to answer grantseekers' questions more purposely.

Grant reviewers are becoming increasingly sophisticated regarding the concept of collaboration. With a fuller appreciation for the different types of collaboration, grant reviewers can more quickly look for specific behaviors that translate into goal sharing and interaction among collaborators. Then reviewers can provide unambiguous feedback on what constitutes a true and engaged partnership when they make their funding recommendations.

STRUCTURE AND CONTENT

Collaborative Grantseeking is designed to complement our existing books about grants in order to better meet the emerging needs of today's grantseekers in an era of increased competition for limited resources. Collaboration is not a fad in the grants world; it's the new reality, the new norm. In this book you will find many concrete examples, strategies, tools, and step-by-step instructions to guide your project planning, proposal writing, and program implementation.

Framework for Sustainability

One of the nagging questions with which proposal writers wrestle is "What do we do when the grant funds run out?" That is, grantmakers usually want to know how a project will be sustained. Our presentation of the fundamentals of collaborative grantseeking in the first four chapters lends itself directly to proposal language you can use to answer this question, to let sponsors know that the issue of future funding has been considered. We identify different types of collaboration before, during, and after the grant period (in chapter 1), lay the groundwork for analyzing sponsor RFPs and writing a collaborative grant proposal (in chapter 2), describe the facilitating and constraining factors of collaborative grantseeking (in chapter 3), and explore strategies for generating ideas for collaborative projects (in chapter 4).

More Sample Proposals

Our book readers and workshop participants repeatedly tell us they want more examples of successful proposals—and we've listened. Four samples of funded collaborative grants, complete with annotations, are presented—two private proposals and two government proposals, including reviewer comments—and provide a springboard from which you can begin to develop your own fundable collaborative proposals. By topic, the proposals represent a technology acquisition and integration project, a literacy and reading service project, a curriculum development project in special education, and a mental health conference grant. By type, the proposals represent a coexistence collaboration (chapter 5), a coordination collaboration (chapter 6), a cooperation collaboration (chapter 7), and a coalition collaboration (chapter 8).

Assessment and Evaluation

Most grant writers recognize that assessment and evaluation are increasingly important proposal components. Accordingly, we present a significant discussion on assessing the effectiveness of collaborations, including describing the types of evaluations, qualitative and quantitative methods, evaluation steps, how to choose an evaluator, and specific tools for measuring participants' attitudes and satisfaction (in chapter 9). When evaluations spot problem areas and potential stumbling blocks, it will be valuable for you to have strategies for effectively handling difficult people and situations. For five scenarios commonly encountered in the conduct of collaborative grants, we offer a situational analysis, annotated dialogue scripts, and reflections on the psychological strategies used to smooth the road to success (in chapter 10).

THE INFAMOUS BOTTOM LINE

Whether they are called "principal investigators," "program directors," "project managers," or some similar name by sponsors, in this book we use the term "grant leaders." The grant leader is anyone who bears a major responsibility for ensuring that goals and outcomes are met. Grant leaders have a deep passion for and sustained commitment to their projects. They channel their powers of influence to motivate project partners to action. They are lantern carriers who shed light on the pathway through the grants gauntlet.

The RFP guidelines, funded proposals, and reviewer comments presented in this book are real. Though some identifying information has been changed to preserve confidentiality, we did not correct *ex post facto* any errors in grammar, spelling, and punctuation. In some cases, the sponsors made minor mistakes; in other instances, we did. We preserved these mistakes in their original forms to demonstrate to you that proposals do not need to be perfect in order to attract funding. Persuasion is the key to successful grantseeking. Your collaborative proposal must demonstrate that a credible individual at a credible organization is proposing a credible project.

Successful grant leaders are often individuals who are so dedicated to their ideas that they will find the means to carry them out with or without extramural support. Sponsors have clear objectives and expectations that they hope to realize by providing financial support to such dedicated persons. A persuasively written grant proposal is the link between them. This book helps you forge that link. Let's begin.

NOTE

1. Visit the Miner and Associates, Inc., Web site for a list of grants workshops, workshop calendar dates, grantwriting tips, and clients—http://www.MinerAndAssociates.com.

PART I

FUNDAMENTALS OF COLLABORATIVE GRANTSEEKING

In part I, we operationally define collaboration as *an interaction between two or more persons or organizations directed toward a common goal that is mutually beneficial* and recognize one of the core tenets of successful collaborative grantseeking; namely, different types of collaborations exist. Four common types of collaborations—coexistence, coordination, cooperation, and coalition—vary in the degree of goal sharing and interaction among partners during the project period (this is discussed in chapter 1).

A three-step RFP Analysis Process aids grant leaders in determining whether a sponsor's Request for Proposal is a good match for their organization and what type of collaboration will be needed to develop a competitive application. And because collaboration should be a strong theme that is woven throughout the complete grant application, we offer specific tips on how to integrate collaboration into the cover letter, application form, project summary, proposal, budget and budget narrative, and appendixes (in chapter 2).

Before a collaboration is agreed upon and a proposal is drafted, grant leaders should go through four specific pre-collaboration steps. These steps identify the requisite attitudes and actions you should follow to prepare for and form a successful collaboration (see chapter 3). Focus groups represent one strategy for effectively engaging partners in a process of generating great project ideas (see chapter 4). An honest assessment of your leadership characteristics and a solid understanding of the dynamics that make collaborations work will strengthen your ability to influence, motivate, and enable others to contribute toward a common cause.

CHAPTER 1

Types of Collaboration

Two heads are better than one.

—Old English proverb

This chapter introduces you to a detailed analysis of the concept of collaboration and differentiates among four different types of collaboration, which vary among two key dimensions: goal sharing and interaction. Also discussed are styles of grantseeking leadership and characteristics that contribute to success when managing people and projects. The chapter concludes by summarizing the specific behaviors that exemplify the different collaboration types and identifying common mechanisms to achieve them.

WHY COLLABORATE?

Consider the following example. Jane Thompson is the executive director of the ABC for Health Agency, a new nonprofit organization dedicated to providing health services for people living in poverty. Jane knows that, as a new organization, ABC lacks credibility to be successful in grantseeking. Her solution: partner with other organizations that have an established track record.

Here's another example: Frank Wilkie is an associate professor of chemistry at Midwest University. He specializes in conducting research on flame retardants and is currently working on a project that would improve the fire-resistant coating on pajamas for infants. To conduct his research project, he needs access to a specialized instrument that he lacks. His solution: submit a collaborative research project with a colleague at another university who has the required equipment.

Whether you are in the nonprofit world like Jane or in academia like Frank, you may be turning your attention to collaborative grantseeking. The motivation for the rapidly growing interest in collaboration comes from both internal and external sources. Internally, the boss may be nudging you to partner up with one of his friends in another agency. Perhaps your revenue stream is running low and you foresee that a collaborative grant will be a new way to improve your financial situation. Maybe you lack the resources you need to fulfill your mission and you hope that by joining forces with other organizations you can have a greater impact on your local community.

Externally, you may form a collaboration because a grantmaker requires it, something that is happening with increasing frequency in the world of grants. Grantmakers are seeking ways to get a "bigger bang for their buck." As another motivator, you may be part of a group of community organizations who realize that the problems needing to be addressed are simply larger than any one organization can handle. Accordingly, everyone agrees that a collaborative approach is required, recognizing that the whole is greater than the sum of its parts.

Right now, you may be like many U.S. nonprofit organizations—there are nearly two million—or academic institutions—there are over 100,000—who pursue grants. You may see grantseeking as essentially a competitive process. You "close ranks" and put forth the most creative ideas that you can generate using your own internal resources that you control. You recognize that many others will also be applying for the same grant, but you hope that your proposal will be successful. You don't expect others to share your goal; rather, you focus on your mission, your needs, and you have little interaction with your competition. You are promoting your organizational interests over those of other groups. Often, grantseeking is like a competitive intellectual sport.

While your current grantseeking baseline may be competition-oriented, you may wish to expand your expertise in collaborative grantseeking for a variety of internal and external reasons. That's what this book is all about. If you are just sticking your toe into the pool of collaborative grants, we want to share with you the benefits and barriers affecting collaborative grantseeking, identify the different types that exist, and discuss the leadership skills needed to ensure successful collaborations. On the other hand, if you are already into the collaboration pool but wish to move on to the deeper end (without drowning), we want to equip you with an array of means to keep you afloat.

Let's jump in.

BENEFITS OF COLLABORATIVE GRANTSEEKING

The concept of collaboration, of course, is not new. It exists in various forms throughout society and has for years. For instance, we find collaborative relationships between husband and wife, physician and patient, teacher and student, and parent and child. When grantseeking relationships are going smoothly (and they don't always), many benefits accrue, including those listed below.

- strengthened infrastructure
- better ideas
- bigger ideas
- clearer ideas
- expanded service delivery
- greater capacity utilization
- larger response capability
- superior facilities
- easier access to capital
- enhanced market positioning
- improved recruitment potential
- increased market share

- lower distribution costs
- additional research results
- more efficient management
- new research findings
- shared resources
- avoidance of duplicated efforts

Quite simply, collaboration is a practical way to get bigger "wins." In most collaborations, multiple benefits result from working together.

BARRIERS TO COLLABORATIVE GRANTSEEKING

Husbands and wives don't always agree, and in extreme cases the result is divorce. If physicians and patients become disconnected, the results may be fatal. When teachers and students fail to respect each other's academic, social, and emotional needs, learning suffers. When parents and their children continually struggle against each other, it leads to turmoil. In like manner, well-intended grant collaborations don't always turn out to be successful. Some common barriers to collaborative grantseeking are summarized next.

- insufficient goal sharing
- absence of leadership
- inadequate interaction
- lack of trust
- poorly matched partners
- faint levels of commitment
- few tangible rewards
- shortage of enthusiasm
- multiple administrative structures
- unskilled group dynamics
- territorialism
- no shared recognition
- unwillingness to change
- weak internal controls
- heavy workloads
- limited accountability
- competing time demands
- insufficient funding

Despite their potential, grant collaborations can produce bigger "losses," especially when multiple barriers are encountered.

LEADERSHIP IN COLLABORATIVE GRANTSEEKING

The key factor in determining whether your grant collaborations produce "wins" or "losses" is leadership. Effective grant collaborations are led by individuals who not only understand the benefits and barriers affecting collaborations but are skilled in managing them. Specifically, we note four different styles of grantseeking leadership. The first two focus on conceptualizing and planning collaborative projects, while the last two focus on organizing and moving people into action.

- **Visionaries** understand the problems that need to be solved and can describe a clear picture of what could exist in the future. They can powerfully articulate needs and the goals of a project.

- **Strategists** describe the specific action steps necessary to fulfill a vision. The methodology needed to solve the problem is clear and grounded in reality. They ensure schedules are met on time and on budget.

- **Team Builders** assemble a group of talented individuals to implement an action plan. They develop process and operating procedures with input from key stakeholders. They ensure infrastructures are properly supported.

- **Motivators** provide focus and instill confidence in team members, inspiring them to achieve mutual goals. They optimistically cheer people into action and calm anxieties. They serve as role models and become "lantern carriers" who go down the path first.

Because managing projects and managing people require different kinds of skills, successful grant leaders often surround themselves with individuals who can offset any shortcomings in their personal leadership style. This inclusive and participative approach connects leaders with their collaborators and provides a clear sense of direction and purpose. In this way, grant leaders can make change happen.

The challenge for grant leaders is to create a situation where all participants feel that they know what is going on and how to affect it, regardless of whether they choose to exercise those rights. In many respects, leadership is not about the leader; rather, it is about how leaders build confidence in others and move them into action. This confidence building occurs on multiple levels: self-confidence; confidence in the leader and other collaborators; confidence in the grant goals, objectives, and methods; and confidence that project outcomes will make a difference. Successful collaborations brim with confidence.

Leadership is so crucial in collaborative grantseeking that we discuss the roles, responsibilities, and characteristics of leaders throughout this book, and especially in chapter 3.

DEFINITION OF COLLABORATION

Collaboration is a seductive buzzword in grantseeking. It is a word—like most—that has multiple meanings. Personally, we've seen at least 33 different synonyms, noted in exhibit 1.1.

Synonyms usually contain slight nuances in meaning, and that is the case with the alternate terms for "collaboration" in exhibit 1.1. A critical analysis of these synonyms reveals that while these terms vary in semantic gradations, they contain two common features: goal sharing and interaction. Accordingly, we operationally define collaboration as *an interaction between two or more persons or organizations directed toward a common goal that is mutually beneficial.*

In successful collaborations, the interaction among partners and their shared goal orientation represents a complex process that requires attention to planning, goal setting, communication, decision making, problem solving, interventions, incentives, and recognition. Individuals or organizations who collaborate agree that change is needed and commit to change through varying types of interaction and goal-oriented behaviors. Without those two elements, collaboration is arguably absent and the result is not collaboration but rather competitive grantseeking.

affiliation	combination	interrelation
aid	conglomeration	lift
alliance	connection	mega-merger
assistance	consortium	mutuality
backing	cooperation	pact
benefit	coordination	participation
boost	engagement	partnership
co-action	ensemble	reinforcement
coalition	federation	relation
coexistence	furtherance	service
co-evolution	helping hand	shared governance

EXHIBIT 1.1   Alternative Terms for "Collaboration"

ONSET OF COLLABORATION

Our operational definition of collaboration recognizes two key elements: goal sharing and interaction. Grant leaders know that varying degrees of goal sharing and interaction occur before, during, and after the grant period; that is, collaboration represents a process that changes with changing circumstances. Each type of collaboration is discussed below, beginning with the nature of grant relationships prior to the formation of a collaboration.

Before the Grant Period

Before deciding to pursue a grant opportunity, the potential collaborators may have no prior history of working together; to be precise, they have been in competition in the past and lack a history of goal sharing and interaction to take up a common objective. Often (but not always), this situation represents the baseline prior to developing a collaborative proposal.

With the competitive strategy, people and organizations are rivals seeking to pursue their own interests and improve their own circumstances. Rather than partner with other organizations to promote larger desirable social ends (one of the benefits of collaboration) the underlying theme of the competitive approach is the promotion of organizational isolation.

Sometimes, collaborators who pursue RFPs (Requests for Proposals) have some sort of relationship other than a competitive one. Perhaps they have worked together before, although not on a grant project. Collaborative grant applications are more persuasive when you can write, "We have worked together previously on three similar grants" or "This collaboration presents a systematic continuation of our prior efforts in working together" or something that highlights any crossover experience you have had with projects of comparable magnitude or complexity—for instance, managing a large group of people or handling a complex budget. Reviewers always like to know that the collaboration being proposed is not a knee-jerk response to a grant opportunity.

Obviously, you can't justify a claim that you and your proposed collaborators have worked together previously if—in fact—you haven't. How, then, do you convince reviewers that your collaboration will be successful? The root issue at stake is one of credibility. If you haven't worked previously with other collaborators, then perhaps you could include some partners who have worked together in the past; maybe one could even serve as a project co-director. In essence, if you lack credibility, you might "borrow" it.

Finally, a strong option for demonstrating that your collaboration will be successful is to write a well-reasoned proposal, including a detailed timeline, thereby letting your reviewers know you have a solid plan to solve a pressing need. Spell out in your proposal how you worked with your collaborators during the development of the grant application. Include such information as the number of planning meetings held or e-mails exchanged, drafts circulated, and any other pertinent forms of interaction (e.g., the results from conducting a community needs assessment together).

In short, before the grant begins, you can let reviewers know that you have collaborated previously on other non-grant-funded projects or, alternatively, that you have collaborated extensively on the preparation of the current proposal and will do so on the proposed project.

During the Grant Period

With collaborative grants, you will be proposing some degree of goal sharing and interaction to take place during the funding period. The vectors of goal sharing and interaction could cross, theoretically, at an infinite number of points. However, thinking in terms of high versus low levels of each, four possible types of collaboration exist during the grant period.

- **Coexistence** means the collaborators have a minimal amount of interaction and goal sharing. While some collaboration exists, it is the least of the four types. This situation often occurs when partners from two or more groups continue to work independently but realize that a token collaboration may help them achieve their own goals. The participants remain relatively independent and self-focused but have a cordial and open relationship, meaning that they will work nominally with others to attain their desired outcomes. Both partners share in the project but not necessarily equally.

- **Coordination** means the collaborators have brought the project components together as a result of appropriate interactions to ensure a successful outcome. This situation often exists when relationships among collaborators build to achieve individual goals through a relationship of codependency. As part of their tactical and calculated partnership, the collaborators have defined roles, identified key leadership, and often share in decision making, such as setting and monitoring performance targets. Communication flows regularly among all collaborators through frequent formal and informal mechanisms.

- **Cooperation** means the collaborators see their futures as linked together and agree upon rules to create stable, purposeful relationships. When partners help create objectives and plans, they are more likely to understand and implement them. A genuine trust exists and is a key element to gain a broader outcome. This situation often occurs when the partners recognize that working together at least moderately will help to achieve their overlapping goals. A strategic, mutually interdependent relationship exists, and each collaborator contributes essential resources to ensure project success.

- **Coalition** means the collaborators have established and are dependent upon a high level of goal sharing and interaction. The elements of both coordination and cooperation collaborations exist to generate new ways of working together. All partners explore together and contribute their unique perspectives toward a shared purpose; they are forthcoming and responsive to each other. Often, coalitions are formed to tackle problems when old ways don't work and a broader approach is required. Solutions are co-designed for a shared purpose that goes beyond consensus to a new level of functioning.

The four types of collaborative grantseeking are represented in exhibit 1.2.

Mathematicians will recognize exhibit 1.2 as a classic XY graph and might quickly point out that an unlimited number of points exist on the XY coordinates. While they are correct, we take a more practical view and note from past experience that, during the grant period, collaborations tend to cluster into four quadrants. The clusters reflect combinations of low and high levels of interaction and goal sharing. As you proceed along the horizontal axis, the extent of interaction increases, in essence, from playing side-by-side to operating together in harmony. Likewise, as you move up the vertical axis, the amount of goal sharing increases, akin to moving from individual thinking to collective thinking.

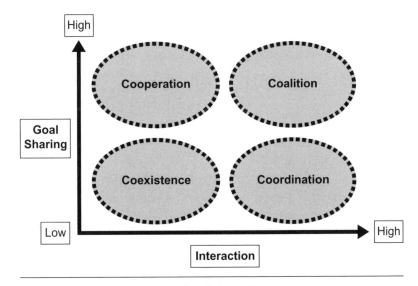

EXHIBIT 1.2   Four Types of Collaboration

After the Grant Period

What happens to a collaboration after the grant period is over? It depends. A collaboration may take on a life of its own. Even without the benefit of grant funding, partners may set aside some of their individual goals in favor of permanently supporting the joint group goals. At heart, the collaboration that existed during the granting period may have co-evolved into a new and permanent organization whose goals become the enduring focus. For instance, after the conclusion of the grant period, partners may decide to continue operating despite the loss of funds, because they see considerable value in collaborating. Each collaborator continues contributing at the same level—effort, personnel, resources—for the foreseeable future.

When partnerships co-evolve, individuals from multiple organizations, while still retaining their affiliation with their parent organization, become a part of a new joint organizational structure to which they are prepared to subordinate some of their individual and organizational behaviors. This joint structure is responsible for reaching agreement about goals and how to achieve them as well as setting performance targets and then monitoring them.

On the other hand, sometimes collaborations will continue after the grant ends, but the scope of effort decreases. That is, the amount of goal sharing or interaction scales back. In practical terms, there may be fewer communications, or some resources may be unavailable. If all collaborative resources are withdrawn and group interaction ceases, then partnerships may revert back to the pre-grant position of "competition."

Grantmakers often request information about project sustainability in proposals, because they want to know what will happen after the grant is over and the funds are spent. As you develop your proposal, in addition to describing plans for the continuation of key activities, be sure to discuss how your collaboration itself will be sustained after the granting period ends. Do you anticipate continuing the project and perhaps co-evolving? Or will you scale back to some lesser level? To what extent will the same resources and communications exist afterward? Grantmakers seek answers to questions like these.

DIMENSIONS OF COLLABORATION

To this point we've discussed the concept of collaboration and pointed out that the term—by itself—is too broad to describe successful collaborative grantseeking. Instead, we identified four types of collaboration—coexistence, coordination, cooperation, and coalition—that may occur during the grant period, types that center on varying amounts of goal sharing and interaction.

When Gustave Flaubert uttered, "The devil is in the details," he probably wasn't thinking about collaborative grantseeking—but he could have been. What are the details of goal sharing and interaction? Both are broad concepts but can be translated into specific, observable behaviors so that people would agree and say, "Yes, when that happens, I accept that as evidence of goal sharing," or "Yes, when I see that, I recognize it as positive interaction among collaborators." In other words, it's time for some operational definitions.

Goal Sharing

Goals represent idealized dreams, the "big picture" vision of what you aspire to accomplish. They are usually presented in terms of hopes, wishes, or desires. They communicate global purposes and typically relate to an improved state of affairs for a target audience.

When two or more individuals (or organizations) have similar or overlapping visions, they might be willing to work together to achieve bigger "wins." Because of their respective commitments to a shared cause, they may agree to engage in a mutual exchange, portioning out some of their resources—people, materials, and dollars—in order to reap benefits such as bigger ideas, expanded service delivery, easier access to capital, and avoidance of duplicated efforts.

For collaborative grantseeking purposes, what then are the resources that might be shared? Our view of past collaborative grants has produced a list of six categories of resources that could potentially be shared as a means of reaching project outcomes.

1. **Tangible Property:** specialized equipment, instrumentation, furniture, space, unique specimens or samples, databases, software, computers, other technologies

2. **Project Personnel:** laboratory technicians, graduate students, work-study students, statisticians, computer specialists, marketing and communications experts, evaluation consultants, medical specialists, access to networks of potential collaborators

3. **Target Populations:** minorities, people with disabilities, people with health disparities, homeless, frail elderly, children with special needs, persons living in poverty, animals (such as spiny mice, which are hypertensive), laboratory specimens (such as those used in basic science research)

4. **Business Office Services:** printing services, paper and envelopes, meter postage for mailings, shared wireless minutes to minimize telephone expenses, use of conference rooms, food, other items that facilitate the administration of collaborative projects

5. **Intellectual Property:** patents, copyrights, trademarks, novel ideas, unique protocols, similar shared materials

6. **Financial Resources:** cash and in-kind contributions such as volunteer time, use of vehicles, value of frequent-flier miles, complimentary lodging, used furniture, loan of executives or technicians

The examples in each category represent specific, observable behaviors on the part of organizations. You can easily determine whether a computer or a technician, for example, has been shared by a collaborator to achieve project outcomes. Shared goals translate into shared resources for purposes of collaborative grantseeking.

Interaction

Positive interaction represents a form of mutual exchange. For collaborative grantseeking purposes, the "mutual exchange" typically is some type of communication, formal or informal, in person or virtual, verbal or nonverbal, oral or written, print or electronic. The list of communication methods and tools that connect collaborators and target populations is lengthy.

1. **Print Media:** journal articles, newsletters, pamphlets, press releases, interim working papers, executive summaries, conference papers, reports

2. **Electronic Media:** e-mail, Web sites, webcasts, faxes, text messages, instant messages, video on demand

3. **Social Media:** Twitter, LinkedIn, Facebook, MySpace, Ning, wikis, podcasts, blogs, RSS feeds, mashups, social bookmarking, widgets

4. **Audio/Visual Communications:** instructional materials, teleconferences, video conferences, Webinars, displays, poster sessions

5. **Interpersonal Communications:** meetings, telephone calls, workshops, colloquia, seminars, site visits, demonstrations, conference presentations

Of note, these goal sharing and interaction lists are not meant to be discrete or exhaustive. Certainly overlaps do exist, and any individual item might be sorted into multiple categories. The intent here is to suggest kernel ideas for grant leaders to use to forge new and stronger collaborations.

COLLABORATION TYPES AND GRANT OPPORTUNITIES

As you review announcements of grant opportunities from public and private grantmakers, you will invariably find ones that explicitly state a collaborative approach is preferred or implicitly suggest one is appropriate. Some RFPs remain silent about a sponsor's interest in supporting collaborative endeavors. Your collaborative approach might be enough to position your project as distinctive from other applications, thus catching the sponsor's attention.

The choice of collaboration type will vary depending upon your project's purpose, your grant leadership, and the extent of goal sharing and the amount of interaction devoted to the project. Organizational differences will exist among collaborators, and those differences are not easily overcome. Different collaboration types will suit different people and projects.

As the grant leader, you might be in the middle of it all and wonder which type to choose. Fortunately, you do not need to select *a priori* your desired type of collaboration and then force it to fit your grant application guidelines.

Rather, begin by making a list of your core values, aspirations, and resources (goal sharing) and your communication options (interaction). As you hold your initial meetings with potential collaborators and conduct your pre-collaboration steps (see chapter 3), literally inventory what each collaborator might bring to the table.

If your inventory list is relatively meager or the grant announcement requires only token collaboration, then you might have a coexistence collaboration. If your inventory list is long on resources and shorter on occasions to communicate, then you might form a cooperation collaboration. Alternatively, if the inventory pendulum swings the other way and you are long on communication options and short on resources, then you could form a coordination collaboration. If you have a relatively hefty supply of both collaboration requirements—resources for goal sharing and communication tools for interaction—then you could form a coalition collaboration.

That is to say, only *after* your grant resources and options are determined do you label the type of resulting collaboration.

Now that you have a perspective on the different types of collaboration and understand the two key elements of collaboration—goal sharing and interaction—we turn our attention in the next few chapters to how these types of collaboration apply to grantseeking (chapter 2), the dynamics of collaborations (chapter 3), and generating winning ideas for collaborative grant proposals (chapter 4).

CHAPTER 2

Collaborations:
Applications to Grantseeking

The greatest obstacle to discovery is not ignorance—it is the illusion of knowledge.

—Daniel J. Boorstin

Chapter 1 introduced the concept of collaborative grantseeking and differentiated among four types of collaboration that occur during the granting period: coexistence, coordination, cooperation, and coalition.

In chapter 2, we apply these different types of collaborations to various aspects of grantseeking. We begin with a broad view of collaborations that have been funded by public and private sponsors. Next, we examine how grantmakers communicate their interest in collaborative grants through RFPs. Then we discuss how to integrate the concept of collaboration throughout the complete grant application. Finally, we present actual comments from grant reviewers who evaluated collaborative proposals.

FUNDED COLLABORATIONS

Collaborations occur within and between organizations. Within an organization, individuals can collaborate within a unit, such as a department, or across units, such as a division. Individuals can also collaborate across organizations. Multiple organizations can and do collaborate.

Exhibit 2.1 highlights the more common categories of collaborators—educational, religious, health care, nonprofit, and government—though they are not mutually exclusive. Nonprofits, for example, encompass a broad range of organizations, including private charities, and may well render educational, health care or faith-based services. Nevertheless, they all receive grant funding from private and public sponsors for collaborative initiatives.

Examples of actual grant awards are provided below for each of the five categories of recipients. Specifically, we provide the name of the grantmaker, the grantee, the dollar

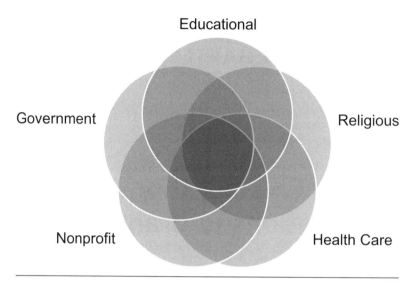

EXHIBIT 2.1   Common Collaborator Grant Recipients

amount, the geographic area, and a general description of the collaborative purpose of the award. The available information does indicate clearly that some type of collaboration was involved; indeed, many of the grant titles include the word "collaboration" or some variant.

Educational Recipients

The educational category includes the following, whether public or private: day care and pre-school programs; elementary, middle, and secondary schools; technical schools; and colleges and universities.

- The Children's Theatre Company and School and in Minneapolis received $160,000 from 3M (in Minnesota) to collaborate with area elementary schools to enhance the performing arts abilities of young children.

- Muhlenberg College (in Pennsylvania) was awarded $85,910 from the National Science Foundation (in Virginia) for a collaboration between the departments of biology, chemistry, and mathematics and computer science to integrate bioinformatics into the biology curriculum.

- The University of New Hampshire received $10,000 from the Byrne Foundation (in New Hampshire) for a collaboration with 12 high schools in New Hampshire and Maine on advanced secondary education topics.

- San Diego State University received $651,718 from the National Institutes of Health (in Maryland) to conduct a neurobehavioral assessment as part of a multi-disciplinary, collaborative initiative on fetal alcohol spectrum disorders.

- The Tukwila Community Schools (in Washington) Collaboration received $15,000 from the Marguerite Casey Foundation (also in Washington) to hire a bilingual/bicultural person as a new site coordinator, to be matched by the Tukwila business community.

Religious Recipients

Collaborative grants are awarded across all faiths and to many interfaith organizations.

- The Lynde and Harry Bradley Foundation (in Wisconsin) granted $90,000 to the Catholic Committee for Cultural Collaboration (in Rome, Italy) to support international student exchanges among many Roman Catholic agencies and churches.

- The U.S. Department of Health and Human Services, Office of Population Affairs (in Washington DC) awarded $350,000 to The Night Ministry (in Illinois) to provide case management services, shelter, family life and parenting education, and support services to at-risk youth who are homeless or in danger of becoming homeless.

- The Cleveland Foundation (in Ohio) awarded $29,000 to the Inter Religious Partners in Action of Greater Cleveland (also in Ohio) for collaboration to create a community food pantry.

- The U.S. Department of Health and Human Services, Administration for Children and Families (in Washington DC) awarded $1,500,000 to Bethany Christian Services (in Michigan) to collaborate with the faith-based community to develop adoption services and supports for youth who wish to retain contact with family members in order to improve permanency outcomes.

- The William T. Grant Foundation (in New York) awarded $20,000 to the Fuller Theological Seminary (in California) for a collaboration among the Applied Developmental Science Institute at Tufts University, Stanford University, Search Institute, and the THRIVE Foundation.

Health Care Recipients

Health care is one of the largest recipients of grant dollars.

- The John Wayne Cancer Institute (in California) received $500,000 from the Avon Foundation (in New York) to collaborate with the Center for Healthy Aging to provide breast cancer education, screening, and treatment services to women over age 65.

- Seattle Children's Hospital received a $644,942 grant from the Centers for Disease Control and Prevention (in Georgia) to collaborate with six clinical sites across the country and study diabetes in children and youth.

- The CAMC Health Education and Research Institute (in West Virginia) granted $125,000 to the West Virginia Nursing Leadership Institute for collaboration with the West Virginia University School of Nursing to start-up a leadership development program.

- Mount Sinai School of Medicine, Center for Children's Environmental Health and Disease Prevention Research (in New York) was awarded $3,136,392 from the Environmental Protection Agency (in Washington DC) to identify linkages between environmental toxicants and neurodevelopmental dysfunction in inner-city children.

- The California Community Foundation awarded $546,586 to the Children's Hospital Los Angeles for planning and start-up support of a model telemedicine collaboration between the hospital and the Dr. Claudia Hampton Clinic.

Nonprofit Recipients

There are many types of nonprofit organizations. The educational, religious, and health care categories are major types and segmented out for illustrative purposes. The examples below highlight additional types of nonprofit organizations.

- The AT&T Foundation (in Texas) awarded the Children's Museum of Indianapolis $20,000 to collaborate with inner-city schools to develop a Communications Center for Youth.

- The National Endowment for the Arts (in Washington DC) awarded the Springfield Library & Museums Association (in Illinois) $65,000 to support a visual arts touring exhibition of American masterpieces.

- The Otto Bremer Foundation (in Minnesota) awarded the Twin Cities Public Television (also in Minnesota) $20,000 to lead collaborative efforts on a statewide anti-racism project.

- NASA (in Washington DC) selected the HDF Group (in Illinois) to receive $1,040,569 to provide hierarchical data format support for the Earth Science Data and Information System project and the Earth Observing System Data and Information System standard data format.

- The California Wellness Foundation granted $150,000 to Domestic Violence Solutions for Santa Barbara County (in California) to conduct teen-relationship violence prevention education in middle and high schools, in juvenile justice facilities, and in collaboration with other community-based organizations throughout Santa Barbara County.

Government Recipients

Government agencies at all levels—local, county, state, and national—can be awarded collaborative grants, as illustrated in these examples.

- The National Conference of State Legislatures (in Washington DC) received $100,000 from the Carnegie Corporation (in New York) for collaboration with National Hispanic Caucus of State Legislators on immigrant issues at the state level.

- The Wisconsin Division for Libraries, Technology and Community Learning was appropriated $2,962,815 from the Institute of Museum and Library Services (in Washington DC) to support statewide initiatives, services, and information sharing between libraries and between libraries and other community services.

- The State of Georgia, Department of Human Resources received $150,000 from the Annie E. Casey Foundation (in Maryland) for collaboration with a residential treatment program for troubled and abused youth.

- The City of Philadelphia, Department of Records was awarded $108,882 by the National Endowment for the Humanities (in Washington DC) for a digital partnership project with the Free Library of Philadelphia to increase access to significant historical records.

- The North Carolina Department of Health and Human Services received $350,000 from the Duke Endowment (in North Carolina) to reform aspects of the child welfare system in North Carolina by focusing on enhanced community collaboration, prevention, and family support services in targeted counties.

Whether it is two colleagues within one department or multiple organizations working together across continents, successful collaborations represent a dynamic process for creating a power-sharing partnership for education, outreach, training, service delivery, and research grants.

REQUESTS FOR PROPOSALS

An RFP (Request for Proposal) is an invitation by a sponsor to submit a grant application. RFP guidelines spell out the details you need to develop a proposal. They generally provide an overview of what the funding announcement is all about, the background or problem that led to this invitation, priority funding areas, sample methodological approaches, timelines, deadlines, evaluation criteria, funds available, and acceptable uses of grant funds.

Throughout this book, we use the term RFP to refer to an announcement of a grant opportunity, though some sponsors use other terms such as Funding Opportunity Announcement (FOA), Grant Announcement (GA), Request for Application (RFA), Program Announcement (PA), Broad Agency Announcement (BAA), or Notice of Funding Opportunity (NOFA). In some RFPs, sponsors explicitly state their preference for collaborative proposals; in others, sponsors' preferences are not addressed at all or are only subtly implied.

Further complicating the issue, even when RFPs require or "strongly encourage" collaboration, only infrequently do sponsors specify the type of collaboration they desire to support. This may be intentional, to allow for flexibility in project design; or it may be unintentional, because they did not consider the full implications of their own guidelines. Regardless, by including specific details about the type of collaboration you will employ, you are, in effect, making your proposal stand out from other applicants who simply describe their collaboration in general terms.

The RFP Analysis Process described next can help you determine not only whether to submit a proposal but also how to increase your chances for success. While sponsors may not specify a preferred type of collaboration, their RFPs may offer linguistic clues as to their minimum performance expectations. If you can meet or exceed these expectations, then you may be well on your way to submitting a collaborative proposal. If you cannot meet their minimum threshold, then you may have a considerable amount of networking to do prior to proposal submission.

THE RFP ANALYSIS PROCESS

Analyzing RFP guidelines means asking a lot of questions and thinking strategically about the many dimensions of collaboration. The process described here enables you to effectively analyze an RFP to assess whether it is a good match for your organization and what type of collaboration will be needed to develop a competitive application.

To effectively analyze an RFP, read it in multiple passes with increasing scrutiny. The three-step RFP Analysis Process will help you answer questions about relevance, feasibility, and probability:

- Step One: **R**elevance—Do we want to do this?
- Step Two: **F**easibility—Can we do this?
- Step Three: **P**robability—Will we be competitive?

Together, these three steps provide you with the details necessary to develop a persuasive proposal if you decide to apply.

Step One: Relevance—Do We Want to Do This?

At this most basic level, read the RFP guidelines and develop a short list of bulleted points that summarize the main ideas, paying particular attention to the role that collaboration might play in the proposal. This process will help you understand exactly what this grant is all about and quickly assess its relevance, determining whether or not it is a good match for your organization—answering the question, "Do we want to do this?"

Step Two: Feasibility—Can We Do This?

Assuming that the RFP appears initially to be a good match for your organization and that you intend to develop a collaborative proposal, examine the RFP for technical aspects of the application procedure and for the stated evaluation criteria. In addition, read between the lines of the RFP for hot buttons and distinctive features—primary and secondary concerns of the sponsor—that must be addressed to satisfy the sponsor's logical and psychological needs. This analysis will begin to answer the question of feasibility— "Can we do this?"—and give you an indication of how much effort will be necessary to develop a collaborative proposal.

Step Three: Probability—Will We Be Competitive?

To develop a highly competitive proposal, this third part of the analysis will force you to examine your individual, organizational, and collaborative strengths and weaknesses in relation to the values of the sponsor. As you begin to prepare a proposal, strategic thinking with your colleagues and potential collaborators is essential. Combine this with feedback from preproposal contact with program officers, past grant reviewers, and past grant winners as you attempt to answer the question, "Will we be competitive?" or more bluntly, "Is it *really* worth our time and effort to develop an application?"

ANALYSIS OF COLLABORATIVE RFPS

This next section puts forward representative RFPs from eight sponsors—four government agencies and four private foundations—all seeking some form of collaborative effort. In general, the level of collaboration detail is less in private than in public RFPs. This does not mean, however, that foundations value collaborative grantseeking less than their government counterparts; rather, it merely means that they have not infused such language into their RFPs.

The eight RFPs are presented in condensed form, to highlight operative direct and indirect references to collaboration types. You will quickly note that the RFP from only one sponsor, the Robert Wood Johnson Foundation, explicitly specifies a preference for a coalition collaboration. For the others, we draw from linguistic clues in the RFP about goal sharing and interaction to infer the sponsor's minimum performance expectations for collaborations. That is to say, collaborative proposals may propose higher levels of goal sharing and interaction than what the sponsor indicates, but collaborative projects with lower levels will not be as competitive.

Coexistence RFPs

With coexistence RFPs, goal sharing and interaction are minimal; the connections with collaborators are often loose and informal. Practically speaking, the collaborators pursue their ways separately, but their paths may touch tangentially. For example, a collaborator who provides a simple letter of support is essentially saying, "I will help you by vouching for the merits of your organization and your work, but I will continue to do my own thing." Collaborators recognize that there are times to—like a good neighbor—stop briefly and give each other a hand.

It should also be stressed that when interaction and goal sharing with other organizations or individuals is somewhat limited, this is, not inherently "bad." Many scientific breakthroughs have occurred when grant leaders have done valuable incremental work. Jonas Salk did not "discover" the polio vaccine; he principally synthesized a paradigm from the basic science research conducted by individual investigators over several decades.

The Corporation for National and Community Service

The Corporation for National and Community Service is a federal grantmaking agency with a mission to "improve lives, strengthen communities, and foster civic engagement through service and volunteering." Their Learn and Serve America Higher Education grants leverage the human talents of colleges and universities—namely, their faculty and students—to address local community needs. To help foster a culture of social responsibility and citizenship, they issued an RFP for a "College Student Social Media Initiative" (www.learnandserve.gov):

> The purpose of the Corporation for National and Community Service's "College Student Social Media Initiative" competition is to facilitate better engagement of college students in service through the use of social media. Some examples of social media include: social networking (i.e., Facebook, MySpace, Ning, or integrating social networking capacity into existing sites), wikis, podcasts, blogs, RSS feeds, mashups, social bookmarking, and widgets. Successful applicants must demonstrate how their program can use these tools to engage increased numbers of college students, especially in partnership with other nonprofit or for-profit

entities. One-time awards of approximately $100,000 to $750,000 will be made for a project period of up to three years.

Eligible applicants include higher education partnerships, defined as one or more public or private nonprofit organizations, or public agencies, including States, and one or more institutions of higher education. Thus, all partnerships must include at least one institution of higher education. Examples of such partnerships include: a national service-focused organization and colleges and universities where it has affiliated chapters; a national non-profit partnering with a Business School to run a national subgranting competition; a regional group of non-profit student organizations working with an institution of higher education which would serve as the legal applicant.

Note that the RFP is silent on the type of collaboration preferred but requires one partner to be an institution of higher education; in essence, this is a forced coexistence collaboration. The institution of higher education could involve a few students in a service learning project, serve as the fiscal agency for the applicant, conduct the evaluation component of the project, or provide space for a meeting. It is quite possible that a nominal form of collaboration might, over time, spark even greater goal sharing and interaction in the future, resulting in a shift from coexistence to a different type of collaboration, such as coordination or cooperation.

Aid to Artisans

Aid to Artisans, founded in 1976, is an established international leader in economic development and environmental sustainability for the craft sector. Their mission is to "offer practical assistance to artisan groups worldwide, working in partnerships to foster artistic traditions, cultural vitality, improved livelihoods, and community well-being. Through collaboration in product development, business skills training, and development of new markets, they provide sustainable economic and social benefits for craftspeople in an environmentally sensitive and culturally respectful manner." In the regions of the world where they work, their "Small Grants Program" makes a big impact (www.aidtoartisans.org).

Aid to Artisans' "Small Grants Program" makes modest awards of $500 to $1,500 to groups of craft producers such as cooperatives and community organizations for the purchase of materials, tools, and equipment to improve or increase their craft production. Only established artisan groups or cooperatives will be considered; newly formed organizations and individual artists are not eligible for grants under this program. And only grant requests accompanied by a letter of recommendation from organizations already known to them or part of their network will be considered. Examples of groups known to Aid to Artisans include IFAT, OXFAM, United Nations agencies, Fair Trade Federation, and U.S. Peace Corps Volunteers.

The requirement that applicants must include a letter of recommendation from an organization known to the sponsor makes this a coexistence collaboration. The artisan groups do not need to share goals or interact with the known organizations; rather, they simply need to have a relationship—personal or professional—that would allow them to secure a letter vouching for their character. In this case, whom you know may be more important than what you propose to do.

Coordination RFPs

Coordination RFPs emphasize hefty interaction among collaborators; that is, they promote frequent communication among partners through a variety of informal and formal means. While no yardstick exists to measure "hefty interaction," the frequency and effectiveness of communication among collaborators are indices to determine collaboration effectiveness.

Grant reviewers seek assurance that the promise to coordinate project efforts has some substance behind it and does not represent proposal puffery. Details regarding the coordination strategy are usually presented in the methodology section of the proposal, often in a subsection titled "Management Plan."

U.S. Department of State

The U.S. Department of State, Bureau of Democracy, Human Rights and Labor leads the nation's efforts to "promote democracy, protect human rights and international religious freedom, and advance labor rights globally." Nearly 70 percent of the bureau's annual budget is distributed in an array of foreign assistance efforts. In light of world events, it issued an RFP for "Human Rights and Democracy Initiatives in the Democratic Republic of the Congo" (www.state.gov):

> Creative approaches are needed in the Democratic Republic of the Congo to ensure that citizens reap the benefits from the country's recent historic electoral advances. Having an elected government (including elected local governments) is a new reality for the country, and there is a need to provide citizens greater information and to foster substantive citizen interaction with local government, particularly so citizens can make their interests known (effective mechanisms might include public hearings, town hall meetings, call-in radio programs, and public policy debates with university officials, private sector representatives, NGOs, etc).
>
> The following issues have been identified as priorities for projects in the Democratic Republic of the Congo:
>
> • Increase civic participation through greater access to information on public policy (such as on decentralization, asset declarations by public officials, new legislation, etc.), new governance structures, human rights, and negotiation and advocacy tools.
>
> • Facilitate anti-corruption reforms to combat impunity at the community level.
>
> • Link citizens to provincial and national elected authorities to facilitate access and dialogue.

The bulk of project activities may last between 1 and 3 years and awards of between $500,000 and $1,000,000 will be made to support the program and administrative costs required to implement programs.

In this example, to increase civic participation and link citizens with various authorities, multiple channels of communication are necessary. The channels of communication are placed in the broader context of the entire communication cycle, including senders, receivers, channels, and messages. This wider view encapsulates multiple international collaborators and provides them with scaffolding to coordinate their communications.

The Tinker Foundation

The Tinker Foundation was established in 1959 and honors Dr. Edward Larocque Tinker's lifelong interest in Antarctica and in the Hispanic traditions of Spain, Portugal, and Latin America. The Tinker Foundation issued an RFP for "Institutional Grants," which support a variety of research activities, conferences and workshops, and special projects that are geographically focused on these areas of the world (http://foundationcenter.org/grantmaker/tinker/index.html):

> Tinker Foundation "Institutional Grants" are awarded to organizations and institutions that promote the interchange and exchange of information within the community of those concerned with the affairs of Spain, Portugal, Ibero-America and Antarctica. (For the Foundation's purposes, Ibero-America is defined as the Spanish- and Portuguese-speaking countries of the Western Hemisphere.) Programmatically, the Foundation funds projects addressing environmental policy, economic policy or governance issues. Projects should have a strong public policy component, offer innovative solutions to problems facing these regions, and incorporate new mechanisms for addressing these programmatic areas. Activities may include, but are not limited to, research projects and conferences related to the Foundation's areas of interest. The Foundation encourages collaboration between organizations in the United States and Iberia or Latin America and among institutions in those regions. Awards typically range from $10,000 to $100,000.

The RFP articulates a clear preference for collaborative projects between domestic and international partners that aim to facilitate information sharing. To meet the sponsor's communication preferences, the coordination collaboration must do more than simply disseminate information; the grantseekers must demonstrate how information is interchanged and exchanged. Communications should flow openly and freely in all directions, among partners as well as interested and affected parties.

Cooperation RFPs

Cooperation RFPs seek to make an impact by supporting partners working toward shared goals. When collaborators are committed to a common cause, they bring a wealth of resources—people, materials, and dollars—to advance their purposeful and deliberate relationship.

A few sponsors seek evidence of a commitment to a collaborative project by requiring cost sharing. In this way, sponsors can directly and indirectly influence the specific resources brought to bear on the project. For instance, budget constraints in the RFP—such as a cash-matching requirement and a prohibition against using grant funds to support personnel salary, laptop computers, and indirect costs—ensure that collaborators commit these resources themselves to the success of the project. Cost sharing may also be viewed as evidence of project sustainability. Sponsors' attitudes toward cost sharing vary widely and, though rarely indicated in an RFP, it is possible to cost share too much.

The National Endowment for the Humanities

The National Endowment for the Humanities (NEH) was established in 1965 as an independent grantmaking agency of the U.S. government "dedicated to supporting research, education, preservation, and public programs in the humanities." Approximately 80 percent of the NEH's annual budget is awarded in program grants, matching funds, state and territorial humanities councils, and special other initiatives. To help strengthen the institutional base of the humanities and facilitate original research and scholarship, the NEH issued an RFP for "Collaborative Research Grants" (www.neh.gov):

> NEH Collaborative Research Grants support original research undertaken by a team of two or more scholars or research coordinated by an individual scholar that, because of its scope or complexity, requires additional staff and resources beyond the individual's salary. All grantees are expected to communicate the results of their work to the appropriate scholarly and public audiences. Awards are made for one to three years and normally range from $25,000 to $100,000 per year. In most cases, NEH Collaborative Research Grants cover no more than 80% of project costs. The balance of the costs is to be borne by the applicant's institution or other non-federal sources.
>
> All collaborators should be identified, regardless of whether NEH funds are requested to support their participation in the project. Project directors must devote a significant portion of their time to their projects. All persons directly involved in the conduct of the proposed project—whether or not their salaries are paid from grant funds—should be named, their anticipated commitments of time should be indicated, and the reasons for and nature of their participation explained.

This RFP expects a significant commitment of resources: the highly specialized intellectual talents of a team of two or more investigators; a considerable amount of time—up to three years—dedicated to the proposed research; and at least 20 percent cost sharing. Cooperation collaboration proposals that are well-written but do not demonstrate this resolute level of dedication are unlikely to be selected for funding.

The John Templeton Foundation

It is the mission of the John Templeton Foundation to "serve as a philanthropic catalyst for discovery in areas engaging life's biggest questions." New frontiers in science are developing at the interface of disciplines. The Foundation is particularly interested in bringing together multiple areas of physical, life, and human science to explore, in an open-minded and empirical way, their boundaries with philosophy and theology. One of their core funding areas is "Science & the Big Questions" (www.templeton.org).

> Sir John Templeton stipulated that most of the Foundation's resources would be devoted to research (and disseminating the results of research) about the "basic forces, concepts, and realities" governing the universe and humankind's place in the universe. Grant awards range from $1,000 to $5,000,000 depending on the project and range in duration from a few months to three years or in some instances four or five years.
>
> In posing the Big Questions, Sir John stressed the need for humility and openness, and he saw the possibility of important contributions from various modes of inquiry. He especially wished to encourage researchers in the natural and human sciences to bring their rigorous methods to bear on the sorts of subjects that he identified, but he was also enthusiastic about the insights that might come from new approaches in philosophy and theology. Whatever the field, he expected research supported by the Foundation to conform to the highest intellectual standards.
>
> For Sir John, the overarching goal of asking the Big Questions was to discover what he called "new spiritual information." This term, to his mind, encompassed progress not only in our conception of religious truths but also in our understanding of the deepest realities of human nature and the physical world. As he wrote in the Foundation's charter, he wanted to encourage every sort of opinion leader—from scientists and journalists to clergy and theologians—to become more open-minded about the possible character of ultimate reality and the divine.

When you read phrases in the RFP such as "various modes of inquiry," "insights that might come from new approaches," and "deepest realities of human nature and the physical world," an intense meta-message surfaces: the John Templeton Foundation invests in big questions in a big way. The Foundation is deeply passionate about advancing human progress through breakthrough discoveries and expects its grantees to be the same. The work of cooperative collaborators is not just about the here and now; it is about building a legacy of discoveries for the next 100 years.

Coalition RFPs

Coalition RFPs combine substantial amounts of goal sharing and interaction; that is, they join the essential elements found in both coordination and cooperation collaborations. In coalition collaborations, all partners explore together and contribute their unique perspectives toward a shared purpose; they are forthcoming and responsive to each other; and they are focused and persistent in their efforts to improve the state of affairs for a target audience.

In established coalitions, multiple elements of interaction and goal sharing exist. They have strong leaders who know how to recruit, influence, and motivate others. They are committed to achieving results that are larger than individual accomplishments. They believe in inclusive participation and take time to build trust. They facilitate information sharing and discuss major issues thoroughly. They help design new solutions to complex community problems.

The Environmental Protection Agency

The Environmental Protection Agency (EPA), created by Congress in 1970, has a mission to "protect human health and to safeguard the natural environment—air, water, and land—upon which life depends." Annually, about 50 percent of this independent agency's budget is disbursed as grants to state environmental programs, nonprofits, educational institutions, and others for a wide variety of projects, ranging from environmental technology research to community action cleanups of toxic pollutants. For instance, in working toward a cleaner, healthier environment for the American people, the EPA issued an RFP for "Performance Partnership Grants" (www.epa.gov):

> Improving EPA's partnership with the states and tribes is critical to accelerating environmental outcomes. Performance Partnership Grants (PPGs) are the cornerstone of the National Environmental Performance Partnership System (NEPPS), EPA's strategy to strengthen partnerships and build a results-based management system. PPGs are innovative grant delivery tools that allow states and tribes to combine up to 20 eligible program grants into a single grant with a single budget. PPGs can reduce administrative transaction costs, provide the flexibility to direct resources toward the highest priority environmental problems, and support cross-media approaches and initiatives.
>
> EPA's overarching goal is to optimize the leveraging power of PPGs to strategically focus on the joint priorities of EPA, states and tribes. EPA's ongoing goals for the PPG program are to: (1) strengthen partnerships between EPA, the state, tribes, and interstate agencies through joint planning and priority setting to more effectively deploy resources; (2) provide states, tribes, and interstate agencies with the flexibility to direct resources where they are needed most to address environmental and public health priorities; (3) link program activities more effectively with environmental and public health goals and environmental outcomes; (4) foster implementation of innovative approaches such as pollution prevention, ecosystem management, and community-based environmental protection strategies; and (5) provide savings by streamlining administrative requirements.
>
> There is no low-end limit for PPG awards to tribes. EPA may make awards as small as two programs and thousands of dollars to tribes. EPA may award PPGs that combine up to 19 categorical grants to states. PPGs for larger states exceed $10 million. State PPGs generally contain six or seven categorical grants, with award amounts averaging around $5 million.

The EPA recognized that it must secure the collaboration of many individuals and organizations to protect the environment. Its "Performance Partnership Grants" attempt to forge partnerships with local and state-level organizations to create safe havens where new approaches to environmental protection can be developed without fear of violating regulation agency requirements. Given the complexities of multiple partnerships and ecosystems management, this would require a coalition collaboration to ensure project success.

The Robert Wood Johnson Foundation

The Robert Wood Johnson Foundation has a 10-word mission statement: "to improve the health and health care of all Americans." To realize this ambitious aim, the Foundation likes to field-test promising ideas and evaluate the results; take proven ideas and approaches to scale; give heightened visibility to an issue, idea, or intervention; cause coalitions of like-minded or disparate individuals and groups to form and act around a problem or issue; and reach and engage organizations and institutions that would not otherwise seek philanthropic support. To help children lead healthier lives, the Robert Wood Johnson Foundation issued an RFP for "Faith-based Advocacy: Galvanizing Communities to End Childhood Obesity" (www.rwjf.org):

> America's vastly diverse faith community is active at the national and local levels, within Christian, Jewish, Muslim, Buddhist, interfaith and other settings. Collaborations across faith communities have a rich history of working together for social change. They successfully have advanced policies that improve the health and wellness of communities, and their growing role in prompting policy and triggering action is evident across all states. Faith-based coalitions have been at the forefront of local and state efforts on social issues such as homelessness, tobacco use, hunger and poverty. Today, there is emerging energy among faith-based coalitions to advocate for improved food, nutrition and environmental policies.
>
> Through this solicitation, we are interested in supporting faith-based coalitions to advance community policies or environmental changes that improve access to healthy foods and/or opportunities for physical activity. We are particularly interested in efforts that reach children at greatest risk for obesity, including African-American, Latino, Native American, Asian American and Pacific Islander children who live in low-income communities or communities with limited access to affordable healthy foods and/or safe opportunities for physical activity. Policies and environmental changes should focus on improving the availability of affordable healthy foods and improving access to safe places for children to play. Awardees receive up to $225,000 for a grant period of 24 months in duration.

For this RFP, not only does the Robert Wood Johnson Foundation have an interest in supporting collaborative projects, but as part of the eligibility criteria it also indicates that applicants must be a faith-based coalition. Further, the coalition collaboration must have at least two years' experience in policy advocacy to promote social change. Said differently, coalitions newly formed in response to this RFP need not apply. The Robert Wood Johnson Foundation is vitally concerned about sustainability and thus will allow 15 percent of the total budget to support organizational or collaborative capacity building. The most competitive proposals will demonstrate that project efforts can continue over time without additional Foundation resources.

Collaboration Options

Seldom do RFPs specify the desired level of collaboration—that is, for instance, coexistence, coordination, cooperation, or coalition. Rather, they mention collaboration, and the grant leader must decide what type of collaboration to form *after* inventorying available resource and communication options. To illustrate, consider this operative paragraph from an RFP issued by the Allied Arts Fund, a private foundation based in Harrisburg, Pennsylvania.

> The Fund provides financial support of projects for the purpose of fostering innovative artistic and multicultural opportunities in Central Pennsylvania. The fund also promotes understanding of different cultures through arts, attracts young people to the arts, and promotes collaboration or organizational resources for artistic outcomes. Grants generally range from $500 to $2,000.

While the Allied Arts Fund "promotes collaboration," no further requirements or expectations are articulated. In responding to this RFP, the grant leader has options for forming a collaboration, depending on circumstances. Let's consider examples of how the grant leader might accomplish different types of collaboration.

1. **Coexistence:** The grant leader agrees to paint a series of watercolors on "Life in Rural Appalachia," and a local art gallery agrees to exhibit the paintings. The artist and gallery owner operate independently but reach agreement to collaborate during the exhibition, which is mutually beneficial.

2. **Coordination:** The grant leader convinces other artisans to put on an Appalachian Art Fair one weekend with the help of local radio and TV publicity. The grant leader had extensive communications with both the artists and media personnel to make the event a success.

3. **Cooperation:** The grant leader decides to attract young people to the arts by reaching out to area schools and youth organizations to create an "Awesome Art" after-school program. With the cooperation of teachers and local youth organizations and parents, a 12-week training program is launched that exposes youth to multiple art forms.

4. **Coalition:** The grant leader assembles a community-based Appalachian Arts Advisory Board, whose charge is to raise the community profile through the arts. Multiple initiatives are launched, including art exhibits in local galleries, a Summer Art Fair, after-school programming, and periodic workshops using various media.

Now that you have examined the ways in which RFPs call for collaborations, both explicitly and implicitly, our attention turns to planning and writing your collaborative grant application.

APPLYING COLLABORATION TO THE COMPLETE GRANT APPLICATION

A complete grant application generally includes six basic components: a cover letter, an application form, a project summary, a proposal, a budget and budget narrative, and appendixes. The tendency when writing collaborative grants is to describe the collaboration in only one area, the methods section of the proposal. Here key partners, their qualifications, and their contributions to the project are identified. This approach to proposal writing, however, does not demonstrate the full potential of the collaboration. Collaborative proposals are more persuasive when you take the next step and show how collaboration applies in all areas and sections. In other words, collaboration should be a strong theme that is woven throughout the complete grant application.

Below are some tips on how you might integrate collaboration in each part of the complete grant application, as well as some questions for you to consider. These are just a few suggestions, to get you oriented. With a little thought, you'll be able to come up with further ideas that apply to your next collaborative application.

The Cover Letter

The cover letter is usually the first read but one of the last written components of your grant application. Although a cover letter is generally not long—one to two pages—it affords you an initial opportunity to tell the sponsor about your collaboration as well as your project. A few words or sentences here describing your collaboration will set the stage early on for reviewers, letting them know that yours represents a true collaboration, not one that exists in name only.

Does the cover letter highlight the uniqueness of the collaboration as well as organizational and individual qualifications and capabilities to conduct the project? If there are multiple co-directors for the project, is contact information listed for each one? Have you considered whether to develop special letterhead that includes the logos of collaborating organizations or names of partnering individuals? Do collaborators feel there would be value in having multiple signatures on the cover letter, such as of the highest-ranking individuals from each unit or agency represented? Use the cover letter to connect to the sponsor's interest in supporting collaborative initiatives as well as to overview the purpose of the project.

The Application Form

Some sponsors require you to submit an application form along with your proposal. The elements and formats of application forms vary widely within and among public and private sponsors. At first blush, completing an application form may seem to be a relatively unimportant step in a bureaucratic paperwork process. The reality is that application forms establish and present your credibility—and that of your collaboration—in condensed format.

When these elements are requested and space allows on the application form, have you:

- Given a title to your project that reflects its collaborative nature?
- Listed the names and affiliations of project co-directors?

- Included a summary statement that underscores the breadth and depth of your collaboration?

- Provided a total number of staff and volunteers who will participate in the project?

- Identified that matching funds have been contributed from multiple partners?

- Secured the signatures from top administrators who have the ability to legally commit their respective organizations to the conduct of the project?

Taken collectively, these multiple indicators send a powerful message to reviewers that your commitment to collaboration is genuine.

The Project Summary

The project summary, or abstract, serves as a condensed substitute for the entire proposal. It should be carefully written, providing a cogent synopsis of your collaboration and proposed project. It should provide a quick overview of what you propose to do and a rapid understanding of the project's significance, generalizability, and potential contribution. To ensure consistency of presentation, write the project summary *after* you have completed the proposal.

Your summary should include at least one sentence relating to problems, objectives, methods, and benefits that touch on the collaborative nature of your project: How were partners involved in identifying and describing the problem? To what extent were collaborators engaged in developing specific, measurable project objectives? What key resources are collaborators willing to contribute to implement the targeted methodology? How are the resulting project benefits consistent with the mission, values, and priorities of participating partners? Although brevity is of the utmost concern when writing an abstract, answers to these types of questions foreshadow your depth of planning and commitment to collaboration.

The Proposal

Proposal narratives may range from 3 to 300 pages. Most RFPs request similar *kinds* of information, but the level of *detail* requested may vary considerably. Although they may bear different names, proposals usually include the following sections:

- **Problem:** why is this project needed?
- **Goals:** what are you going to do, in broad terms?
- **Objectives:** what are you going to do, in concrete, measurable terms?
- **Methods:** how are you going to do it?
- **Evaluation:** how are you going to measure effectiveness?
- **Dissemination:** who needs to know about the project?

Interestingly, there is very little relationship between the proposal length and the amount of money requested. You may write 100 pages of detail for a $10,000 grant from one sponsor and five pages of detail for a $1 million grant from another sponsor.

Problem

A problem is a gap, a discrepancy between the way things are and the way things ought to be. To persuade proposal reviewers that your collaboration has identified a significant problem, you must document both (a) the frequency and severity of the current problem and (b) the failure of the status quo to address the need. Said differently, changing an existing and unacceptable situation is the common thread that binds your collaboration together.

Have you conducted a needs assessment with your collaborative partners to identify and prioritize problems in the community? Do you have an infrastructure that requires strengthening so you can produce a greater impact collectively than you might individually? Are you presently duplicating efforts that might be streamlined and more effectively redistributed if you collaborate? Will collaborating allow you to serve more people or existing people better? Does current evidence-based research justify your need for a collaborative approach? Answers to questions like these and similar ones will point the way to explaining why the need exists to address the problem you seek to solve collaboratively.

Goals

Goals represent the idealized dream of what you and your collaborators hope to accomplish. They communicate global purposes and embody hopes, wishes, and aspirations. Goals are written in general terms and provide reviewers with a broad understanding of the main thrusts of your project and collaboration.

What is the big picture vision that you share with your collaborators? Have you looked at your mission, vision, and values statements to identify some conceptual threads that might weave the collaboration together? Do partners subscribe to common guiding principles, such as prevention, enhancement to provide a critical margin of excellence, responsiveness to accelerate existing efforts and stimulate new initiatives, efficacy to support evidence-based efforts, or sustainability to invest in transformational programs that can evolve and become self-sufficient? Compelling goal statements encourage partners to willingly give up individual recognition in order to design and realize new, collective solutions.

Objectives

Objectives are the specific, measurable activities that will help you meet your goals and solve the problems. They spell out in precise terms exactly what will be different at the end of the granting period. When your sponsors fund your collaboration, they are literally "buying" your objectives. When you write your objectives, follow the acronymic advice: "Keep them SIMPLE." Objectives should be specific, immediate, measurable, practical, logical, and evaluable.

To what extent do collaborators agree on pursuing the proposed objectives? What procedures did you follow to ensure that the collaboration is based on a mutual decision to engage in the objectives? Once these objectives are accomplished, how will the collaborators benefit? Your objectives represent the conceptual glue that holds your collaboration together.

Methods

Your methods are your action plan to reach your project goals and eventual dream. The methods section of your collaborative proposal tells how project activities will accomplish your objectives, including your project's sequence, flow, and interrelationships. A time and task chart is one common and successful means of clearly communicating these details in your proposal. This one-page visual summary segments your project into organized steps. In essence, it tells reviewers who is going to do what, when it will be done, and how it will be managed.

Will you begin with a training program so all project participants know the rudiments of effective collaboration? Will you prepare a written Memorandum of Understanding that details what each collaborator brings to the table? Will you develop a collaboration communication plan so appropriate internal and external stakeholders are kept in the know? Will you combine resources? Will you develop a strategy for collaborative decision making? Will you periodically evaluate the progress of the collaboration? These are some of the informational bits you can sprinkle in to let reviewers know how collaboration applies to your methodology section.

Evaluation

Evaluations pinpoint what is really happening in your project so you can improve its efficiency, effectiveness, and equity. That is, you can ensure project funds are being spent wisely, the project is making a difference, and project benefits are being distributed across the target population or community. If you collaboratively developed your proposal objectives and methods, you are already well on your way toward a writing a collaborative evaluation plan. Put differently, you have already agreed on what and how the evaluation process will take place, and now your collaborative planning efforts need only to focus on the approach you will take to collect, interpret, and summarize the data for each objective.

To what extent have project partners discussed whether the evaluation should be conducted by internal or external individuals—or both? Do members of your collaboration have the expertise and experience to objectively evaluate a project such as yours? Have collaborators discussed what questions they will be able to answer as a result of the evaluation? Is a subset of your collaboration willing to serve as an Evaluation Steering Committee to oversee the evaluation process and ensure it meets stated proposal objectives? Have steps been taken to assess collaborators' attitudes and performance at the outset, thus providing baseline data against which to compare during and at the close of the project? Do members of your collaboration know any good evaluation consultants who could be brought in to facilitate evaluation planning in anticipation that they would conduct the evaluation if the project is selected for funding? Answers to questions like these demonstrate a depth of thinking and planning; they demonstrate that the proposal is not a knee-jerk response to an RFP but rather the product of a serious commitment by collaborators to improving the status quo.

Dissemination

Dissemination is the means by which you tell others about your project: its purpose, methods, and results. Project dissemination offers many advantages, including increasing public awareness of your program or project, soliciting additional support, locating more clients, alerting others in your field to new ideas, and adding to the stockpile of knowledge. Let reviewers know that you mutually agreed on your collaborative dissemination plan and the role that each partner will play.

Have collaborators collectively determined who needs to know what types of information, when they need to know it, and how it will be disseminated? Do members of the collaboration have distinct relationships, networks, and distribution lists and systems they can tap to get information into the hands of key stakeholders? Have specific individuals accepted responsibility for creating a Web site, preparing a press release, generating the first draft of a journal article, presenting a paper at a convention, holding a teleconference, or distributing an executive summary to policy makers? Including details such as these will make it apparent to reviewers that each action item is a deliberate part of an overall collaborative dissemination plan.

The Budget and Budget Narrative

A project budget is more than a statement of proposed expenditures. It is an alternate way to express your project, establish its credibility, and judge your project's value. Reviewers will scrutinize your budget to see how well it fits your proposed activities: incomplete budgets are examples of sloppy preparation; inflated budgets are signals of waste; low budgets cast doubt on your planning ability. The budget narrative serves as a bridge between the proposal and the budget. It explains precisely who will be getting how much money and what they will be doing with it. The budget narrative shows the basis of budget calculations and is meant to persuade reviewers that sufficient funds are requested to achieve project goals and objectives in a cost-effective manner. In essence, your budget and budget narrative is as much a credibility statement as your project narrative.

Have collaborators considered establishing Memorandums of Understanding or Subcontract Agreements to formalize fiscal dimensions of the partnership? Have project partners offered cost sharing to further underscore the level of collaboration reflected in the budget section of the proposal? Have collaborators double-checked requested budget items to ensure that they are realistic and allowable under both their institutional and the sponsor's policy guidelines and budgeting practices? Does the budget narrative show sufficient detail so reviewers know how all budget items were calculated? The budget is another place for collaborators to demonstrate that they trust each other to be a good steward of their portion of the grant funds.

The Appendixes

Appendixes contain supportive secondary information that will further strengthen your proposal narrative. They can demonstrate that you have logically and systematically documented and addressed all of the essential elements that will contribute to the success of your collaborative project. Sponsors vary in the number and type of appendix information they allow, but listed here are some of the more common ones along with applications to collaborative grantseeking.

Letters of Support and Commitment

Outside of the proposal narrative itself, letters of support and commitment are powerful tools for demonstrating the full potential of the collaboration. Letters of support, in essence, provide unambiguous testimonies that "This is a great project." These letters are nice, but their impact may be limited. Letters of commitment from all key project personnel, on the other hand, are more persuasive to reviewers because they spell out exactly what resources are being committed to the project. Those letters need to be very specific. They should explain the roles that collaborators have played before, during, and after the proposed project.

- **Before:** What have you done to collaborate before the grant was submitted? Have you worked together in the past on other grant-funded projects? Did you participate in the process of collecting and interpreting community-needs-assessment data? Do you buy in to the project goals and objectives? How and how often have you interacted to date—through periodic informal e-mail exchanges, weekly phone calls, monthly face-to-face meetings, quarterly teleconferences, or other means?

- **During:** How will you propose to collaborate during the grant? What resources are you willing to commit to the success of the project? Will you provide collaborators with access to any of the following: *tangible property* (equipment, databases, software, samples), *personnel* (lab technicians, technology specialists, connections to print and media outlets), *target populations* (patients, minorities, individuals with special needs), *business office services* (printing services, postage, calling cards, conference rooms, food), *intellectual property* (patents, copyrights, trademarks, unique protocols), *financial resources* (cash or in-kind, such as volunteers, use of vehicles, frequent-flier miles, complimentary lodging), or *channels of communication* (e-newsletters, webcasts, teleconferences, site visits, press releases)?

- **After:** To what extent are you willing to commit to project sustainability after the grant is over? Will you maintain comparable levels of personnel effort and financial resources? How will you use the resulting evaluation data and feedback to benefit your work situation? For instance, will you now be able to determine if a particular invention is effective with your target population? Will program enhancements be institutionalized and continue to be offered at no additional cost to the target population? Will a new systems capacity ensure that information and managerial decisions flow in a timely and effective manner?

Exhibit 2.2 provides one example of a letter of commitment that addresses the before, during, and after stages of a grant.

Lists of Board Officials

Lists of board officials are mini Who's Who directories. Sponsors examine these lists to see whether they know anyone on your board or those of your collaborators. If so, sponsors then have another means by which to evaluate the credibility of your organization,

Ms. Carrie Amway
Association for Perinatal Health
101 Main Street
Anytown, USA 12345

Dear Carrie:

I write on behalf of Infant Health Care to whole-heartedly endorse your proposal to create a statewide database that captures pertinent perinatal health information.

Thank you for the opportunity to participate in the development of this proposal. The datapoints now included in your database will serve the multiple needs that exist at Infant Health Care, where we continually strive to understand the factors that contribute to high infant mortality rates. Our two organizations have worked together on past projects and this one represents a systematic continuation of our prior collaborative relationships. We will, once again, join others in this unique learning collaborative.

As the database is being developed, we will serve as a beta test site to refine the data-capturing and report-generating processes. To that end, Infant Health Care will commit project personnel in the form of a representative who will serve on the Perinatal Data Committee, the organizational structure that meets at a minimum four times per year to oversee the entire effort from design to full deployment. Rebecca Anderson, a perinatal clinical nurse specialist with our organization, has served consistently on the Committee and will continue to serve through the duration of the project. Ms. Anderson has taken the lead in designing an interface with Infant Health Care's electronic medical record and your newborn module.

Once the grant concludes, we are committed to continuing our full participation in the learning collaborative since the project goal is aligned with our mission to protect and improve the health and lives of infants, their families, and the greater community. Completion of the database will allow us to access information about all newborns delivered at our facilities.

We will use the data resulting from this expansion to fuel additional quality-improvement initiatives within our organization. In addition, knowledge gained from the data collected about all newborns will inform educational and community-based initiatives focused on improving health outcomes for all infants. This project has the highest level of commitment to success. We eagerly await active participation.

Sincerely,
Mikael M. Victoria, Ph.D., RN
President

EXHIBIT 2.2   Sample Letter of Commitment

your personnel and collaborators, and your project. The listings typically include board officials' names, titles, organizational affiliations, and geographic locations.

Have you consulted with your board officials prior to proposal submission to determine whether they have existing relationships with the sponsor that might be of value in stewarding the application? Have lists of board officials been compiled from each partnering agency for inclusion with the grant application? Have you flagged for the sponsor any key officials who serve the boards of multiple partnering organizations? In addition to possible name recognition, when examined as a whole, these lists can provide the sponsor with insight into the values of your organization and collaboration (e.g., when officials serve on multiple boards, it's not surprising that those organizations elected to collaborate on a project).

Maps of Service Areas

Because a picture is worth a thousand words, in some instances you can add major impact to your application by including a map of the proposed service area. For instance, GPS (global positioning system) and GIS (geographic information system) software was used to model the distribution of debris across northern Texas from the space shuttle *Columbia* disaster in 2003. A map can often communicate at a glance what may take pages of narrative to explain: in a single page, reviewers may be able to see, literally, the connection between your identified gap and proposed improved situation.

Do any of your collaborators have the expertise to use GIS software? Is there distinct value in mapping out the targeted service area? Which features are the most essential to illustrate: the character of the target population as clustered or widely distributed; the target population's proximity to or distance from the services offered at partnering organizations; natural features, such as mountains, valleys, plains, lakes, rivers, and vegetation; or artificial features, such as boundaries, roads, bridges, buildings, and utility supply lines? Socioeconomic and demographic analysis, environmental monitoring, and emergency and disaster response are a few subjects among many that lend themselves immediately and directly to mapping.

Organization Charts

An organization chart visually illustrates the structure of an agency and the relationship among its units and personnel. For collaborative proposals, you may consider including the existing organization charts of individual agencies as well as developing a new chart that shows the relationships among collaborative partners. This allows reviewers to understand precisely where your project fits within your organization and across partner agencies.

Do all project participants know where they fit into the collaboration and how their contributions fit into the "big picture"? Can project participants articulate how other individuals fit into the collaboration? Do collaborators recognize and respect the informal as well as formal chains of command? Can project participants see how the organization chart contributes to transparency, communication flows, and decision-making processes? Lines of authority and responsibility become clearer when represented in graphic form.

Résumés

A résumé summarizes your education, training, skills, employment history, and experiences in concise form so reviewers can see that you possess the qualifications necessary to conduct—plan, implement, and evaluate—your proposed project. Most grant applications call for an abbreviated résumé or biosketch, often two to four pages in length. Collaborative partners sometimes select a standardized format for the proposal résumé so that they all look similar.

Have you included résumés for all of the personnel who are named directly in the proposal narrative? Are résumés for other key individuals included so that there is representation from all partner organizations? Do the résumés contain the detail necessary to put your best collaborative foot forward, to persuade reviewers that partners have the experience and expertise to make the project a success? Did you check to make sure that all résumés are up-to-date? Collecting résumés for all key individuals sends an unmistakable message to reviewers (and collaborators!) that project partners are valued members of the team.

With these writing tips in mind, we next examine reviewers' responses to collaborative grant applications. What follows are examples of both positive and negative reviewer reports.

REVIEWER PERSPECTIVES ON COLLABORATION

Grant reviewers are taking an increasingly closer look at the way collaborations are described in proposals. They will judge what they read as persuasive or unpersuasive. Below are actual comments from some reviewer evaluation forms relative to collaboration. Reviewers were instructed to look closely at the proposed collaborations, among other things, in some academic-community partnership grants. Applicants were asked to provide the following:

1. a clear description of the distinct roles and responsibilities of each collaborator

2. clear evidence of appropriate individual and organizational skills and experiences

3. a clear description of how the partners will capitalize on the strengths and unique skills of each collaborator to achieve impact

4. clear evidence of a commitment to and capacity to achieve the project goals and objectives

As reviewers used these four criteria to evaluate a series of collaborative proposals, they noted the following strengths, which are presented here unedited, except to avoid individual identifiers.

- The collaborators bring a wealth of experience and expertise, and the project is designed to harness and share that expertise across all partners. The multiple areas of specialization will both enhance the leadership potential and skills of the experienced partners while using that expertise to train new team members.

- The collaboration is committed to key partnership principles and they are currently working together on a successful project. The skill and strength of its members are clearly described. Because they have worked together on several projects, the roles and responsibilities of each collaborator are clearly understood.

- The roles of the collaborators are clear. Good demonstration of building on prior experience and utilizing expertise to engage new collaborators. Shared oversight is important to achieving success.

- The collaboration aims to have inclusive participation through an advisory group to ensure an economically and culturally-mixed population base.

- Collaborators are identified by name, academic degree, title, and responsibilities. In addition, collaborators have worked together on a previous grant-funded initiative. The lead applicant has a strong reputation for effectively reaching the target population with information, opportunity, and support to improve their quality of life.

- A clear description of the distinct roles and responsibilities of each collaborator is provided. Appropriate individual and organizational skills and experiences are represented. The proposed collaboration plan clearly describes how they will measure both project and collaboration effectiveness.

As you might suspect, reviewer responses are not always favorable. Next we "turn the coin over" and present some feedback from the same reviewers using the same criteria to judge a different set of proposals. Their less-than-enthusiastic reactions include:

- There is no spirit of collaboration in this proposed relationship. The role of one community partner is basically to provide access to the target population; they appear to have had minimal if any input into the design or evaluation of this project. The budget is largely reflective of this imbalance as the community partner receives little funding.

- There is no history of these partners working together and little evidence exists that they have worked together in the preparation of this grant application.

- The application would be stronger if the collaboration was described in greater detail. It's not clear why these two organizations were drawn into a potential partnership in the first place and what administrative procedures will be instituted to ensure active engagement, timely communication, and fiscal and programmatic accountability.

- The affected population is in no way involved in the design or conduct of this study. This does not suggest a strong collaborative relationship.

- There is no mention of having any of the actual target population as collaborators at the table in providing perspective, direction, and insight.

- The Partnership Organization Chart illustrates the partners as being co-equals but the Time and Task Chart does not reflect that same equality.

These positive and negative comments may be helpful as you draft your next proposal. Remember to reflect the perspective of the reviewers. In the following chapters, specific steps and examples are presented to ensure that your proposal is persuasive.

To review: so far we have identified four different types of collaborations, looked at them from the perspective of grantmakers and various categories of grantseekers, and offered suggestions on how the concept of collaboration applies to sections of the complete grant application. We next turn our attention to the dynamics that facilitate or inhibit collaborations.

CHAPTER 3

Collaboration Dynamics

Always bear in mind that your own resolution to succeed is more important than any other.

—Abraham Lincoln

After reading the first two chapters of this book, which laid the foundation for collaborative grantseeking, you now appreciate that the broad concept of collaboration can be defined and implemented in many grants. Within any collaboration, different types may exist among participants. Grant leaders need to distinguish among types of collaboration for two main reasons. First, sponsors are increasingly requiring collaborations in their RFPs, as chapter 2 indicates. Second, many proposal writers either fail to differentiate among types of collaboration or propose what reviewers quickly recognize as a "phantom collaboration." Accordingly, you can gain a competitive edge in grant applications by making such a differentiation.

In this chapter, we will discuss the key details that grant leaders must manage in crafting successful grant collaborations. This includes careful review of collaboration dynamics, completing each of the pre-collaboration steps, meticulous selection of collaborators and team members, outlining the plans for ongoing evaluations, and establishing clear lines of communication. In essence, careful work must be done in advance of developing and administering a collaborative grant project.

Some people see collaboration as the "dream team" approach to solving complex problems. Others observe that such projects often fail and produce fewer results than "going it alone." From our perspective, collaboration is an approach to solving problems whose success or failure is the result of the human dynamics that are brought to bear and the grant leader's ability to manage those dynamics. In the discussion that follows, we examine grant leadership and the human dynamics that make collaborations work successfully and address those that cause them to fail.

DYNAMIC FACTORS OF COLLABORATION

Organizational psychology, business management, health care, and sociology literature identify a number of dynamic factors that positively influence or impede successful collaborations, such as commitment, communication, conflict management, goal orientation, risk tolerance, and trust. For grantseeking purposes, we find it useful to cluster these dynamic factors around our two key dimensions of collaboration—namely, goal sharing and interaction.

Exhibit 3.1 presents 24 dynamic factors that are found in various degrees in grant collaborations. Coalition collaborations have the most interplay of goal sharing and interaction and thus they typically have more dynamic factors and factors of high intensity. Coexistence collaborations represent the least amount of interaction and goal sharing and, consequently, they exhibit fewer dynamic factors or factors of low intensity. Cooperation and coordination collaborations have dynamic factors relating to goal sharing and interaction, respectively.

For example, a cooperation collaboration may demonstrate high levels of goal consensus, growth, intelligence, persistence, priorities, and challenges, and low levels of achievement, conflict management, group affiliation, and thinking orientation. In practical terms, this means that the collaborative partners agree on the project goal, have the know-how to tackle a major undertaking, and are willing to push each other, but they still identify themselves as individuals first and as a team second, so unresolved tensions may eventually cause the project to plateau below its full potential.

Goal Sharing	Interaction
• accountability	• challenges
• achievement level	• change orientation
• commitment	• communication
• effort	• conflict management
• goal consensus	• diplomacy
• goal orientation	• emotion
• growth	• feedback
• intelligence	• group affiliation
• motivation to pursue goal	• social competence
• persistence	• thinking orientation
• priorities	• time management
• risk tolerance	• trust

EXHIBIT 3.1. Dynamic Factors in Collaborations

DETERMINING THE APPROPRIATE TYPE OF COLLABORATION

As a grant leader, you may wonder: Is it worth the effort to collaborate on this project? How do I figure out which type of collaboration I need for my project? Which type of collaboration is best? Do all of my potential partners share the same understanding of what it means to collaborate? How much leadership do I need to exert? Which type of collaboration does the sponsor expect? How do I convey the strength of my collaboration in the grant proposal?

Beginning grantseekers, when they have decided to collaborate, often do not differentiate among types. Or worse, they pick a type of collaboration and then make it fit the proposal requirements. Experienced grantseekers typically do the opposite. That is, they analyze the RFP, carefully select collaborators, and mutually determine the level of interaction and goal sharing they wish to have in order to successfully complete the project. Once those decisions are made, then they identify the type of collaboration that best fits their situation. Said differently, decisions about the appropriate type of collaboration are best made *after* the conceptual shell of the proposal is established, not *before*. Chapter 2 offers suggestions for shaping this conceptual shell.

While all collaborators should help shape the proposal—defining the problem, goals, objectives, methods, evaluation, dissemination, and budget—the grant leader bears a special responsibility to ensure that the requisite dynamic factors work in concert to achieve project success. Clearly, the role of leadership is a major element in successful collaborations.

The Role of Leadership

Grant Leaders

Every grant should be led by an individual—possibly the person who originated the idea for it—who has a deep passion for, and a sustained commitment to, the project. Whether they are called Principal Investigators, Program Directors, Project Managers, or some similar name, grant leaders must have thorough knowledge of all project elements, possess demonstrated management skills, exhibit enthusiasm and drive, and be free from hidden agendas and conflicts of interest.

Robert House and colleagues (1999) put forth a definition of leadership that is particularly suited to the context of collaborative grantseeking: "the ability to influence, motivate, and enable others to contribute toward the effectiveness and success of the organizations of which they are members" (p.13). Grant leaders must take responsibility for partnership formation; inspire people involved in the partnership; empower people involved in the partnership; communicate a partnership vision; foster respect, trust, inclusiveness, and openness; resolve conflict among partners; and combine the perspectives, resources, and skills of partners.

Grant leaders must exert their leadership skills in a manner that ensures an environment of equality among partners. All collaborators must trust the grant leader. That trust is built through a combination of winning behaviors and attitudes, including ongoing communication, mutual knowledge and respect of one another's strengths, the desire to work together to help all parties succeed, and an empowering environment of shared leadership. Without strong leadership, the result is predictably chaos and collaboration failure.

Frequent communication is a powerful trust-building tool for leaders. In many organizational units, communication flows more readily inward and upward than it does outward and downward. Leaders can strengthen their collaborations by increasing top-down communications. For example, you can publish agendas in advance of meetings and minutes after the meetings, and you can publish summaries of key discussions and actions. Collaborators often value having an understanding of the process by which decisions are made, so communications can make clear whether a course of action was determined by the grant leader alone, by the grant leader in consultation with a kitchen cabinet group of advisors, by consensus, or by majority vote.

Failure to communicate regularly and effectively initiates an emotional behavior chain reaction, as Rosabeth Moss Kanter (2004, pp.97–98) notes. Specifically, when communication decreases, it triggers the following negative results.

- Criticism and blame increases.
- Respect decreases.
- Isolation increases.
- Focus turns inward.
- Rifts widen and inequities grow.
- Initiative decreases.
- Aspirations diminish.
- Negativity spreads.

The consequence is low performance or even failed collaborations. The grant leader's job is to establish the right culture for successful collaborations. Leadership is more about building confidence in others than building personal achievements.

Project Co-Leaders

Skilled grant leaders recognize the value of power sharing, which may result in the creation of project co-leaders, depending on the specific form of collaboration. For instance, in a cooperation collaboration, such factors as location and distance, complexity of the project, number of people and service sites involved, and shared resources requiring close local supervision could argue for project co-leadership. On the other hand, in a co-ordination collaboration, its very nature argues more for a single leader who is responsible for monitoring all activities and elements of the project regardless of the location of project participants.

While distributing administrative, fiscal, and programmatic responsibilities may promote ownership and active engagement from multiple partners, some sponsors do not formally recognize project co-leaders. The National Science Foundation, for example, does not infer any distinction between multiple principal investigators or co-principal investigators; the first individual listed on the application form will serve as the point of contact for all communications. Ironically, there are other sponsors who require collaboration as an eligibility criterion in their RFP guidelines but do not allow project co-leaders to be named on their application forms; one person must be named as the overall grant leader.

In cases where sponsors acknowledge only a single grant leader, that specific individual typically retains authority to delegate administrative, financial, and programmatic responsibilities to others, as appropriate, to ensure that the project is completed on time and on budget. That is to say, collaborative partners may recognize the position and status of project co-leaders even if sponsors do not. One major challenge with the project co-leader situation involves communication among collaborators; project co-leaders may forget with whom and what they should be communicating. The bottom line in determining when a project co-leader is needed or will work goes back directly to the insights of the leader who initiated the grant proposal.

PRE-COLLABORATION STEPS

Before a collaboration is agreed upon and a collaborative grant proposal is drafted, grant leaders should go through four specific pre-collaboration steps. These steps identify the requisite attitudes and actions you should follow to prepare for and form a successful collaboration.

1. **Introspection:** Can you lead a collaboration?

2. **Conceptualization:** Do you understand your proposed project?

3. **Identification:** Have you targeted top-quality collaborators?

4. **Selection:** Have you decided on which partners can best contribute to the project's success?

The first two steps focus more internally, on your capacity to lead; while the last two focus more externally, on your interactions with collaborators. Each step is discussed in detail below. The outcome of this four-step process indicates the extent to which goal sharing and interaction are likely to occur during the granting period.

Step One: Introspection

Do you have what it takes to lead a successful collaboration?

John Gardner (1990) observed that no one type of leader fits all situations or contexts. Under the right circumstances and in the right context, almost any competent person can be an effective leader. For instance, a grant leader who would be an outstanding guide for a collaboration between two small, local nonprofit agencies that share common goals might fail miserably as the leader of a statewide multi-institutional collaboration. The contexts are totally different.

Recognizing that approximately half of all collaborative ventures fail, the first pre-collaboration step is the reality-check inventory of your leadership characteristics. An honest assessment of your strengths and weaknesses can help you determine which types of collaborations you are suited to lead and when you might need complementary styles of leadership to make change happen.

In exhibit 3.2 we reorganized Gardner's leadership characteristics as they relate to goal sharing and interaction. It is not necessary to possess high concentrations of all

Goal Sharing	Interaction
• adaptability; flexibility of approach	• ascendance; dominance; assertiveness
• accept responsibility	• capacity to motivate
• capacity to manage, decide, set priorities	• confidence
• courage; resolution; steadiness	• display trust
• intelligence and judgment-in-action	• physical vitality and stamina
• need to achieve	• skill in dealing with people
• task competence	• understanding of constituents and their needs

EXHIBIT 3.2.   Leadership Characteristics

characteristics to be a great leader. To meet the needs of the type of collaboration, you must have the right mix of attributes at appropriate levels.

For example, to lead a successful coordination collaboration you may need high levels of the following: capacity to motivate; skill in dealing with people; understanding of constituents and their needs; and capacity to manage, decide, and set priorities. You may be fine with low levels of physical vitality and stamina; ascendance, dominance, and assertiveness; and courage, resolution, and steadiness. That is to say, once the goal and course of action is framed, you can focus on inspiring collaborators to act rather than attempting to take charge in a forceful way. Other types of collaboration may require different combinations of leadership characteristics.

Step Two: Conceptualization

Can you imagine your project so vividly that it becomes real?

One challenge in preparing a grant proposal is writing clear goals and measurable objectives. The difficulty often lies in the fact that there is only a general understanding of the problem that needs to be addressed. The overarching concept of the proposal and the intended processes and outcomes are unclear because the magnitude of the gap is not fully understood.

Perhaps the problem has grown considerably in a short period of time and there has not been a concomitant growth in your organization's ability to address the need. Collaboration has become a survival imperative. By eliminating duplicated services, partners will be able to reallocate resources to help close the gap. In other words, a well-defined rationale for the project is a means to triggering the vision for an improved future and specific activities to solve the problem.

Before embarking on any type of collaboration, the problems and potential solutions to be presented to prospective collaborators should be as plain and complete as possible, based on the information available at the time. Concepts do and should change with input from others and from changes in circumstances. But identifying a targeted need and preliminary goals will greatly facilitate the process of forging a successful collaboration.

Approaching a potential collaborator and saying, for example, "Let's get together and see if we can design a new reading curriculum," is a waste of time. This statement focuses on the process you want and does not invite the potential partner to engage in a collaborative endeavor. It is better to start with the baseline situation and define the outcome you have in mind—for example, "Like you, I'm concerned about the growing numbers of students who are reading below grade level. Let's see if together we can find a way to raise reading skills by one grade level in six months." Then present your initial vision of what the proposal would entail before deciding what type of collaboration, in your judgment at this time, could work best to achieve the desired result. A shared understanding of the starting and ending points establishes a firm communication ground for continuing conceptual discussions and logistical negotiations with possible collaborators.

Conceptual clarity is achieved through a rigorous goal analysis (Mager 1997). Your project goals represent the "big picture" vision of what you want to accomplish in your grant. Goals come in all shapes and sizes, sound important, and refer to individuals, organizations, and communities, as in the following examples: to build self-confidence, to improve workforce skills, and to provide a healthy environment. Project goals are things you can hope for but can never directly measure.

As part of your goal analysis, you must also identify the performances that represent your meaning of the goal, the evidence you will accept that your goals have been achieved. For example, an individual with renewed self-confidence will be able to look in the mirror and smile, give a speech in a packed auditorium, and negotiate a better price on a major household appliance; an organization with enhanced workforce skills can increase its net revenue, reduce processing errors, and retain 95 percent of its employees for two years or more; a community with a healthy environment stays within federally accepted limits of ozone, offers quality public transportation programs for the elderly, and provides extracurricular activities for children.

The point of the goal analysis is to operationally define your project goals. If the outcomes are achieved, then all partners can readily agree that the goals have been met. Regardless of the type of collaboration—coexistence, cooperation, coordination, or coalition—effective grant leaders have preliminary goal statements in mind as they begin talking to potential collaborators. These goal statements, though they may be refined further as discussions continue, help to focus project energies and unify would-be partners.

Step Three: Identification

Where do you find potential project partners?

Martin Linsky and Ronald Hiefetz (2002) remind us that finding good collaborators inside and outside your organization takes time and effort. In rare instances, an RFP might require specific categories of collaborators to be included: "It is expected that there will be active engagement and participation of core representatives on the coalition, including such groups as: community-based organizations, schools, medical service providers, public health and environmental agencies, academic institutions, childcare providers, businesses, religious organizations, media, voluntary health agencies, and community residents." Even then, it is still up to the grant leader to locate individuals who fit into these groups. It's time to begin consulting your networks.

Consider whether you have colleagues inside your organization and friends outside your organization that might play a role in your project; perhaps you had a positive experience collaborating with some of them on a non-grant-funded project in the past and can build on that relationship of trust. Ask your colleagues and friends for recommendations of other individuals and organizations with whom you could possibly collaborate. In particular, seek out individuals that have a reputation for achieving results, and seek out organizations that have a track record of success.

Leverage relationships with potential sponsors. Talk with your congressional officials and state legislators to see whether they can direct you toward possible sources of public funding and toward other organizations that share similar community concerns; providing these types of constituency services to the public is one way that government officials get reelected. Contact private foundations that you would like to approach in the future and ask them to share the names of a few grantees who they consider to be "star performers." Approach organizations that have already received funding and investigate teaming up with them on a future grant application; in this way, you build off of their credibility to establish yours with a sponsor.

Tap into the networking resources offered through professional associations. Participate in conferences to learn about best practices from a community of professionals who share similar interests, roles, responsibilities, and geographic areas; attendees could become project mentors, advisors, coaches, and volunteers. Engage in discussion groups, summer institutes, and online forums to hear firsthand where your counterparts turn to find collaborators for their projects; in some cases you may be able to adopt similar strategies to identify your own would-be partners.

Take advantage of community resources. Visit area libraries; librarians are information experts who can suggest resources, locate and acquire materials, recommend strategies, navigate technologies, and make connections among disparate ideas and peoples. Consult your nearest nonprofit center to identify other nonprofit leaders and volunteers who may facilitate collective community action. Contact the local chamber of commerce to link up with business leaders and economic drivers who care about making an impact on the future of your region.

Search online for organizations that have missions, values, and services similar to yours. Enter key words into search engines such as Google (www.google.com), Yahoo! (www.yahoo.com), and Exalead (www.exalead.com/search). Explore the Web sites of the Foundation Center (www.foundationcenter.org) and GuideStar (www.guidestar.org) to locate potential nonprofit partners. Look at the Web sites of the Better Business Bureau (www.bbb.org) and ThomasNet (www.thomasnet.com) to find businesses, manufacturers, distributors, and service providers.

Step Four: Selection

How do you know a potentially successful collaborator when you see one?

Getting the right people on the team (and the wrong people off the team) is a top priority and responsibility of the leader (Collins 2001). There is no room in a collaboration for partners who, deep down, don't consider themselves as partners. Grant leaders must ensure that all collaborators feel comfortable, even when confronting each other, and are willing to stand up for each other, as appropriate. It's likely that collaborators enjoy relationships with many other groups and won't abandon their previous commitments, so you must have a litmus test for selecting the right people.

As you screen potential collaborators, your communications might be rather informal (e.g., reviewing online résumés or talking with past collaborators) or they might be somewhat formal (e.g., interviewing candidates or conducting reference checks). These strategies attempt to look at an individual's qualifications, preparation, and accomplishments and are built on the premise that "past behavior is the best predictor of future performance" (Green 1986, p. 12).

Gathering competency-based information means examining both positive and negative situations. The following types of questions are not designed to "trap" individuals; rather, the answers reveal how individuals react to adverse circumstances, their decision-making processes, their respect for rules, and their willingness to ask for help.

- Tell me about a recent problem in which old solutions didn't work. How did you analyze the situation and solve the problem?

- How do you keep your various stakeholders in the loop with regard to issues and strategies that affect them?

- Describe how you have organized activities in order to accomplish the best results when you have multiple competing priorities and requests as well as limited resources.

- Give me an example of a time when a major project did not come through as anticipated. What went wrong?

- Tell me about a time when you were asked to do something you felt was unnecessary and maybe even detrimental to a project. What actions did you take?

Beyond identifying an individual's strengths and weaknesses, your probing should help determine "goodness of fit." You should be able to answer key questions such as "Does this individual reflect sensitivity to my organizational mission and values? Is this someone with whom I could work on a collaborative project? Is this someone with whom other partners could work?" Jim Collins (2001) argues that selecting "the right people" means placing a greater weight on character attributes (e.g., work ethic, basic intelligence, dedication to fulfilling commitments, and values) than on teachable traits (e.g., specific educational background, practical skills, specialized knowledge, or work experience). A strong cultural fit matters more than basic skills.

In reality, collaborators may come and go for many reasons. Relocation, promotion with new responsibilities, limited time to devote to the project, illness, and loss of interest are not uncommon. Circumstances are difficult to predict. Potentially nonperforming or poorly performing partners, however, can be identified with proper pre-collaboration interviewing. Some partners are motivated to "join up" just for the association or prestige of being involved; they never really intend to do much. Others become partners simply as a way to pursue their own interests. Friendly talks, subtle but targeted questioning, and even formal interviewing can reveal these motivations and, at the same time, allow the competent partners to rise to the top of the candidate pool for you to select.

STAGES OF CHANGE

The purpose of the pre-collaboration steps is to examine inclination, capacity, and likelihood for forming a successful collaboration. This includes self-evaluation as well as assessment of potential partners. As the grant leader, you have been thinking about collaboration quite a bit and have already bought in to the benefits that it can produce. On the other hand, for your would-be partners, collaborating—or more specifically, collaborating with you—may be a brand-new idea.

The potential collaborators that you identified in pre-collaboration step 3 and selected in step 4 may range from early adopters, who recognize immediately the benefits of collaboration, to late adopters, who require additional time to warm up to the idea of collaboration. That is to say, it may take several exchanges with some of your potential partners to secure their full buy-in.

In practical terms, your invitation to collaborate asks people to change the way they normally operate, to think and act in a different way. James Prochaska, Carlo DiClemente, and John Norcross (1992) have identified six stages of change, which we have applied to the concept of collaborative grantseeking. These stages represent the process by which individuals change their intentions and behaviors over time.

Pre-contemplation Stage: Individuals have no intent of participating in a collaboration. They may be unaware, unwilling, or unable to collaborate. They may be naïve about the benefits of collaboration. They may be skittish about joining a collaboration because of a negative experience with one in the past. They may not feel empowered or have the authority to commit to a collaboration. They hold an attitude of "Hey, I'm doing fine by myself."

Contemplation Stage: Individuals are aware of both the benefits and challenges of collaborating. They recognize that a problem exists and that something must be done about it. They think about the possibilities change can produce, but they are not sure they want to make a change. Indecision prevents them from taking action, so they procrastinate. Their predominant thinking might be "Hey, maybe something should be done."

Preparation Stage: Individuals have seriously considered joining the collaboration and intend to act in the near future. They have collected the information they needed to make a decision. They have identified the steps to be taken to move forward. They have a plan of action and are motivated to begin implementing it. Someone in this stage might say, "Hey, let's meet next week on Tuesday at two o'clock to figure out how we might work together."

Action Stage: Individuals have committed to participating in the collaboration. They modify past behaviors in order to allocate time and energy to this new partnership. They are excited by a joint approach to solving community problems and want to be actively involved. They consult others to understand roles and responsibilities and the levels of interaction and goal sharing. They ask, "Hey, what are the specific resources and communication options we can all bring to the table?"

Maintenance Stage: Individuals work to sustain the partnership. They recognize the benefit and value of collaborating with others. They offer positive reinforcement and social support. They celebrate successes. They are convinced that working together produces a greater impact than going it alone. New patterns of behavior have replaced the old. They state, "Hey, we've got a good thing going here and we should keep it that way."

Termination Stage: Individuals have adopted a growth mindset for collaboration. They fully embrace and express behaviors that support the group. They are not deterred by minor setbacks. They are in favor of setting aside permanently some of their individual goals and instead supporting joint group goals. They may propose, "Hey, we should form a new and permanent organization with goals that will be our focus for the long term."

More broadly, by recognizing at which stage your potential partners and later your partners are—revealed by their behaviors and expressed intentions—you can respond appropriately to address their concerns and needs. For instance, in the early stages, you may provide information about the magnitude and severity of the problem, facilitate visualization of the consequences of maintaining the status quo, and break down the solution into manageable chunks or steps. In the later stages, you may give group praise and individual recognition, maintain self-efficacy through accountability system reporting, and monitor opportunities for programmatic, administrative, and financial growth. These logical and psychological touch points help potential collaborators see themselves as valued team members.

COLLABORATIVE CAPACITY BUILDING

Successful collaborations don't just arise out of the ashes like the phoenix, replete with vigor and splendor. Rather, collaborations must initially build the capacity for success. If you are starting a new collaboration, regardless of type, you must demonstrate to grant reviewers that you have the know-how to successfully complete the project. If you already have a collaboration in place, you must show grant reviewers that it is being sustained and perhaps even expanded.

Christopher Potter and Richard Brough (2004) point out that the term "capacity building" is too broad a concept to be useful. They view systemic capacity building as a cluster of nine separate but interrelated components, described below. Their broader view of collaboration is particularly useful in identifying the collective resources that must exist in order to manage a collaboration effectively.

Performance Capacity: Are adequate tools and financial resources available to implement the project? Do partners have the requisite equipment, technologies, software, databases, resource manuals, health records, medications, diagnostic tests, and survey instruments? Can collaborators access cash and in-kind contributions, such as office supplies, postage, and transportation?

Personal Capacity: Do collaborators have the knowledge, skills, and abilities to be successful in their work? Are they empowered and confident in their decision making? Is there a need to provide role-specific or general training, such as bloodborne pathogen, cultural sensitivity, information technology, interpersonal skills, managerial skills, or sexual harassment?

Workload Capacity: Are enough collaborative partners available to handle workload requirements? Are people deployed in appropriate areas? Is there flexibility to temporarily reallocate human resources to respond to urgent demands? Do individuals have the necessary skill set to perform agreed-upon duties?

Supervisory Capacity: Have clear lines of authority and accountability been established? Are the means for monitoring, reporting, and evaluating performance understood?

Are there known consequences for poor performance and failure to complete tasks? Conversely, is there opportunity for recognition and reward for a job well done?

Facility Capacity: Is there enough space for projects to be implemented, both programmatically and administratively? Are basic facilities such as classrooms, fitness centers, kitchens, laboratories, offices, training rooms, and storage spaces available for use at the times they are needed? Are the facilities readily accessible by collaborative partners and the target population?

Support Service Capacity: Is there access to the requisite administrative support, financial management, human resource, logistics management, quality assurance, research and statistical support, supply organizations, tech support, and technical assistance services? Can the support services deliver quality results in a timely and cost-effective manner?

Structural Capacity: Are there appropriate executive, finance, fundraising, marketing, and membership committees for making decisions, maintaining records, implementing policy, and ensuring accountability? Has appropriate legal status been obtained to be eligible to apply for and receive grants, such as a nonprofit 501(c)(3) designation with the Internal Revenue Service?

Systems Capacity: Are key decisions and other information shared with collaborators in a timely manner? Are processes and procedures established for accessing internal reports, entering and retrieving database information, and tracking expenditures and filing for reimbursements? Are networks in place to engage the target audience, sponsors, and other key stakeholders?

Role Capacity: Do individuals understand their roles in the collaborative project? Are responsible personnel, activities, and timeframes delineated on the time and task chart? Do formal Memorandums of Agreement exist that specify responsibilities to be carried out, financial and discretionary decision-making authority, channels of communication, and evaluation criteria?

These nine components address the observable aspects of capacity building—tools; skills; staff and infrastructure; structures, systems, and roles—that collaborators can identify as their contribution to the new partnership. The time and task chart can spell out who will do what and when. Obviously, not all elements need to exist before a collaboration can move forward. At the same time, more complex collaborations may have many of these elements in place.

MEASURING COLLABORATIONS

Evaluations ensure a measure of accountability—to the target audience, to the sponsor, and to collaborators. That is, in addition to evaluating project results, collaborative grant projects bear a special obligation to assess the partnership itself. Since partners' perceptions may change due to changing circumstances, it is essential to periodically examine their take on the collaboration.

For assessment purposes, we measure five attributes for each of our two main dimensions of collaboration, namely goal sharing and interaction.

Goal Sharing

1. **Leadership:** The ability to influence, motivate, and enable others to contribute toward the success of shared goals

2. **Commitment:** The combined action of collaborators to achieve something larger than individual accomplishments

3. **Decision Making:** The process of mutually identifying problems and implementing solutions through discussion, negotiation, and conflict resolution

4. **Resources:** The sharing of human, physical, and fiscal resources, goods and services essential for an effective collaboration

5. **Evaluation:** The use of sound measurement tools to determine progress toward goal achievement and make adjustments as necessary

Interaction

1. **Administrative Management:** The collaboration's use of its resources

2. **Incentives:** Factors that motivate involvement in the collaboration

3. **Communication:** Clear, open, frequent communication among project leaders and collaborators

4. **Value of Participation:** Getting something of benefit from participating in the collaboration

5. **Satisfaction with Participation:** The feeling of gratification that comes with participation in the collaboration

Rather than use a generic survey tool that may be insensitive to your needs, we prefer to guide you through the process of developing a tailored instrument that meets your specific situation. Chapter 9 contains a pool of 180 potential questionnaire items, covering these 10 attributes, from which you can select the ones most appropriate for measuring your collaboration.

These questionnaire items can be used for formative evaluation purposes; that is, they can be administered at the *onset* of the project to establish baseline data and then again at appropriate intervals *during* the project to provide immediate feedback for monitoring the collaboration. With slight changes in verb tense, you can administer them *after* the project is completed, thereby providing you with summative evaluation feedback to document the worth of the collaboration. Follow the three-step process in chapter 9 to generate your own questionnaire. Walid El Ansari (1999) and the Center for Advancement of Collaborative Strategies in Health (2006) also provide information about surveys regarding the effectiveness of collaborations.

TERMINATING A COLLABORATOR

Arnold Schwarzenegger made his movie reputation as a terminator, not as a collaborator. A time may come when you, as the grant leader, will need to terminate a collaborator—not in the sense that Hollywood has given us, of course, but rather in terms of meeting your overall project goals and maintaining the overall chemistry of the collaboration.

Most likely, your collaborations will include diverse personalities who will pose occasional difficulties with which you must cope. Rather than pulling the collaborative plug as a first response, use your best people-management skills to deal with what Robert Bramson (1988) calls "difficult people." Below are three common situations that experienced grant leaders refer to as "Prozac periods."

Situation One: Agreeable Abby. Abby is what you would call a "super-agreeable" person. In your collaborative meetings she is so friendly, responsive, and compliant. She'll agree to anything you ask, *until* it comes time for action: a signed letter of support, an introduction to a foundation executive, or documentation of her cost-sharing commitment. Super-agreeables tell you what you want to hear, but later they are apt to let you down.

To cope with Agreeable Abby, tell her directly that you value her as a person, make honesty nonthreatening, be personal when you can, and set deadlines for reasonable commitments. For instance, "I appreciate your enthusiasm and willingness to take this on. You have a pretty full plate already. Will you be able to get it done and e-mail it to me by the end of the day on Wednesday? Otherwise we could ask another volunteer to step forward."

Situation Two: Silent Sam. Sam shows up for collaborative meetings and takes your phone calls but displays little interest or enthusiasm. He doesn't even argue. It's as if he is just putting in his time because someone told him to do so. When you raise ideas or ask questions, you expect a reasonable and relevant response, but Sam just clams up, and it is maddening.

To cope with Silent Sam, ask open-ended questions, wait for a response, avoid filling the silence with conversation, and, if you get no response, comment on what is happening. For example, "We've opened up several issues here and I'm getting little response. Everyone here has good ideas that we need to hear. Speak now, or run the risk of inheriting something you don't agree with or don't like."

Situation Three: Nancy Know-It-All. Nancy knows everything there is to know about your project and how successful collaborations work. She's "been there, done that." She's quick to explain why something won't work—or will. She conveys a belief in her own superiority that often leaves collaborators feeling humiliated, immobilized, and frustrated.

To cope with Nancy Know-It-All, you must do your homework, listen and acknowledge, question firmly without confronting, avoid being a counter-expert, and deal with her in a one-on-one basis, when possible. To illustrate, "You've raised some valid points. Let's take a few minutes after this meeting for the two of us to talk off-line about your viewpoints. Who else from the group would like to share their current thinking about this matter?"

In spite of your best efforts to select appropriate collaborators, things may not always work out as hoped and planned; you may end up with an Abby, a Sam, or a Nancy on your project team. Perhaps your collaborators were selected for reasons that were not as sound as they might be or reasons outside the true interests of the project, such as partnering with individuals solely because of an obligation you felt to a colleague, your boss's commitment, an organization's prestigious reputation, political connections, gender and diversity considerations, or geographic representation. The list could go on, but these examples are not uncommon.

It is true that everyone makes mistakes, and unanticipated circumstances sometimes arise. When a collaborator is hampering the effort, the grant leader must decide whether to end the collaborative relationship or allow a "second chance." If you decide to end the collaboration, this action must be weighed against the consequences of the loss of partners and the impact of their absence on the project's continuation and outcome. Hopefully, circumstances will never reach this point. Careful selection of partners at the outset, monitoring and measuring progress on a regular basis, and frequent communication and contact are the best recipe for insuring against the need for such measures.

Planning for Second-Chance Success

Experienced grant leaders usually devise a plan that allows troublesome collaborators to improve their performance and stay with the project. The aim is to set them up for success. Termination on an impromptu basis may be unfair, and it can undermine the morale and motivation of other people in the project. The partner's friends and colleagues may be negatively affected and the entire project jeopardized, not just the role of the individual.

In planning for second-chance success, grant leaders recognize an important principle of behavior that applies to both humans and animals: *organization prevents reorganization.* Grandma said it better: "It's hard to teach an old dog new tricks."

All of us fall into patterns of behavior in our daily lives and in our work. When faced with a task or multiple tasks, we organize ways of resolving them that seem to work and are within our comfort zone. Once this organization is in place, it is difficult for us to change. In fact, we resist change sometimes to the point of refusing to change. This principle must be kept in mind when trying to help people alter their habits. Losing weight, starting an exercise program, and giving up smoking, for instance, are major and difficult changes with high failure rates.

Planning for a second chance applies at two levels: (1) when initially selecting a potential collaborator and (2) when dealing with unacceptable performance midstream in the project. While your first impression may be to avoid selecting a potential collaborator on the basis of past performance or recent information, it may be necessary to take a second look at a candidate because of special resources or talent, a small candidate pool, or unavailability of other candidates. When the decision is made to give a candidate a second chance, detailed planning of performance expectations is crucial; that is to say, mutually acceptable performance benchmarks must be established to which both partners agree to be held.

The second level of success planning occurs when termination of the collaborator is justified based on performance metrics and observation. Developing the second-chance plan is a combined effort between the grant leader and the collaborator. Some people simply don't have effective self-management strategies and this undermines their performance on a daily basis. Subtle changes, such as getting to work on time, planning an effective workday schedule, keeping appointments, attending meetings regularly, and performing tasks on time can sometimes transform a collaborator whose current performance fails to meet expectations into a solid performer. Exhibit 3.3 lists seven tips for developing a second-chance plan, and a sample retention script is provided in chapter 10.

The last point in establishing a second-chance plan—stating the desired outcome—is vital. If a person's heart really isn't in it, if a very low dedication exists, or if an underlying need exists to get out from under it, then the plan is likely to fail. Otherwise, it is a plan designed to set an individual up to succeed. It is specific in detail.

1. Stay friends, or at least stay in a positive relationship.

2. Avoid blaming, pointing fingers, and finding fault.

3. Refer to documented facts, reports, and progress and lack thereof, but stay focused on the "big picture," the benefits of collaborating, the goals of the project, and, most important, the outcomes described in the proposal.

4. Acknowledge the partner's achievements—no one typically fails 100 percent of the time.

5. Focus in detail on what has been done as well as what needs to be done. Point out the relationships between the two. Often the effort that was needed to complete assigned tasks is not as great as it seemed to be.

6. Review the specifics of the assigned role and responsibilities.

7. Make a plan for success by allowing the partner to decide the answers to the following questions:

   a. What needs to be done next?

   b. When does it need to be done?

   c. Where does it need to be done?

   d. How long will it take to do it?

   e. What resources are needed to do it?

   f. How many times will it need to be done?

   g. How will you know when it has been done?

   h. What outcome do you seek?

EXHIBIT 3.3. Developing a Second-Chance Plan

When the next meeting is held to check progress, the first question for you to ask is "How did the plan work out?" If it didn't work out, don't ask why—it only leads to excuses. Just ask, "When do you plan to do it?" or "What else do you think you could do?" Then make another plan or repeat the original one with some modifications, if necessary. There are two endings: either the partner carries out the plan successfully or, after two or more repetitions, it becomes apparent that the individual has no intention of completing the plan and taking responsibility. Termination of the partnership and separation will be the obvious decision.

Termination without Second-Chance Opportunities

Sometimes a collaborator's performance is so demonstrably ineffective and inadequate that terminating the relationship is the only answer. Nonetheless, this situation requires careful planning based on objective documentation, not on subjective and emotional responses. A sample termination scenario is scripted in chapter 10.

Following are some data sources you should plan to use when conducting a collaborator termination conference:

- the time and task chart from the original grant proposal
- results from your formative survey of collaborators
- notes from one-on-one meetings and phone conversations
- e-mail and other written correspondence
- observations from your site visits and of work in progress
- notes from meetings with key personnel and other partners
- feedback from satisfaction surveys completed by project participants
- progress reports submitted to the sponsor

When building a case for terminating a relationship, it is only fair to both parties that objective data be the basis for decision making. The time and task chart, for example, was the basis for assigning responsibilities and time lines and has been known from the outset of the project. Feedback from surveys, meetings, and discussions with key personnel, other partners, and project participants demonstrates an inclusive understanding of the performance problem.

When possible, the termination meeting should be conducted in person, in a private room where you won't be interrupted. Meeting someone face-to-face, looking that individual in the eye and presenting an objective, fair, and equitable assessment of the situation is always best. Constraints such as distance and available time may, however, influence the decision to communicate via mail, e-mail, telephone, or videoconference. In addition, the effects of the partner's default may be having immediate consequences, thereby creating the need for a quick and expedient separation. Accordingly, strong leadership and good management skills come into play.

Skillful grant leaders have compassion and concern for people, their achievements, and their struggles. They terminate relationships in such a way that individuals are allowed to preserve their dignity. Focus on redirecting behavior; you should neither punish nor vilify the actions of others. Because a former collaborator can be your best—or worst—project advocate, it's always advantageous to attempt to turn the termination into a mutually beneficial resolution. Failed partnerships benefit no one. A smooth transition out of the partnership will allow the individual to move on and allow you to repair damage, correct deficits, and get the project back on track.

Redefining and Adjusting the Project

The loss of a partner may have a serious effect on the project's progress and on other collaborators. A termination will cause individuals to ponder a variety of backward-looking questions such as "What triggered this termination? Who knew this was coming? Was the termination handled fairly?" and forward-looking questions such as "Could this happen to me? Will this cause an increase in my workload? Will a replacement partner be recruited?" The grant leader can minimize the impact of these worrisome questions by meeting with the remaining collaborators in small groups or individually and being honest, direct, and empathetic about the situation.

The grant leader would now call Plan B into play if, indeed, a Plan B had been formulated. More than likely it will not be available in full, because terminations are not anticipated. It takes time to realize that a termination is needed and time to bring it about. Two primary options exist: replace the partner with a new one or adjust the project without replacing the partner. Before that decision can be made, you may first attempt to assess and control damage by considering questions such as the following:

- What resources have been lost—material, space, equipment, personnel, dollars?

- How can what is lost be replaced from existing resources or other resources?

- How much time will be lost toward meeting project time lines and goals?

- Is there another partner available who might have interest in stepping in?

- What is the financial impact of this change?

- Are there any components of the project that could be eliminated or postponed without undue harm to the overall project?

- What is the effect of the loss of the partner on the morale and motivation of the remaining partners and personnel who contribute to the project?

- What forms of retaliation might be anticipated from the terminated partner?

- Does the sponsor need to be notified about the change in project personnel?

- Will it be necessary to request from the sponsor an extension for project completion?

In essence, borrowing from counseling principles, grant leaders are asking versions of the question "What's the worst thing that can happen?" Answers to these questions, and likely many others, lead the way to redefining and adjusting the project. The need for the project still exists, so the project must move on.

WHEN THE PROJECT ENDS

As the collaborative grant project approaches its natural conclusion, partners may experience a mixture of positive and negative reactions, including those noted in exhibit 3.4.

The grant leader has a special task to perform as the project concludes. All partners should go away with a feeling of "closure," one that reinforces their decision to participate in the project. Without a strong sense of closure, people feel discomfort and feel left hanging—that something is incomplete and unfinished. Even collaborators who are "just ready to be done" with a grant project benefit from formal recognition of a job well done; it lets them focus on the future, including the possibility of a future collaborative endeavor.

You can help collaborators achieve successful project closure by holding a final general meeting, complete with food and refreshments, to officially wrap up the project. At the meeting, review the overall accomplishments of the project and their significance to the partnering organizations and target audience. Acknowledge the actions of key individuals and committees, highlighting their contributions to the overall success of the project. Identify additional project dissemination strategies that will be used to share the

Positive End-of-Project Reactions	Negative End-of-Project Reactions
• feeling of achievement	• loss of interest
• sense of accomplishment	• dwindling motivation
• satisfaction in completing a difficult task	• feeling let down
• feelings of personal and professional growth	• feeling the future is uncertain
• establishing new friendships and relationships	• wondering what's next
• anticipating a promotion or new responsibility	• fear of loss of work
• excitement for the next opportunity	• relief that the project is over

EXHIBIT 3.4. Possible Feelings and Reactions When the Project Ends

final results with major constituencies. Talk about plans for the future, if appropriate, and the steps that have been or will be taken for the next collaborative project. Thank everyone for their efforts and dedication. End it all on a high note.

After the final general meeting, hold private meetings with those few individuals who made the most valuable contributions, even if they were already recognized by the group. These individuals did many things right; take the opportunity to learn from them what they think should be done differently on future collaborative grant projects to improve processes and enhance results. Ask, "What do you know now that you wish you would have known when we started this collaborative venture?" Inevitably, people learn from the positive experience of getting a grant and have concrete suggestions about what they would change to strengthen their next project.

When logistical barriers such as geographic distribution of partners and time considerations prevent a final general meeting from being held, you can facilitate project closure in other ways. Conduct a teleconference or videoconference with collaborators to simulate the group setting for recognizing important achievements. Solicit audio- or video-recorded testimonials from a few members of the target audience and post their recordings on your Web site for partners to view. E-mail the partner's supervisor to recount the successes of the collaboration and, more specifically, the valuable contributions made by the individual. Send handwritten notes to collaborators, thanking them for their passion, energy, and commitment to the project and serving the target audience.

These stewardship activities may take an extra bit of time, but the benefits double: as the grant leader, you are validating the individual's choice to take part in this collaborative project and you are predisposing the individual toward collaborating with you again on a future project.

CONCLUSIONS AND BEGINNINGS

By now you might be saying, "This is all too much!" Or perhaps, "A-ha! Now I see how it works." Even, "I see now how to fix some problems we're having in our present situation." This chapter has outlined the dynamics that make collaborations work. Regardless of the type of collaboration—coexistence, cooperation, coordination, or coalition—it is made successful through using sound management practices to direct people and things toward focused goals.

An awarded grant is an agreement between you and the sponsor. If you treat it as you would any other business deal (and you should), good management skills must prevail. There must be strong and competent leadership, sound planning, careful selection of partners and other personnel, constant monitoring and measuring of progress, the ability to make changes when necessary, and the ability to work with people in a fair and equitable manner. This includes recognizing both success and failure and responding appropriately to them.

CHAPTER 4

Generating Ideas for Collaborative Grants

Lack of money is no obstacle. Lack of an idea is an obstacle.

—*Ken Hatuka*

In the highly competitive world of grantseeking, plenty of *good* project ideas exist, but only rarely does an idea less than *great* receive funding. Collaborative grantseeking represents a significant opportunity to formulate great ideas. Because high-quality ideas are so crucial to obtaining grants, this chapter examines the process of generating such ideas through focus groups. In particular, we distinguish between two formats—brainstorming and round-robin—and discuss the activities that need to occur before, during, and after the focus group sessions in order to garner meaningful feedback and use it effectively.

GENERATING IDEAS

Where do grant leaders find great ideas?

Great ideas come from a variety of internal and external sources. One way to come up with a great idea may be to sit down at your desk and methodically think through a situation, systematically reviewing the literature to see what's been done in the past and analytically examining ways to improve the system. That is, generating ideas can be the result of hard work. Or, you may find inspiration while in the shower, on the commute to work, exercising, sitting in a boring meeting, or falling asleep. These "a-ha!" moments occur when your subconscious mind elevates thoughts into your conscious mind. Precisely because you were not actively thinking about developing great ideas, they had time to formulate on their own. These are internal methods of generating ideas.

Externally, you can seek the advice of consultants who are experts in the field; they often have vast intuitive knowledge of problems and issues and can communicate that information in an immediately usable form. More often, however, ideas arise from existing staff and people who are in the trenches on a daily basis. Their observations may emerge during informal conversations, such as around the water cooler, or they may be the product of more formal focus group sessions.

Most people know about focus groups, and some have participated in them. In broad terms, this popular social science technique is designed to explore the attitudes, feelings, and ideas of a small group via a formal group discussion technique. It is a very structured way to gather specific information in a short time. From the perspective of the grant leader, conducting effective focus groups means selecting an appropriate format and following through on essential activities before, during, and after the session.

FOCUS GROUP FORMATS

A focus group is a qualitative technique in which a small corps of people—typically 8 to 20 individuals—engages in a roundtable discussion of selected topics in an informal setting. For collaborative grant projects, the conversation is usually directed by the grant leader, or a moderator, who guides the session in order to obtain the group's opinions about or reactions to specific issues of shared interest—for example, defining priority problems, project goals, methodological approaches, or resource allocations.

By inviting qualitative input from collaborators and constituents, focus groups can aid in project planning and decision making. Often, focus groups are used in collaborative grants to determine attitudes and feelings. They may also generate new and original thinking about project processes and outcomes.

Focus groups are usually conducted in either a brainstorming or a round-robin format. Whether sessions are led by you or a moderator, a key to success is being able to impose rules and control the discussion without offending or intimidating the group.

- **Brainstorming focus groups** are used to reveal ideas about broader topics, including opinions, opposing ideas, agreements, and attitudes. Participants' comments are directed to the group; members are allowed to interact with each other and the grant leader.

- **Round-robin focus groups** are designed to elicit objective and constructive ideas, drilling down on the multiple dimensions of a few concrete issues. Participant's comments are directed to the grant leader, and participant interaction is discouraged.

The difference between the two formats is essentially breadth versus depth. The brainstorming focus groups cover a wider range of topics and allow for interaction between participants, whereas the round-robin focus groups are more focused and severely limit participant interaction. In a brainstorming session, a participant talks out an idea for two to three minutes before time is called and the next group member gets a turn. In round-robin sessions, the pace is much quicker: each participant takes one minute to summarize one idea at a time.

Neither focus group format is inherently better than the other. They are just different techniques for generating ideas. Brainstorming focus group advantages and disadvantages are summarized in exhibit 4.1. Round-robin focus group advantages and disadvantages are presented in exhibit 4.2.

Advantages	Disadvantages
• The concept of brainstorming is easy for participants to understand.	• The unpredictable nature of the session can be intimidating to participants.
• The group as a whole has the opportunity to express themselves.	• Capturing group discussion verbatim is challenging; audio and video recordings take time to transcribe.
• A variety of thoughts and perspectives emerge and can even be reconciled.	• Determining exactly where the group stands at the end of the session is difficult.
• Multiple topics can be explored in a limited time period.	• Valuable ideas go unheard when group members exceed their individual 2-3 minute time allotments.

EXHIBIT 4.1. Advantages and Disadvantages of Brainstorming Focus Groups

Advantages	Disadvantages
• Participants feel they have an equal chance to speak and be heard.	• Participants feel some pressure to speak.
• Spread across topic areas, an average of two ideas per minute can be generated.	• Sidebar discussions among group members interrupt the flow of the session.
• Opposing views and other topics may emerge that need to be explored in a future session.	• Participants are uncomfortable not having the opportunity to explain or expound on their ideas.
• The majority of the comments are useful for future planning.	• The time limit may be viewed as too short to generate numerous ideas of high quality.

EXHIBIT 4.2. Advantages and Disadvantages of Round-Robin Focus Groups

BEFORE THE FOCUS GROUP

What you get out of a focus group is a function of what you put into it. So before convening a focus group, you will need to make a number of methodological decisions about how you will organize and manage the session. This includes defining the focus group's purpose, participants, environment, materials, and seating arrangement. Each point is addressed below.

Purpose

The more clearly you can define the purpose of the focus group, the more valuable the results will be. For instance, your purpose may be to explore the various dimensions of a broad topic, in which case a brainstorming format would be appropriate. Or your purpose may be to garner specific feedback on several narrowly defined topics, in which case a round-robin format would be appropriate. Regardless of the format you choose, getting at a breadth or depth of information, a participant's level of spontaneity and innovative thinking is typically limited to an hour or two.

Because closed-ended questions, which can often be answered with "yes" or "no," do not encourage a free exchange of ideas, you should develop open-ended questions for each of your topics. Open-ended questions may be far-reaching, such as "What's not happening in this area that should be happening?" and "What are the key features of an ideal solution?" Or they may be narrow, such as "What are the biggest sources of dissatisfaction with our current approaches to training?" and "What can be done to increase community engagement?" Prioritize your topics and questions to ensure that the most significant ones are asked and answered first.

Participants

Focus groups should have 8 to 20 participants. Groups with fewer than 8 may experience sluggishness from a shortage of creativity and energy to fuel the exchange. Groups with more than 20 may become unwieldy, particularly as you try to ensure that all voices are heard and responses are recorded. Rather than letting a group get too large, it is preferable to run multiple sessions with a manageable number of participants in each group.

It's also important to consider the composition of the group. As you are selecting participants, think about whether you want representation from people of varying age, race, ethnicity, gender, disability, religion, and socioeconomic status. And if you plan to conduct multiple sessions, depending on the purpose of your focus group, you may need to cluster participants strategically. A heterogeneous group may give you a breadth of surface-level responses. A homogeneous group may provide responses of a limited range but of greater depth.

Environment

Select an environment where participants will feel comfortable sharing their ideas freely. Use a quiet room with ample space and sufficient ambient lighting. Ideally, the room will be relatively neutral—for instance, free from art, signs, large windows, and other potential distractions. Also check whether the temperature of the meeting room can be adjusted easily to accommodate participants' preferences. A room that is too hot or too cold can also be distracting.

Materials

The materials needed for your focus groups depend on variables such as the number of participants, the number of topics, and the length of the sessions. There are low-tech and high-tech options for recording, displaying, and voting on participants' ideas. The following materials work for the optimal participant size for both brainstorming and round-robin focus groups.

For Recording Information

The low-tech approach to recording information involves flip charts, an easel, and markers. Use several flip charts to record participants' responses, one for each topic area and one extra for capturing thoughts that are important yet not immediately relevant to the topic at hand. Ideas relegated to the "parking lot" can be revisited at a later time. The easel should be tall enough for participants to see it easily and sturdy enough to allow you to write on and tear off flip chart sheets effortlessly. While markers come in many colors, dark-colored ones are best because they are easy to see from a distance; you might use black, blue, and brown to write down thoughts and red, green, and purple to draw connections among ideas.

The high-tech approaches could range from using laptop computers, smart boards, and audio-video tools to record information. You may capture key ideas and type them directly into your laptop computer. Participants using tablet PCs can type or write down their ideas and share them with you wirelessly or via a flash drive. You can record participants' responses on a smart board, save them, and print them out or distribute them electronically immediately at the end of the session. The computers and smart boards allow you to change type styles, font sizes, and colors very quickly to differentiate between speakers and to visually represent relationships between ideas. You might even use audio-video tools to record the session for later transcription.

For Displaying Information

The low-tech approach for displaying information entails using tape, pushpins, or poster tack to hang flip chart sheets on a wall, bulletin board, or portable display board. Some brands of flip charts have self-stick adhesive built in, which holds securely to most wall surfaces and removes cleanly. Masking tape comes in different grades of stickiness or "tack"; select a low-grade tack so the tape won't pull paint or wallpaper off the meeting-room wall. Bulletin boards and portable display boards should be large enough so that several flip chart sheets on one topic can be viewed simultaneously. This will help prevent ideas from being repeated identically by multiple participants and help associations to be made among ideas.

The high-tech approach could mean that you use a projector to display content on your laptop computer for all to see; transmit wirelessly to a Listserv or secure Web page the observations you keyed in on your laptop for participants to view on their tablet PCs; employ a smart instructor console to override participants' computers and share information directly on their individual screens; or record participants' responses on a smart board at the front of the meeting room. Again, it's best when the display allows for all of the recorded thoughts on one topic to be viewed at once. When ideas are spread across several pages that must be viewed in series rather than in parallel, it's difficult to see patterns that might otherwise emerge immediately.

For Voting on Information

The low-tech approach to voting for the ideas considered to be the most important could include markers, sticky notes or dots, or a show of hands. In some cases, it is valuable to rank the ideas that have been generated by the focus group. You can supply participants with markers and ask them to make a check next to their top few preferences. Similarly, you can invite participants to place a sticky note or dot by their favorite responses. Whether voting with markers or sticky notes or dots, it is valuable for participants to be able to see all of the options at once so that they can choose among alternatives. You can also go through each recorded thought individually and poll participants via a show of hands.

The high-tech approaches could include inviting participants to come up to your laptop computer one at a time to place an "X" next to the statements they feel are of the greatest significance; asking participants to approach the smart board and check their top choices; having participants use their tablet PCs to log on to a secure Web site and complete an online poll to rank responses; or encouraging participants to vote using audience response systems or wireless "clickers." Web-based polls and audience response systems offer the advantage of allowing participants to make their selections simultaneously and anonymously. And because results can be tallied and displayed immediately, if it is necessary to a break tie vote, a run-off can take place right away.

Seating Arrangement

The seating arrangement will depend on the size of the group and the available furnishings. Any tables—rectangle, round, or square—will provide a hard surface for participants to write on and a place for their coffee, water, snacks, and notepads; however, rectangle tables in a U-shaped arrangement offer the dual advantage of keeping you connected to the group and the group members connected to each other.

In particular, a U-shaped seating arrangement facilitates discussion because participants can see each other and can be brought together easily for consensus agreements. It allows you to walk down in the midst of the group, where you can engage participants one-on-one to draw out ideas that need further explanation or, conversely, to wrap up discussions that have gone on too long. This arrangement also provides group members with an unobstructed view of the front of the room where their ideas are being recorded and displayed.

DURING THE FOCUS GROUP

As the grant leader, it is your job to explain the "rules of the game" to focus group members so they know what to expect and can participate effectively in the session. You should introduce participants and orient them to focus groups, familiarize them with the nominal group technique, and make closing remarks and adjourn the meeting. Your limited time together will go by quickly. Be sure to monitor the clock regularly so that you stay on track and on schedule.

Introductions and Orientation

Begin the focus group session with introductions. Beyond good social etiquette, these few minutes of small talk will help to create an environment that is open and trusting. Making eye contact and offering a warm smile as participants say their names and affiliations will also make people feel comfortable and welcome. Then you can take a moment to address any logistical issues—reminding participants to turn off their cell phones, encouraging them to help themselves to refreshments and snacks, and pointing out the location of the restrooms, for instance.

Even when individuals have participated previously in other focus groups, it's worth a few moments of time for you to explain what a focus group is, how it will work, and how long it will last. You can define roles in their simplest terms: as the leader, your job is to promote energy and engagement among group members; as participants, their job is to come up with as many ideas as they can to the questions posed and, as appropriate, to rank the ones they feel are the most important. Let them know that you intend to respect the allotted time and thus occasionally may need to move the session along. Thank them for their willingness to take part in the focus group. Exhibits 4.3 and 4.4 contain sample orientation scripts you can use with brainstorming and round-robin focus groups.

As part of the orientation to a brainstorming focus group, the grant leader might say:

You know that we have agreed to operate on a consensus basis. The topic is written on the board. Kelly will help me record responses. You may respond at any time with a word, phrase, or statement presenting your position or ideas. No lengthy speeches, please! We want spontaneous, off the wall, creative, imaginative, and even crazy ideas. For now, anything relevant to the topic is acceptable. Really way-out ideas can go in the parking lot, if the group decides. While we're not taking turns, let a speaker finish before you jump in. We'll keep going until time runs out or there are no more responses. Try not to get into sidebar discussions with your neighbor. The group needs to hear and record everything. So have fun, and let's begin. Who has a first thought to share?

EXHIBIT 4.3   Orientation Script for Brainstorming Focus Group

---

As part of the orientation to a round-robin focus group, the grant leader might say:

You know that we have agreed to operate on a consensus basis. The topics are on the charts in front of you. They are not in any particular order. I'll begin with Heather, on my left. She will give us her statement in one word or a short phrase for any one of the topics. Don't worry if your response is right or wrong, appropriate, or stupid. It's important that you had the thought now, so let's get it down before we lose it. If you have a thought and are having trouble stating it, I will ask the group to help. You will have final approval before we record it. We will move quickly around the room, ending over here with Bob. Then we'll begin again with Heather. If you have nothing to contribute when your turn comes, just say "Pass." I'll move on, and you can contribute something during your next turn.

The session will end when either the time expires or everyone has passed. Please be patient as I record your responses. Be sure your response is recorded accurately. My job is to keep the process moving, so if I seem to cut you off when you begin to make a speech, don't take it personally. I suggest that you not take notes. You may, however, write down your thoughts that you want to contribute. Try to listen to each person while you wait your turn. Are there any questions about the topics and what we're going to do? Okay, let's start.

EXHIBIT 4.4   Orientation Script for Round-Robin Focus Group

Nominal Group Technique

Once you've completed introductions and orientation, then you move into the heart of the focus group: the questions and answers. Nominal group technique is a process that encourages active input from all participants and, equally significant, generates consensus. There are four steps:

1. **Generating Information:** After you put forth a question for consideration, participants independently take a few moments to quietly reflect on its various dimensions and then generate as many ideas as they can in the time allowed, ordinarily 10 minutes.

2. **Recording Information:** Ask participants to share, in turn, their top responses. Ideas are recorded, usually in short phrases that capture the concept clearly and accurately, until participants have exhausted their lists; it's not necessary to record duplicate responses.

3. **Discussing Information:** Group members are allowed to make comments, ask questions, and offer clarifications about any of the ideas recorded. Both you and the participants are permitted to propose that closely related ideas be combined.

4. **Voting on Information:** Based on the quantity of ideas recorded, agree on the number of votes each participant must cast (e.g., 5, 10, or 20) and whether multiple votes can be cast for a single idea. Tally the votes to rank the top ideas as determined by the whole group.

Nominal group technique aims for consensus, not "majority rule." Multiple voting helps avoid the conflict outcome of majority rule winners versus losers because a greater likelihood exists that each participant will agree with at least one idea on the final list. Operating by consensus means that *everyone* in the group agrees to support the group's decisions and actions even if they disagree with some or all of the other members. What's more, when you ask the group to re-confirm its consensus position, the group members come closer together. The naysayers have a more difficult time trying to filibuster or otherwise disrupt the progress of the group.

Closing Remarks and Adjournment

At this point, you will have generated a lot of important information in a very short period of time. You should take a moment to congratulate the group on their productivity and thank them for following the rules and participating openly. Acknowledge the difficulty of the task and yet point out that, as they have experienced firsthand, a focus group is an effective way to learn from each other. Remind them that the information generated will form the basis for future plans and actions.

Depending on your circumstances, while you have the group together, there might be value in identifying some actions that constitute logical next steps. For instance, you could set a date by which the focus group feedback will be transcribed and disseminated to all participants. You might schedule a future meeting to make decisions and chart a course of action. You could solicit a few volunteers to delve into the items relegated to the "parking lot." You might appoint some individuals to committees that will study the ranked responses and come back with recommendations. Otherwise, thank group members one last time as you adjourn the meeting.

AFTER THE FOCUS GROUP

You should plan to transcribe the focus group feedback while it's still fresh in your mind. In addition to elaborating on the telegraphic phrases captured during the session, you may wish to include your own observations and reflections. For instance, you might note ideas that were immediately embraced without much dialogue, ideas that should have emerged but didn't, and ideas that evoked much discussion but were ultimately rejected. These types of details are particularly valuable in collaborative grantseeking when an RFP asks you to include in your methodology section "a description of the various feasible alternatives that were considered."

Once the focus group feedback has been transcribed, you can analyze the results more critically. Look for patterns, trends, and themes that might not have surfaced during the focus group session. Perhaps a specific phrase elicited wildly opposite responses from select participants. Maybe a number of key words really relate to a larger but unidentified umbrella concept. Conceivably, inconsistencies and discrepancies exist in the feedback because group members had different understandings or operational definitions of core concepts.

In cases like these, you may decide to follow up with some or all of the participants to clear up remaining ambiguities. Whether you make a few telephone calls, send a letter or e-mail message, administer a print or Web-based survey, or convene a new focus group, the information you gather will bring even more conceptual clarity as you begin turning your ideas into actions. The focus groups established a shared understanding of the problems that exist and potential solutions that are available. Now, as the grant leader, you are in a position to inspire, motivate, and empower others to act. Your collaborative grant proposal provides the roadmap to success.

PART II

EXAMPLES OF SUCCESSFUL COLLABORATIVE GRANTS

In part II, we turn our attention from understanding the fundamentals of collaborative grantseeking to examining examples of successful collaborative grants. In each of the following four chapters, after a brief introduction to the grant sponsor and analysis of the RFP guidelines, an actual funded proposal is presented in its entirety. The proposals are real—only identifying details such as names and contact information have been changed—and they illustrate each type of collaboration.

- **Chapter 5:** a coexistence collaboration request to a private foundation for a technology acquisition and integration project in higher education
- **Chapter 6:** a coordination collaboration request to a private foundation for a literacy and reading project serving elementary school children
- **Chapter 7:** a cooperation collaboration request to a government agency for a curriculum development project in special education
- **Chapter 8:** a coalition collaboration request to a government agency for a conference grant to heighten awareness about mental health issues and best practices

Further, we annotate key dimensions of the collaboration, grant leadership, and proposal in call-out thought bubbles. We also include verbatim comments from the grant reviewers, when available (chapters 7 and 8). This in-depth look at the integrated process of planning and writing these proposals will provide you with a framework that you can use to develop your own successful collaborative grant proposals.

CHAPTER 5

Coexistence Collaboration: HP Technology for Teaching

The HP Technology for Teaching Grant Initiative, launched in 2004, aims to increase student achievement in K–12 schools and higher education settings by integrating technology into the learning environment. Educators apply for funding to collaboratively redesign a core course in mathematics, science, engineering, or information systems, and awards include a fixed combination of cash and in-kind computer equipment and accessories.

Integrating technology into the classroom reflects a change in styles of teaching and learning. To effectively reach today's students, educators can no longer act as the all-knowing "sage on the stage" who transmits knowledge to a passive audience; rather, educators must position themselves as a "guide on the side" who facilitates knowledge construction through active engagement. Technology fosters the discovery process: with direction from educators, students can rapidly access information and manipulate data as they seek to answer the questions they helped to formulate.

The HP Technology for Teaching Web site, at http://www.hp.com/go/hpteach, provides a wealth of information, including a program description, grantmaking priorities, funding levels, application processes, a list of past grant recipients, best practices, and online communities.

For a list of the latest education grant programs offered through the HP Office of Global Social Innovation, visit http://www.hp.com/go/edgrants.

In this chapter we examine a successful application to the HP Technology for Teaching Grant Initiative. The RFP guidelines made clear the sponsor's preference for collaborative endeavors in redesigning a core course in higher education: they requested information about campus involvement and indicated, "We encourage projects that involve multiple professors." This broad statement allowed applicants to decide which type of collaboration would be most effective for their projects. In this case, the purpose of the coexistence collaboration was to revise one section of a yearlong General Chemistry sequence. Using technology to better integrate classroom lecture and laboratory experiences, the goal was to enhance students' academic achievement.

HP Technology for Teaching Grant Initiative
Transforming teaching and learning through technology

» Company information

» Global citizenship

» HP Global Social Innovation
» HP Social Innovation - US

Video: Empowering education tools and HP

About HP Technology for Teaching

In 2008 we celebrated 5 years of commitment to innovative educators who are transforming teaching and learning through the effective use of technology as part of the HP Technology for Teaching program. HP believes that teaching excellence, combined with the right technologies, has a positive impact on student achievement.

The HP Technology for Teaching Grant Initiative is designed to support the innovative use of mobile technology in K-16 education, and to help identify K-12 public schools and two- and four-year colleges and universities that HP might support with future grants.

The HP Technology for Teaching initiative encompasses a total investment of nearly $60 million from 2004 to 2008, impacting over 1000 educational institutions in 41 countries.

- K-12 HP Technology for Teaching Grant Recipients (US)
- Best practices for technology integration in K-12 classrooms (lessons learned from HP Technology for Teaching grant recipients)
- Higher Education HP Technology for Teaching Grant Recipients (worldwide)

HP continues to build on the successes of the HP Technology for Teaching program, through new education initiatives. More information on HP Social Innovation education programs can be found at www.hp.com/go/edgrants.

NEWS

» Students from 14 European countries generate amazing ideas through HP supported Social Innovation Camp

» HP supports National Lab Day for students across America, to inspire hands-on learning in science, technology, engineering and math.

» HP launches three global initiatives to support innovative education: HP Catalyst Initiative, HP EdTech Innovators Award, HP Learning Initiative for Entrepreneurs.

HP Social Innovation blogs
» Teaching, Learning and Technology in Higher Education
» CSR in Europe, Middle East and Africa
» Follow us @HP_OGSI on Twitter!

FIGURE 5.1 Screen image from the HP Technology for Teaching program (2004–2008) used with permission of the HP Office of Global Social Innovation (www.hp.com/go/socialinnovation).

A careful reading of the RFP guidelines revealed three hot buttons and two distinctive features that influenced the design, shape, and direction of the proposed project. The hot buttons, listed below, were given importance over other criteria because of their repetition throughout the RFP.

- **New Models of Success on Campus:** key phrases included "new models of success on campus," "broader deployment of mobile technology solutions," "on-going student impact," and "sustainable advances in teaching and learning."

- **Assessment and Outcomes:** key phrases included "positively impact student learning," "improved student outcomes," "progress measurement and documentation," and "indicators of advancement in student learning."

- **Widespread Dissemination:** key phrases included "foster publication, demonstration, and presentation opportunities," "communicating the project outcomes, on campus and beyond," and "project visibility."

Distinctive features raised in the RFP guidelines were related to the terms and conditions of gift acceptance:

- **IT Infrastructure and Support:** recipients agree to "provide the proper IT infrastructure and support to ensure program success, including installation and proper maintenance."
- **Technology Conference Participation:** recipients agree to "participate in a Worldwide HP Mobile Technology Conference in the fall. (Funding for travel and accommodations for one participant will be provided by HP)."

Responding to distinctive features will not guarantee funding success; however, failing to acknowledge them may be viewed as a project weakness. In other words, to increase the competitiveness of the proposal, these hot buttons and distinctive features—logical and psychological needs—must be strategically addressed in the narrative.

For this coexistence collaboration, represented in exhibit 5.1, the grant leader remained relatively independent and focused on revising his one section of General Chemistry; however, some interaction did occur with the instructors of two other sections of the course. And because General Chemistry is a gateway course for students majoring in other fields such as geology, biology, and environmental science, a geology instructor was enlisted to provide input on the course redesign. In short, the science instructors all recognized that nominal involvement in the project would ultimately help them to achieve their own course and academic program goals.

The proposal is presented in its entirety on the following pages. What's more, we provide a nuanced analysis of key dimensions of the proposal in the call-out thought bubbles, so you can gain insight into the process of planning and writing a successful collaborative grant.

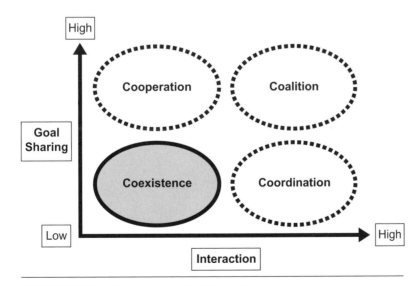

EXHIBIT 5.1 Coexistence Collaboration

HP TECHNOLOGY FOR TEACHING

1. Technology Vision (150 words): Describe your campus or school vision on the role of mobile technology in learning environments.

The Griffin University vision for mobile technology is driven by the principles of *infusion* and *interaction.* In a university setting, students learn wherever they go, not just in classrooms and labs. Students study in their dorms, at the library and campus center, and under trees in the courtyard. They learn in lively exchanges with peers, faculty, and community members. A campus infused with state-of-the-art technology empowers faculty and students by expanding connectivity, promoting flexibility, and encouraging interaction. Wireless, mobile technology fosters active teaching and learning through collaborative classroom activities, research projects, and field-based experiences. Inquiry-based exercises develop students' critical-thinking and problem-solving skills and prepare them for lifelong learning. The University is in an early stage—level 2—of achieving its mobile technology plan, having begun in 2002 when a federal grant allowed us to acquire 65 laptops to support curricular developments in our Teacher Education program.

> The opening sentence of the first paragraph foreshadows the collaborative nature of this project; that is, from an institutional perspective, faculty members share a common goal to enhance student learning by changing their pedagogy from a passive teacher-centered to an active student-centered style.

2. Synergy (150 words): How will the project you're proposing for this grant help you make a substantial contribution toward achieving the educational technology vision on your campus?

This project will serve as a model for curricular reform in the Natural Science Division and as a catalyst for advancing our mobile technology vision across the University. Wireless, mobile computers are changing the way educators think about technology—and the way students think about education. As our Teacher Education program learned when they piloted curricular reforms in 2003, one of the greatest advantages of instructional technology is the ability to offer information in several modalities at once. For instance, when students have the ability to use digital video in learning, they tap into literacy skills, higher order thinking skills and a rich level of creativity inspired by the medium. Building on this momentum, this science initiative will: (1) increase student and faculty awareness of and access to mobile technology; (2) encourage the expansion of wireless networks across campus; (3) support faculty in curricular developments; and (4) enhance students' academic achievement.

> This paragraph appeals to the hot button of creating "new models of success on campus" and acknowledges past and future collaborations. Namely, the proposed chemistry course revisions will benefit from the lessons learned during recent curricular reforms in another discipline—teacher education—that piloted instructional technologies. Revisions in chemistry also hold the potential to be adopted by several other disciplines in the natural sciences.

3. Academic Leadership (150 words): Describe how you have demonstrated academic leadership, as evidenced by the adoption of your teaching methodologies, pedagogy, or curricula, or by other tangible evidence.

Griffin University has the necessary academic and administrative leadership to enhance teaching and learning in the sciences. In 2001, the

University embarked on the most ambitious fundraising campaign in its history to help ensure the centrality of its mission and strengthen academic programs. Concurrently, Dr. Neva Shelby and other science faculty and administrators began participating in Project Kaleidoscope, an informal national alliance working to build strong learning environments for undergraduates in the sciences. Tangible results include: (1) an audit (2002) of the physical conditions of our science facility; (2) a campus master plan (2003) that includes renovating the science facility; (3) a revised strategic action plan (2003) for all academic programs; (4) a consultant assessment (2004) of science facility plans and proposed curricular improvements for majors and non-majors; (5) a review of our general education program (2005) and possible alternative models; and (6) a programmatic vision for the future of the sciences (2005).

> The third sentence in this paragraph helps to establish the credibility of the institution, the grant leader, and the project by describing a partnership with a national alliance of organizations working toward a shared goal of enhancing learning environments.

4. Instructional Leadership (150 words): Describe how you have demonstrated instructional leadership, as evidenced by course changes you have made, in response to student needs, that have improved student outcomes in your courses, or by other tangible evidence.

Dr. Shelby, principal investigator, has the experience and expertise to make this project a success. She provides indispensable academic leadership as the Project Kaleidoscope "Project Shepherd," guiding the planning process for a renovated science facility that will meet the needs of students and faculty for decades to come. Additionally, Dr. Shelby is co-investigator on a 2-year grant recently awarded by the National Science Foundation for planning an undergraduate research center. Alongside colleagues from the University of the South and the University of Western State, this spring semester she began creating curriculum models that will increase students' exposure to the scientific process. Science majors and non-majors alike will have the opportunity to engage in research experiences during the academic year/summer and to participate in an undergraduate research conference. Mobile technologies will play a vital role in hands-on, inquiry-based learning; an Internet-access shared instrumentation program will allow students to conduct experiments in real time.

> This paragraph describes the characteristics of the grant leader, as they relate to goal sharing and interaction, that will contribute to collaborative grantseeking success: need to achieve, task competence, understanding of constituents and their needs, and confidence.

5. Project Executive Summary (200 words): Provide a high-level overview of your project in an executive summary. Describe how students will benefit from the course redesign and the application of mobile technology.

Griffin University is at a unique point in its evolution where faculty and administrators are ready to redesign the science curriculum. The goal is to enhance students' academic achievement by better integrating classroom lecture and laboratory experiences. Wireless, mobile technologies are an integral part of curricular reforms. The chemistry curriculum beings with a year-long sequence of General Chemistry (CHEM 105 and CHEM 107). For this project, one section of General Chemistry will be revised to give forty students greater exposure to scientific research by incorporating semester-long inquiry-based projects into laboratory experiences. As in the research world, students will take an active role in asking questions, designing experiments, and using computer technology to collect and analyze data, organize spreadsheets and graph molecular structures, and present results in multimedia formats. Electronic laboratory notebooks will allow students to access these research tools virtually anywhere on campus. Mobile technology will facilitate a seamless transition from data collection in the laboratory to data analysis and discussion in the classroom. After the pilot year, curricular revisions will be expanded to all sections of General Chemistry, thus impacting 120 students/year and, ultimately, expanded to the entire chemistry curriculum (200 students/year) and the Natural Science Division (500 students/year).

6. Teaching and learning issues (200 words): Describe the fundamental learning and teaching issues that the project addresses (i.e., why is this project important for your students and instructors?).

Advanced technologies are causing a remarkable transformation in learning environments. Traditionally, in the introductory chemistry sequence, a sharp distinction existed between classes and labs: classes were for *learning* while labs were for *doing.* This apparent separation leaves students with the impression that science is performed in short, well defined segments and always produces the "correct" result. Even when laboratory activities are directly aligned with the lecture, students feel that labs are for completing tasks rather than for experiencing the scientific process; often, students do not recognize the connection between lab exercises and lecture topics. Wireless, mobile technologies offer an innovative solution to this pedagogical problem. An interactive class with a research-based laboratory component allows students to work on projects that cannot be completed in a single period and that may not result in the same "correct" answer for every student. Tablet PCs let students easily transport their work from laboratory to classroom and, more importantly, allow them to take ownership of their research projects. By requiring students to design experiments, rather than just follow the directions of a traditional experiment, they learn that science is a continual process of asking and answering questions and that the "answers" frequently generate new questions.

7. Goals, objectives and outcomes (200 words): Describe the project goals, objectives, and anticipated outcomes from the perspective of impact on student learning.

By design, project goals, objectives, and outcomes are synergistic and interrelated. The goal of this project is to redesign the year-long introductory General Chemistry sequence to better integrate classroom

The first and last sentences of this paragraph emphasize the commitment administrators and faculty collaborators have made toward their shared goal of enhancing students' academic achievement. Starting with the redesign of one section of General Chemistry, collaborators are ready to work together to incrementally expand the curricular revisions to all sections of General Chemistry, then to all chemistry courses, and finally to other courses in the natural sciences. Identifying the number of students demonstrates that the course enhancements will have a broad impact.

This paragraph appeals to the hot button of creating "new models of success on campus." The proposed course redesign changes the use of class time with students, from a series of discrete 50-minute lectures and labs to a semester-long project experience.

lecture and laboratory experiences; strategically infusing mobile technologies and research-based activities will produce rich student-faculty interactions.

Four specific, measurable objectives will drive project activities: (1) develop web-based polls to measure student knowledge and comprehension of class lecture; (2) identify a cadre of semester-long, inquiry-based research experiments from which students can select to investigate in the lab; (3) introduce students to Tablet PCs and software for collecting, analyzing, and sharing research data in class and in the lab; and (4) evaluate the effectiveness of curricular reforms and disseminate the results on campus and beyond.

A growing body of evidence in the chemical education field documents that student academic performance is enhanced by learning environments which allow for student involvement in the educational process. Wireless, mobile technology fosters active teaching and learning through collaborative classroom activities, research projects, and field-based experiences. Targeted student learning outcomes include:

- Improved mastery of key chemistry concepts and basic research tools.
- Enhanced exposure to and application of the scientific method.
- Increased quality of laboratory notebooks and reports.

8. Measures (200 words): What indicators of advancement in student learning will be measured and how will they be documented?

Advancement in student learning will be measured at individual and holistic levels through a combination of quantitative and qualitative, direct and indirect measures. Although not mutually exclusive, the following indicators will document students':

(1) mastery of chemistry concepts and basic research tools.

- Examine results from web-based polls administered during classes;
- Compare mid-term and final exam results against classes taught in previous years and against course sections taught in traditional formats by other instructors;
- Compare performance on the American Chemical Society exam against other course sections and against national norms.

(2) exposure to and application of the scientific method.

- Compare pre/post surveys of attitudes toward science and understanding of the scientific method;

The fourth objective touches on two hot buttons that are addressed more fully later on in the proposal: "assessment and outcomes" and "widespread dissemination." Including an objective related to evaluation and dissemination demonstrates its importance to the success of the project. Collaboration is planned, not accidental.

The entire grant application process was managed online, which posed a slight document design challenge because the text box fields did not allow bullet points, graphics, tables, or special characters. Thus, asterisks were used in place of bullet points in the third paragraph.

80

- Examine performance on virtual experiments/simulations;
- Compare ability to collect and analyze data against classes taught in previous years.

(3) quality of laboratory notebooks and reports.

- Compare research projects/reports against those from previous years;
- Examine the frequency and type of interaction with laboratory notebooks;
- Examine the types of interactions between students and with the instructor in class and in labs.

Student reactions to the course overall are reported on the teaching surveys administered at the end of the semester.

9. Project timeline: Describe the project timeline and milestones (Projects are to be implemented in the school year; evaluations can extend beyond this timeframe by several months). Please enter text only into this field (no bullets, graphics, tables, or special characters), e.g., date followed by milestone description.

As Principal Investigator, Dr. Shelby, a full-time chemistry faculty member, will be responsible for coordinating all project activities and reaching the milestones identified in the following timeline.

Summer (June–August) 2005:

June—assemble the team of science faculty, administrators, and students to clarify roles and responsibilities; test current software packages on Tablet PCs; research and select electronic notebook software; and test functionality of wireless systems in labs and classrooms.

July—image Tablet PCs; install software on network server; expand wireless access to labs and lecture classrooms; and identify a cadre of semester-long inquiry-based research experiments for students.

August—have undergraduate students field-test research experiments with wireless technology; work with the Institutional Research Office to develop assessment tools for the courses; and train faculty and laboratory assistants in the use of wireless technology and new software.

Fall (September-December) 2005: Modify one section of General Chemistry (CHEM 105) to implement wireless technology and test the applications; develop web-based polling questions; perform first assessment of course; and attend Worldwide HP Mobile Technology Conference.

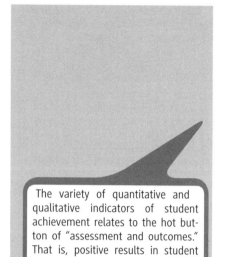

The variety of quantitative and qualitative indicators of student achievement relates to the hot button of "assessment and outcomes." That is, positive results in student learning, as demonstrated through comparisons against previous years, other course sections, and national norms, will promote wide-scale adoption of course enhancements by other instructors.

As the senior-most member in the chemistry department, the grant leader was confident that a team of science colleagues could be assembled in summer to organize the pilot. The instructors have a cordial and open relationship, thus they are willing to share their expertise on the proposed curricular redesigns. Collaborators have not yet committed, however, to making any changes in their own courses. They will wait to see what works first.

Winter Break 2005: Analyze assessment data from first semester and modify course based on evaluation results; identify additional inquiry-based research experiments for students; and continue to develop web-polling questions.

Spring (January–May) 2006: Implement wireless technology in second semester General Chemistry (CHEM 107); perform second assessment of course; and present a workshop at the University of the South for college professors and high school teachers on incorporating inquiry-based research activities into the science curriculum.

Summer (June–August) 2006: Analyze assessment data and modify course as necessary; disseminate project results on and off campus (e.g., the annual Research Day at Griffin University and the Conference on Chemical Education hosted by Pepe University); introduce curricular revisions to all sections of General Chemistry; begin planning curricular reforms in upper division chemistry courses and in laboratory-based courses in physics and geology.

10. Technology Integration (200 words): Describe how you plan to use the granted HP products to support the goals of your project and how will the granted HP technology contribute to resolving the fundamental problem or opportunity this project addresses.

HP wireless, mobile technology is vital to our goal of integrating classroom lecture and laboratory experiences so that the science curriculum is more responsive to the changing needs of students. Piloting this technological integration in the General Chemistry sequence will provide a model for reform throughout the chemistry curriculum and throughout the sciences. The use of electronic laboratory notebooks has become commonplace in industrial and major research settings; their use in educational lab settings with inquiry-based experiments will allow students to experience firsthand how research is conducted. Equally significant, Tablet PCs will allow us to address one of our major concerns: the apparent separation of the lecture and laboratory. Students will now be able to come to class and discuss and analyze their *own* data, rather than simply observe the instructor illustrate the data analysis process. Research shows that providing immediate feedback has a positive impact on students' future performance and motivation. Mobile technologies allow students to take their research wherever they go, between the classroom, laboratory, library, and dormitory. Students will be able to manipulate data and observe chemical structures on their own. This individualization allows students to take ownership of their education and enhances the learning experience.

11. Course impacted (100 words): Describe the course or courses that will be re-designed for this project (begin with course number).

The initial courses that will be redesigned include the first-year sequence of General Chemistry (CHEM 105 and CHEM 107). Students enrolled in

To address the hot button of "assessment and outcomes," plans for measuring and documenting progress are integrated throughout the project time line: developing assessment tools, analyzing first-semester feedback, analyzing second-semester feedback, and assessing the yearlong sequence.

The time line addresses the distinctive feature of "technology conference participation" by confirming attendance at the Worldwide HP Mobile Technology Conference in the fall.

The final two paragraphs touch on the hot button of "widespread dissemination." They identify one on-campus and two off-campus venues where results will be shared with other educators.

Preproposal contact with a past grant winner revealed that, while it was important to have an understanding of the best practices in educational technology and science pedagogy, it was not necessary to cite the literature. Thus, the sixth sentence simply refers to "research shows that..." without attributing the specific sources.

The RFP states that project proposals must focus on redesigning a "core course," and this paragraph confirms General Chemistry meets that criterion: this yearlong introductory sequence is required for students majoring in chemistry, biology, and geology.

The final two sentences of the paragraph hint at the hot button of "new models of success on campus." Technology enhancements will not only be integrated across the curriculum, they will be infused into a new science building. Thus, advances in teaching and learning will be sustainable over the long term.

While the onus of redesigning the one General Chemistry course section will fall to the grant leader, involving other instructors in minor ways during the planning process—meeting to secure their buy-in and input—sets the stage for a greater degree of interaction with these partners after the granting period as they adopt enhancements in their courses.

In addition to placing restrictions on document design features, the online grant application process limited the content allowed in each text box. In this case, only a number was allowed, which meant that details about the other partner instructors, such as names, titles, and roles, could not be included.

these courses are primarily undergraduate science majors with a few non-majors. This introductory sequence is required for chemistry, biology and geology majors. Upon successful completion of course modifications, we anticipate adopting similar models and technology throughout the chemistry curriculum and, eventually, throughout the other laboratory-based courses in the Natural Science Division. Courses of this type, based on mobile technology, will become an integral part of the scheduled renovation of our science facility, which is currently in the planning stage.

12. Course redesign (200 words): Describe how the course will be altered to take advantage of the technology.

The major change in the redesigned General Chemistry sequence is the introduction of a research experience for students. Specifically, the new sequence model will replace traditional directed laboratory exercises with semester-long guided-inquiry projects. Wireless mobile technologies will serve as the centerpiece of students' experience with the scientific method. Students will be introduced to electronic research tools that allow them to ask questions, design experiments, collect and analyze data, search scientific journals, graphically represent molecular structures, and present results in multimedia formats. Tablet PCs will also allow students to use electronic notebook software, effectively replacing the traditional paper lab notebook. Mobile technologies will support a greater degree of *interaction*—among students and with their electronic notebooks. Course lecture will be reduced so students can work in class on problems using their own data, rather than simply observing examples presented by the instructor. Further, because interactivity is vital to a meaningful lecture period, web-based polls will be developed to assess basic knowledge, attitudes, and misconceptions. Web-based polls process information instantaneously and provide instructors with a simply way to diagnose student understanding and, in response, adapt during a class. HP technology will help integrate laboratory work and lecture experience, facilitating a shift to active learning that emphasizes critical-thinking and problem-solving skills.

13. Department where course resides. This is a core course in one of the following departments:

Science

14. Faculty: How many professors/faculty will be directly involved in this project?

8

15. Students: Approximately how many students will be impacted during the first full year of this pilot project implementation?

40

16. On-going student impact: Approximately how many students will be impacted per academic year when this course design is fully implemented?

120

17. Student Financial Need: What percentage of your degree students receive need-based assistance under Title IV of the Higher Education Act?

17%

18. Ethnic Representation: Please indicate the ethnic representation of students at your institution?

African American: 1%
Asian/Pacific Islander: 1%
Caucasian/White: 90%
Hispanic: 1%
Native American: 1%
Other: 6%

19. Campus Involvement (100 words): How will your campus educational technology and instructional leadership be involved in this project? What other departments or functions, if any, will provide support to the project?

Griffin University's Technology Services enthusiastically endorses and will support this science initiative; indeed, the University's core information technology has historically been supplied by HP/Compaq. The Academic Dean provides administrative leadership for initiatives that will enhance teaching and learning in the sciences. Within the Natural Science Division, the Associate Dean will ensure the continuity of curricular reforms with the strategic action plan, and faculty members in physics and geology have demonstrated great interest in adopting the chemistry model for integrating mobile technology into research experiences. The Director of Institutional Research will ensure that assessments of student learning are high quality. Of note, two science students will also be involved in the planning and implementation processes.

This collaboration exhibits dynamic factors relating to goal sharing, including goal consensus and intelligence, and to interaction, including group affiliation and change orientation. As colleagues within a small department and within the same division, there exists a shared affinity to one another as well as a fidelity to their students; collaborators understand the implications of maintaining the status quo and will test an innovative approach to enhancing student learning experiences.

Grant awards included a modest but fixed amount of cash and a significant and specific combination of in-kind technologies (i.e., laptop computers, docking stations, digital projectors, inkjet printers, and digital cameras). This paragraph addresses the distinctive feature of "IT infrastructure and support," reassuring the sponsor that the technical expertise is available and willing to support project implementation.

20. IT Infrastructure: The environment where my project will be deployed has an IT infrastructure with Internet access that can accommodate an 802.11 b/g Access Point.

Yes

21. IT Support (50 words): Describe the support the IT department has committed to providing this project (such as support for networking, Tablet PC imaging, onsite help, etc.).

Griffin University's Technology Services will provide network access, network support, and general computing support to the project. They have experience with Tablet PCs and can provide standard images and onsite support as needed. Wireless networking is integrated into our data network and has 802.1x authentication and WEP encryption.

22. Project Visibility (100 words): Please describe your interest in and method for developing visibility for the project on your campus and beyond (publications and presentations at academic events, industry events, etc.).

Project results will be disseminated locally, regionally, and nationally. In addition to posting information on the University website, press releases will be issued to local media and the statewide Association of Independent Colleges and Universities. Poster displays will be set up at campus-wide events such as the annual Research Day, which celebrates student-faculty collaborative endeavors. An article will be prepared for *The Journal of Chemical Education* and results will be presented at the Conference on Chemical Education and the University of the South's annual Science Research and Education conference.

This paragraph addresses the hot button of "widespread dissemination," identifying specific local events and national conferences that will be targeted as well as a specific journal that will be targeted for publication of an article.

23. Contact Details: Please provide the following contact details for the Principal Investigator, the secondary contact, and up to three additional team members. Please provide information about your institution.

Principal Investigator: Dr. Neva Shelby, Professor; Chemistry; 2207 Ivalo Way, Louis, TX 06199; phone: (555) 444–3333; fax: (222) 111–0000; email: Neva.Shelby@griffin.edu

Secondary Contact: John Calder, Director of Technology Services; 2207 Ivalo Way, Louis, TX 06199; phone: (555) 444–5555; fax: (222) 111–2222; email: John.Calder@griffin.edu

Additional Team Members:
Dr. Cameron Nicholaus, Assistant Professor of Chemistry; 2207 Ivalo Way, Louis, TX 06199; phone: (555) 444–7777; fax: (222) 111–4444; email: Cameron.Nicholaus@griffin.edu

Dr. Patrick Ignatius, Assistant Professor of Chemistry and Environmental Science; 2207 Ivalo Way, Louis, TX 06199; phone: (555) 444–9999; fax: (222) 111–6666; email: Patrick.Ignatius@griffin.edu

Dr. Dominic Michael, Associate Professor of Geology; 2207 Ivalo Way, Louis, TX 06199; phone: (555) 444–3579; fax: (222) 111–0246; email: Dominic.Michael@griffin.edu

Institution Name: Griffin University, 2207 Ivalo Way, Louis, TX 06199

Institution Mission Statement: Griffin University is a private institution of higher education that is committed to providing an educational environment that is intellectually, spiritually and personally challenging.

Consistent with our set of core values, students will develop skills in critical and analytical thought, quantification, synthesis, problem solving and communication, and will learn to apply these as responsible citizens of a diverse, interdependent, changing world. Students will identify, test and strengthen their moral convictions, act with personal integrity, develop meaningful personal goals, and build relationships based on mutual respect.

Institution Tax ID number: 39–1234567

This final section requests the names, titles, and contact information for up to three additional team members and is the only place in the proposal where individuals other than the grant leader are listed. Because the online grant application form does not allow for a description of their roles in the project, it is only apparent by title that collaborators represent individuals within chemistry and within the natural sciences.

CHAPTER 6

Coordination Collaboration: Target Store Grants

As part of its role as a responsible corporate citizen, nationwide department store Target awards local Store Grants to support nonprofit programs that impact the arts, early childhood reading, and family violence prevention.

For 65 years, Target has been giving 5 percent of its income to enhance the communities in which it conducts business. In 2010, that translated into more than $3 million per week.

Target accepts Store Grant applications between March 1 and May 31 for projects taking place between October 1 of the same year and September 30 of the following year. Only grant applications submitted online are considered, and most awards average between $1,000 and $3,000. The Target Web site provides information about its history, commitment to social responsibility, funding priorities, eligibility criteria, application guidelines, and e-submission processes. Visit http://www.target.com/community.

In this chapter we examine a successful application to Target Store Grants. While the RFP guidelines do not require projects to be collaborative, Target values forming partnerships. For instance, to make an even bigger impact in its priority giving areas, Target partners with a variety of national organizations to make art more affordable and accessible, assist students with educational needs, and help people with their most basic and urgent needs. Aptly, this project represents a coordination collaboration between an institution of higher education and an elementary school to provide literacy tutoring and mentoring to disadvantaged youth.

By carefully reading the key ideas and concepts in the RFP, as well as reading between the lines, three hot buttons and one distinctive feature became apparent. The hot buttons, listed below, were given importance over other criteria because of their repetition throughout the RFP.

- **Disadvantaged Youth:** key phrases included "children from birth through age 9," "age groups," "babies/toddlers (under 5 years old)," "children (5–14 years old)," "diverse populations," "ethnic groups," "disabled," and "economically disadvantaged."

FIGURE 6.1   Screen image from Target Community Outreach Web page (www.target. com/community).

- **Community Relationships:** key phrases included "team members that currently serve on your organizations' board," "community volunteer opportunities," "geographic area served is local," "store closest to your organization," and "current board of directors list."

- **Program Evaluation:** key phrases included "measurement," "anticipated outcomes," "benefit the people served," and "complete a program evaluation form."

A distinctive feature noted in the RFP guidelines was the expectation of *recognition opportunities.* While many sponsors encourage the dissemination of project results, through which they gain acknowledgment for their financial support, in this case the publicity of the grant award seemed to take a front seat to the project's accomplishments. Persuasive proposals strategically address hot buttons and distinctive features in the narrative.

For this coordination collaboration, represented in exhibit 6.1, the partners aim to achieve individual goals through a codependency relationship. That is, the institution of higher education has a vision to engage students in a wide range of meaningful co-curricular leadership and service experiences that expose participants to current social

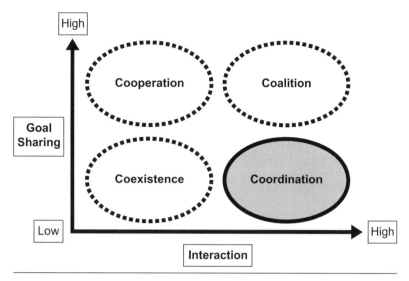

EXHIBIT 6.1   Coordination Collaboration

issues. The elementary school has a vision to help children reach their full potential in reading. The grant leader and school principal recognized that a calculated partnership would meet both their needs: connect college students with elementary children as volunteer tutors and mentors in an after-school literacy program.

The proposal is presented in its entirety on the following pages. What's more, we annotate key dimensions of the collaboration, leadership, and proposal in the call-out thought bubbles, so you can gain insight into the process of planning and writing a successful collaborative grant.

TARGET STORE GRANTS

Organization Information

Organization Tax ID: *399876543*

Organization Legal Name: The Legal Name as identified in the IRS database based on the Tax ID entered above.
Abigail Grace College

Organization Name: *Abigail Grace College*

AKA Name: *None*

Street Address or P.O. Box: Please include your street address in the first line & if applicable, the P.O. Box or Suite Number in the second line.
333 Lucky Street

City: *Winona*

State: *MN*

Zip Code: Please provide the full 9 digit ZIP code (www.usps.com is a helpful resource).
98765-4321

Main Phone Number: Please use this format (xxx) xxx-xxxx.
(210) 867-5309

Main Fax Number: Please use this format (xxx) xxx-xxxx.
(210) 867-5300

General E-Mail Address: *info@grace.edu*

Website: *www.grace.edu*

Which Best Describes The Organization? [multiple choice]
EDUCATION-Higher Education

Mission Statement:
Abigail Grace College is a higher education community that strengthens character, sharpens competence, and prepares Christians for service.

What Year Was the Organization Founded?
1937

Have You Ever Received a Target Grant? Please answer Yes or No.
Yes

While both collaborating organizations are eligible to apply for grant funding under the RFP guidelines, the partners agreed that the institution of higher education should be the lead applicant because the majority of work would be performed by and the majority of funding would go to the college student volunteers.

This one-word answer helps to establish the credibility of the lead applicant and the grant leader, who have received funding from this sponsor previously for a literacy project. The fact that they have been good stewards in the past suggests that they are trustworthy to manage another grant award. It also reduces the need for pre-proposal contacts.

Please List any Target Team Members that Currently Serve on Your Organization's Board: Please provide only the first and last name of each Target team member (i.e., John Doe) separated by commas.

None

Contact Information

Primary Contact for this Funding Request:

Prefix: *Ms.*

First Name: *Jessica*

Middle Initial: *A.*

Last Name: *Kwasny*

Suffix: *None*

Title: *Director of Service*

Street Address or P.O. Box: Please include your street address in the first line & if applicable, the P.O. Box or Suite Number in the second line.
333 Lucky Street

City: *Winona*

State: *MN*

Zip Code: Please provide the complete 9 digit ZIP code (www.usps.com is a helpful resource).
98765-4321

Direct Phone Number: Please use this format (xxx) xxx-xxxx.
(210) 867-5555

Fax Number: Please use this format (xxx) xxx-xxxx.
(210) 867-4001

E-Mail Address: *Jessica.Kwasny@grace.edu*

Organization Primary Contact: *(e.g., Executive Director, President)*

Prefix: *Dr.*

First Name: *Brychan*

Middle Initial: *D.*

Last Name: *William*

Suffix: *None*

Title: *President*

This "negative" response was not the preferred way to address the hot button of "community relationships." As a practical issue, it was just not realistic to try to recruit a member of the sponsor's team to serve on the board merely to increase the odds of funding success. Possibly, this detriment of absence was, in effect, neutralized by having received a literacy grant previously from the sponsor.

Street Address or P.O. Box: Please include your street address in the first line & if applicable, the P.O. Box or Suite Number in the second line.

333 Lucky Street

City: *Winona*

State: *MN*

Zip Code: Please provide the complete 9 digit ZIP code (www.usps.com is a helpful resource).
98765-4321

Direct Phone Number: Please use this format (xxx) xxx-xxxx.
(210) 867-3003

Fax Number: Please use this format (xxx) xxx-xxxx.
(210) 867-4004

E-Mail Address: *Brychan.William@grace.edu*

Proposal Information

Proposal General Information:

Request Amount: *$2,800*

Project/Program Title: Please limit your response to 25 words or less.
Abigail Grace College Tutoring Program at Aidan Tyler Elementary School.

Project/Program Start Date: *August 15, 2008*

Project/Program End Date: *May 15, 2009*

Proposal Detail: Which Best Describes the Primary Focus of the Project/ Program? [multiple choice]
EDUCATION-Before/After School Reading Programs
Please Provide a Summary of the Project/Program.

In 1993, Abigail Grace College became a site for the U.S. Department of Education "America Reads" literacy program, a national initiative that seeks to have all children reading proficiently by the end of the third grade, and the program has since expanded to include math tutoring (America Counts). Since 2005, Abigail Grace College students have tutored in the after-school mentoring program at Aidan Tyler Elementary School, a K-5 school in the Winona Area with 90% of its 175 students eligible for free/ reduced lunch and 66% racial/ethnic diversity. The neighborhood surrounding Aidan Tyler Elementary School has a Community Disadvantage Index of 8 (on a 9 point scale) according to the SMART System and is ranked in the top 5 most disadvantaged community tracts in Winona.

One of the most significant challenges in our primary education system is ensuring that children can read at appropriate levels. In the most recent

In less than 10 words, the project title conveys that this is a collaborative endeavor that will reach the sponsor's preferred age group of children.

The first paragraph confirms that the lead applicant has been addressing literacy issues in the community for more than a decade and that the partners have a history of working together over the past several years. This grant request, then, represents a systematic continuation of prior efforts to, in the sponsor's words, "foster a love of reading."
The opening paragraph also addresses the hot button of "disadvantaged youth." The free/reduced school lunch counts provide internal data to document that students come from economically disadvantaged families and the community survey provides external data to document that the surrounding neighborhood faces sizeable challenges.

statistics available (November 2006), 80% of third graders statewide are scoring at the proficient or advanced level in reading on the Aptitude and Concepts Examination. However, the same year's data shows that only 43% of Aidan Tyler Elementary School third graders are proficient or advanced in reading. The Helping to Trigger Talent Program (HTTP), a balanced literacy intervention that builds skills in the basic components of reading, accelerates vocabulary acquisition, and enhances students writing and critical thinking skills, is intended to help close the achievement gap at Aidan Tyler Elementary School.

In 2008–09, 12 Abigail Grace College students, as part of the fourth cohort of Campus Compact Citizen-Scholar Fellows, will continue to tutor/mentor 45 students at Aidan Tyler Elementary. Each of the tutors spends a few afternoons each week mentoring and tutoring students in Aidan Tyler's HTTP reading enhancement program. In addition to providing essential reading skills, Fellows, who are primarily low-income and/or first generation college students, also demonstrate that students from all academic brackets can succeed academically.

Abigail Grace College is requesting $2,800 help children to develop crucial reading skills, encourage families to read together, and help foster a lifelong love of reading. Funds will be used to transport tutors to children ($1,500); one dinner event ($400) to bring tutors, parents, and children together to celebrate accomplishments in reading; tutor training ($400); and books for children to take home to read with their families ($500).

Please Describe How the Project/Program Fosters a Love of Reading in Children.

Your contribution will enable tutors to travel to these at-risk children—at no cost to the children—and provide books for the tutored children to take home, encouraging them to read together with their families and to develop a lifelong love of learning. According to a recent survey of the Aidan Tyler Elementary HTTP students, 80% (28 out of 35) said they liked coming to the HTTP program, 97% (34 out of 35) said the HTTP program helped them to read better, and 88% (28 out of 32) said they read more now as a result of the program. Providing children with tutors after school and books to take home will give them both the skills and the practice they need to succeed. By involving the parents in the celebration and reading as families, children can see that reading is a lifelong pleasure that lasts beyond the school years.

What is the Average Age of Program Participants?

The second paragraph hits the hot button of "program evaluation." Namely, standardized baseline data exists that can show local student progress and be compared against state averages on reading test scores. Because the sponsor cares about the local community, this data is more persuasive than national student achievement data.

The third paragraph establishes the credibility of the grant leader, who was able to secure funding from a different sponsor in four consecutive years to support the college volunteers. Part of the program's success is based on the grant leader's ability to recruit students from disadvantaged backgrounds to serve children with similar situations.

The second sentence of this paragraph appeals to the hot button of "program evaluation." In addition to student achievement data, satisfaction surveys are being administered to assess student attitudes and behaviors. These results help to justify the costs of books for the children to take home and read with their families, a stated value of the sponsor.

What Year was this Project/Program Implemented?

2005

Please List Recognition Opportunities for Target: i.e., production/show alignments, newsletters, website, etc.

Your contribution would be highlighted on the Abigail Grace College's Campus Compact Citizen-Scholar Fellows web page (http://www.grace. edu/service). The College would also include you in our annual Wall of Donors and publicize your contribution through press releases to various media outlets.

This paragraph touches on the distinctive feature of "recognition opportunities" by identifying specific print and electronic publicity vehicles that are commonly used at the institution. Of note, this distinctive feature was confirmed in the grant award notification: the sponsor provided a CD-ROM with logo art, program ads, and a sample press release for the recipients to use.

What Community Volunteer Opportunities are Available?

An Abigail Grace College education is designed to be transformative, providing students with the skills they need to change themselves, their communities and their world. It allows students to explore the connections among formal learning, citizenship and service to the community. Thus, the College's service and volunteer mission engages students in a wide range of service opportunities and exposes them to current social issues. The Campus Compact Citizen-Scholar Fellows, as participants in the AmeriCorps Education Award Program, embody this dedication by serving 300 hours in the Greater Winona Area Community and in their home communities, and by each recruiting at least 5 other Abigail Grace students to assist with tutoring and other service projects. Community members are welcome to volunteer their time, talents, and treasure as appropriate.

This paragraph addresses the hot button of "community relationships." The grant leader manages a cadre of students who volunteer significant hours directly in the community as well as recruit others to assist with service projects. The final sentence is an open-ended invitation to members of the sponsor's team to join in and serve as literacy tutors and mentors.

Please Indicate your Best Estimate of the Percentage of those Served by this Project/Program for each of the Ethnic Groups Listed Below. Please input whole numbers only (no decimals), do not input percentage signs, and ensure that your allocations total 100%.

Asian or Pacific Islander	44
Bi/Multi Racial	0
Black or African American	29
Latino or Hispanic	0
Native American	0
White or Caucasian	27
Other Ethnic Group Not Specified Above	0

These population estimates touch on the hot button of "disadvantaged youth." Locally, these percentages demonstrate that high levels of diversity exist among school children in a small urban city that is not known for its diversity.

Please Indicate your Best Estimate of the Percentage of those Served by this Project/Program for each Gender Listed Below. Please input whole numbers only (no decimals), do not input percentage signs, and ensure that your allocations total 100%.

| Female | 47 |
| Male | 53 |

Please Indicate your Best Estimate of the Percentage of those Served by this Project/Program for each of the Age Groups Listed Below. Please input whole numbers only (no decimals), do not input percentage signs, and ensure that your allocations total 100%.

Babies/Toddlers (Under 5 Years Old)	0
Children (5–14 Years Old)	100
Youth (15–19 Years Old)	0
Young Adult (20–25 Years Old)	0
Adults (26–64 Years Old)	0
Senior Citizens (65 Years Old and Over)	0

Please Indicate your Best Estimate of the Percentage of those Served by this Project/Program for each of the Diverse Populations Listed Below. Please input whole numbers only (no decimals), do not input percentage signs.

Disabled	11
Economically Disadvantaged	76
Gays/Lesbians (GLBT)	0
Veterans	0

These population estimates address the hot button of "disadvantaged youth" and reveal that this literacy project is targeting the children in the greatest need: more than 75 percent are from economically disadvantaged families.

Other Proposal Attributes:
Which Best Describes the Geographical Area Served by this Project/Program? [multiple choice]
Local

Target Store Location: Please select the Target store closest to your organization from the dropdown list below.
Store #17, 601 Curry Blvd, Winona, MN 98765

Target Division to Fund Grant Request: Please select Target
Target

Type of Support Requested: Please select Grant
Grant

Type of Grant Request: Please select Project Support
Project Support
Measurement

How Many People do you Anticipate will be Served by this Project/Program? Please enter one whole number only.

45

What are the Anticipated Outcomes of the Project/Program? How will this program benefit the people served?

The goal of the project is to help close the achievement gap at Aidan Tyler Elementary by improving the reading skills of students in grades two through five. Abigail Grace College's outcome is to provide 12 well-trained tutors who will provide 2–3 hours of service per week from September 2008 through May 2009 at Aidan Tyler Elementary School. The College tracks the hours worked by tutors and assesses tutor effectiveness via site visits and individual supervision meetings.

As part of the tutoring partnership, the HTTP program (at Aidan Tyler Elementary School) examines the reading level of participating program before and after tutoring. For example, Samantha Ayla, the Learning Specialist for Winona Area Public Schools, stated in April that HTTP students at Aidan Tyler this year have made a 1.08 academic year's growth at semester, which means that they have gained (on average) over a year's growth in half a year's time. This is especially significant when we add in the special factors that surround many of the students including poverty, English Language Learning needs, and Special Education needs.

For the 2008–09 Target Grant Program Evaluation Form, Abigail Grace College will share the relevant tutor evaluation and will report data collected from the HTTP program.

In 2008/2009 we will be Asking All Grant Recipients to Complete a Program Evaluation Form.

The final three paragraphs address the hot button of "program evaluation." Systems and procedures exist locally to assess student achievement immediately in addition to feedback from standardized state tests. This data will be used to complete the sponsor's new required program evaluation form.

This collaboration exhibits dynamic factors relating to goal sharing, including effort and persistence, and to interaction, including communication, emotion, feedback, time management, and trust. Partners understand that they need each other in order to realize their individual goals. Thus, they put forth good-faith efforts and interact regularly for the benefit of the students and children.

The grant leader possesses leadership characteristics related to goal sharing and interaction including capacity to manage, decide, and set priorities; adaptability and flexibility of approach; capacity to motivate; outward display of trust; understanding of constituents and their needs; and skill in dealing with people. Recruiting, training, placing, and evaluating college student volunteers requires extensive communication and coordination with collaborative partners.

CHAPTER 7

Cooperation Collaboration: National Science Foundation Research in Disabilities Education

The National Science Foundation (NSF), with a congressionally mandated mission "to promote the progress of science; to advance the national health, prosperity, and welfare; and to secure the national defense," supports education and research across all non-medical fields of fundamental science, technology, engineering, and mathematics. From its modest beginnings in the early 1950s when a $225,000 budget allowed it to make 100 grant awards in a year, this independent agency now has a $6.9 billion annual budget (FY2010) and makes 10,000 new grant awards per year through more than 50 offices, directorates, and divisions.

To realize its vision for "advancing discovery, innovation and education beyond the frontiers of current knowledge, and empowering future generations in science and engineering," the NSF invests in fundamental and transformational research, leading-edge technologies and instrumentation, training and mentoring for promising researchers, and scientific literacy for K–16 students and the general public. Because invention frequently occurs at the intersections of disciplines, many NSF offices and directorates participate in crosscutting programs that promote collaborative endeavors exploring high-risk ideas, complex systems, and emerging fields.

The NSF Web site (http://www.nsf.gov) presents detailed information about the NSF's mission, strategic plan, budget, partners, funding trends, grant guidelines, electronic submission processes and procedures, special reports, and publications. It also provides searchable databases of grant awards, research discoveries, and science resource statistics.

In this chapter we examine a successful proposal to the Research in Disabilities Education program within NSF's Directorate for Education and Human Resources, Division of Human Resource Development. While the RFP guidelines did not specify a preferred type of collaboration, the program promotes "inclusiveness." Specifically, the "outcomes of the program's diverse areas of support seek the proportionate and fully inclusive participation of persons with disabilities in the nation's STEM [Science, Technology, Engineering, and Mathematics] workforce."

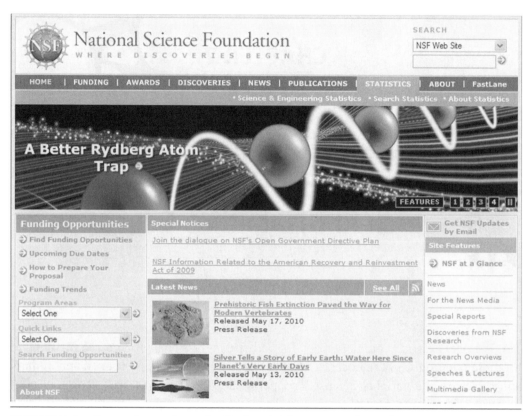

FIGURE 7.1   Screen image from the National Science Foundation home page used with permission (www.nsf.gov).

Simply stated, the following cooperation collaboration project attempts to answer one prime question: "How do you teach algebra to high school students who are blind?" The grant leader recognized that algebra is a "gateway" mathematics course to most STEM careers and knew from past experience that blind students, though they are perfectly capable of learning algebra, face many challenges because it is such a visual language. Accordingly, the grant leader assembled an interdisciplinary and inter-institutional team of educators, math instructors, and technology specialists with the aim to simplify the learning process, thereby increasing participation and achievement in mathematics by youths with disabilities.

Two hot buttons—intellectual merit and broader impacts—cut across all NSF programs and are the primary criteria on the reviewer's evaluation form. Intellectual merit refers to the significance of the proposed activity to advancing knowledge and understanding. Broader impacts refers to the ability of the activity to promote teaching, training, and learning. These hot buttons are so weighty to the NSF, in fact, that even the project summary must address both of them specifically: "Proposals that do not separately address both merit review criteria within the one-page Project Summary will be returned without review."

In addition to intellectual merit and broader impacts, following are hot buttons particular to the RFP guidelines for the Research in Disabilities Education program:

- **Demonstration:** key phrases included "increase participation and achievement," "engaging education," "promote accessibility to STEM disciplines and career experiences," "full participation," "science-enrichment activities," and "support services for recruitment and retention."

- **Enrichment:** key phrases included "availability of student-enrichment resources," "mentoring activities," "counselors," "tutorial centers," "summer internships," "career-development activities," "enhance STEM learning experiences," "broadening opportunities," "supportive and relevant experience," "nurture," "laboratory experiences," and "bridge programs."

- **Information Dissemination:** key phrases included "disseminate information," "instructional materials," "exceptional products," "successful research methods," "proven education practices," "widespread use," "information exchange," "commercialization," "inform the public," and "broad national audience."

- **Evaluation:** key phrases included "evaluation," "outcome measures," "techniques and/or instruments to be used for measuring," "program-level evaluation," "assess quantitative gains," "qualitative assessments," "formative and summative evaluations," "process of change," and "collecting and analyzing data."

Distinctive features noted in the RFP guidelines include:

- **Best Practices:** previous projects designed to recruit, train, and retain students with disabilities have consistently identified common elements such as hands-on science experiences, fostering student self-advocacy, encouraging peer interaction, mentoring by successful STEM professionals and students who have disabilities, and bridge programs.

- **Assistive Technology:** it is expected that "appropriate Assistive Technology (AT) will be integrated into the learning activities of students involved in the projects," and "an evaluation of the effectiveness of the AT, with recommendations for further improvement and universality of design" should be conducted.

These distinctive features influenced the shape and design of the project, but they are not repeated throughout the RFP guidelines like hot buttons. While integrating best practices and assistive technologies is a natural part of designing a comprehensive project for students with disabilities, quite simply, the sponsor wants explicit assurance that it will be done.

For this cooperation collaboration, represented in exhibit 7.1, a high level of goal sharing existed among partners and manifested itself in specific terms through their extensive exchange of resources. Though collaborators were physically located in three different states, they all knew each other, and most had worked together on other projects prior to the development of this proposal. In addition to their shared passion for addressing the needs of blind students, partners committed specific resources to this project, including haptic systems and other instructional technologies, educational materials, access to blind student populations, specialists in mathematics and education of the blind, and business office services.

The proposal is presented next, in its entirety. Note that bibliographic citation numbers were retained in the proposal to remain true to the original document, although the references themselves and other appendixes are not included. More significantly, key dimensions of the collaboration, leadership, and proposal are highlighted in the call-out

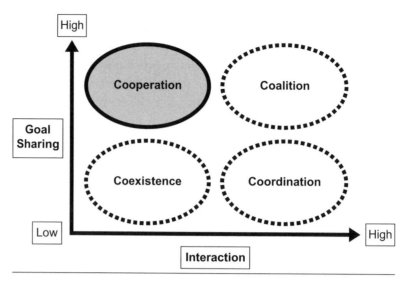

EXHIBIT 7.1   Cooperation Collaboration

thought bubbles, so you can gain insight into the process of planning and writing a successful collaborative grant. Following the proposal are verbatim comments from three external reviewers. Each NSF reviewer independently evaluated the intellectual merit and broader impact of this proposal as well as provided a summary statement. Our reactions to the reviewers' evaluations are also noted in call-out thought bubbles.

NATIONAL SCIENCE FOUNDATION RESEARCH IN DISABILITIES EDUCATION

Project Summary

Overview. This proposal is a $100,000 three-phased project over 12 months to develop, implement, and evaluate an introductory algebra course for blind students. The project is entitled VROOM: Visualizing the Real Operations Of Math.

Need. Mathematics is a visual language that poses major barriers to blind students considering careers in science, engineering, technology or mathematics (STEM). The learning challenges are further attenuated by federal law, parental advocates and educators who seek better tools and techniques. Presently, there is a dwindling supply of teachers properly trained to serve the blind students seeking STEM careers. As a result, there is a spiraling gap between the number of blind students needing training and those adequately trained to provide the requisite instruction.

Objectives and Methods. *Phase One* of the Project VROOM will produce a workable Math 101 (Introductory Algebra) curriculum under the guidance of an interdisciplinary team of mathematicians, engineers, instructional technologists, and special educators. *Phase Two* will field-test the Math 101 curriculum during a six-week summer workshop for blind high school students. Finally, *Phase Three* will evaluate the effectiveness of the Math 101 curriculum and disseminate the results to stakeholders concerned about educating blind students. The ultimate project outcome will be the creation of an evidence-based Math 101 curriculum, one that is technologically appropriate for the blind, and ready for further analysis and research.

Evaluation and Dissemination. Formative and summative evaluation measures will examine baseline and changes in knowledge and attitude among students and teachers. The formative data will ensure the effectiveness of the project during the granting period and allow for any needed "mid-course" corrections. The summative evaluation will judge the ultimate success of the completed project using both quantitative (test scores) and qualitative measures (focus groups and attitude surveys). Six different dissemination strategies will employ a blend of active/passive and visual/verbal dissemination approaches.

Intellectual Merit. The development of Math 101 and its demonstration through a summer mathematics workshop are unique. The key project staff has a cumulative 125 years of experience providing education, evaluation, technology and support services that directly impact the blind. This project is distinctive because no existing program provides

"VROOM: Visualizing the Real Operations of Math" is a catchy project title, one that would appeal to teenagers.

The opening sentence sets the stage that this project represents a collaboration among an interdisciplinary team of experts in content, pedagogy, and technology.

This paragraph appeals to all four program-specific hot buttons—"demonstration," "enrichment," "information dissemination," and "evaluation"—and both distinctive features—"best practices" and "assistive technology." Namely, an evidence-based, technologically appropriate introductory algebra course for blind students will be developed, field-tested, evaluated, and shared with others.

This paragraph provides even more detail about the hot button of "evaluation." The evaluation design includes gathering quantitative and qualitative data to assess formative and summative results. Test scores demonstrate student achievement, and focus groups and surveys reflect teacher and student attitudes toward activities.

an interdisciplinary, evidence-based approach to teaching Math 101 to the blind.

Broader Impacts. Blind students will receive algebra instruction in accessible formats, establish relationships with mentors for follow-up support and encouragement, and learn about STEM-based career options. **School systems** serving the blind can implement lesson plans for teaching math to blind students, improve existing techniques for teaching graphical information, and use CD-ROMs to teach existing students and future teachers. **University training programs** will acquire a replicable, evidenced-based model for teaching Math 101; adopt field-tested training materials; and deliver improved techniques for presenting science, mathematics, and engineering concepts to students with visual impairments. **Society** will nurture an early interest in mathematics and coordinate bridge programs between academic levels.

I. Work Statement

I.A Objectives

Rationale. The broad goal of Project VROOM is to develop, implement and evaluate a Math 101 course for blind students.

Five major factors underpin the rationale for selecting this goal. First, mathematics is a visual language that represents an enormous stumbling block to the more than 53,200 blind students in the U.S. educational systems, according to the American Printing House for the Blind[1] (FY03). Because of the visual barriers to learning, few blind students choose science, technology, engineering, or mathematics (STEM) careers at a time when the workplace requires increasingly advanced computation and technological skills.[2]

Second, our educational systems are becoming increasingly taxed in their ability to address the educational needs of blind students. For instance, in Louisiana, the demands on special educators, classroom teachers, and schools to provide services to students who are legally blind have grown in recent years, not only because of the mandates of federal laws, but also because of the rising sophistication among parent advocates, the continuing development of adaptive technology, the passage of a state Braille law which requires that Braille instruction be provided to all appropriate students, and state mandated achievement tests.

Third, many states have a severe shortage of certified teachers and resources to meet the needs of blind students. Teacher shortages for blind students are particularly acute in Illinois, Missouri, New York, Tennessee, Pennsylvania, Maryland, Virginia, Montana, and Florida.[3] The situation in Florida is so severe that they have adopted a loan forgiveness program

As required in the RFP guidelines, the project summary addresses separately the NSF-wide hot buttons of "intellectual merit" and "broader impacts." Further, the program-specific hot buttons and distinctive features are all covered underneath these umbrella hot buttons: for "demonstration," a new math course will be developed; for "enrichment," mentoring, career planning, and bridge programs will occur; for "information dissemination," lesson plans will be made available to schools; for "evaluation," a replicable model for teaching will exist; for "best practices," evidence-based approaches will be adopted; and for "assistive technology," accessible formats of instruction will be used.

The boldface headings used in the narrative matched the sponsor's grant proposal guide at the time the proposal was prepared. This kind of attention to document design facilitates the jobs of reviewers because they can find information quickly and easily.

The opening sentence states the overall goal of the proposed project, touches on the program-specific hot buttons of "demonstration" and "evaluation," and speaks to the sponsor's concern for increasing achievement of people with disabilities in STEM fields.

The RFP guidelines did not require a problem statement, yet the grant leader included "needs" data anyway to help justify the selection of the project objectives. This added detail increases the persuasiveness of the narrative.

whereby teachers of the blind with an outstanding student loan will have it forgiven, provided they remain serving blind students.

Fourth, "Introductory Algebra," Math 101 on most college campuses, is the "gateway" mathematics course to most STEM careers, an essential prerequisite to more advanced mathematics courses such as calculus or differential equations. Presently, a growing gap exists between the number of blind students who could take Math 101, and the number of math educators who are prepared to teach it to the blind. Specifically, the number of blind students has remained relatively constant while the number of math educators available to address the special needs of the blind continues to decrease, thereby accounting for the spiraling disparity between competence and performance.

Fifth, no evidence-based, field-tested, technology-based algebra curriculum exists that has been specifically adapted for the blind. Since appropriate curriculum materials are lacking and current evaluation and dissemination strategies are less than robust, this project addresses three broad goals.

1. To develop a Math 101 curriculum
2. To implement a Math 101 curriculum
3. To evaluate and disseminate a Math 101 curriculum

To produce a discernable impact on these three broad goals, specific measurable objectives are necessary for each of the three project phases.

Phase One Objectives: To Develop a Math 101 Curriculum.

The following objectives will develop a workable Math 101 curriculum.

1. Between November 2004 and December 2004, synthesize existing literature review and anecdotal information regarding Math 101 learning barriers
2. Between January 2005 and April 2005, develop technologically appropriate pedagogies for Math 101
3. Between April 2005 and May 2005, compile and critique the draft Math 101 curriculum
4. Between April 2005 and June 2005, revise Math 101 curriculum

The outcome of phase one is a "good-to-go" Math 101 curriculum.

Phase Two Objectives: To Implement a Math 101 Curriculum.

The following objectives will field-test the implementation of the Math 101 curriculum during a summer workshop for blind high school students. All objectives occur during the June-July 2005 period. Different objectives exist for each of four personnel categories.

The genesis of this project can be traced back to the grant leader, who recognized the gap in mathematics achievement among blind students and the inability of educational systems to fulfill their legal obligation to provide Braille instruction to students when deemed appropriate by Individual Educational Programs. Because this problem situation is so complicated and is widespread to many states, the grant leader assembled an interdisciplinary, inter-institutional team to devise a workable solution.

Collectively, these need arguments foreshadow the necessity of a collaborative approach because the problem is far-reaching: it affects students, teachers, administrators, parents, educational technologists, and policy makers.

The current lack of an evidence-based, field-tested, technology-based algebra curriculum touches on the distinctive features of "best practices" and "assistive technology." That is, the grant leader begins to establish credibility by demonstrating knowledge of and familiarity with the tools and techniques being used with blind students.

Given the complexity of the problem, collaborators agreed to break the solution into chunks: three different phases with four different target populations. Hence, objectives address developing, implementing, and evaluating and disseminating a math curriculum and address teachers, students, mentors, and math educators.

Workshop Teacher Objectives

1. Conduct Math 101 classes using newly developed curriculum
2. Maintain daily journal of classroom experiences
3. Provide semi-weekly formal feedback to math educators

Student Participant Objectives

1. Complete Math 101 at Louisiana Tech University with a passing grade
2. Master ten strategies for solving algebra homework problems
3. Share Math 101 learning experiences with 10 student peers

Workshop Mentor Objectives

1. Attend Math 101 classes
2. Be accessible for homework tutoring and personal mentoring at least two hours daily
3. Maintain a log of student questions and academic or personal concerns

Math Educator Objectives

1. Coordinate project administration
2. Collect formative and summative evaluation data
3. Solve unanticipated instructional technology problems

Collectively, these phase two objectives cover the summer workshop experience and provide crucial evaluation and dissemination data.

Phase Three Objectives: To Evaluate and Disseminate a Math 101 Curriculum

1. Between June 2005 and July 2005 conduct formative and summative evaluations
2. Between August 2005 and October 2005, post on Web site, www.instituteonblindness.latech.edu, the project status reports: purpose, outcomes, educational materials, evaluation results
3. By September 2005, submit for publication an article to the Journal of Visual Impairment and Blindness
4. Present conference papers at the American Society of Engineering Education (by June 2006) and the American Educational Research Association (by April 2006)

The objectives appeal directly to the program-specific hot buttons of "demonstration," "enrichment," "information dissemination," and "evaluation." Together they show strategies for increasing academic achievement in and out of the classroom and strategies for assessing and sharing the results in local and national contexts.

By the end of Phase Three an evidence-based Math 101 curriculum will exist, one that is technologically appropriate for the blind, one that should increase the participation and achievement of blind persons in science, technology, engineering, and mathematics (STEM) education and careers. As a next step, this demonstration project will be ready for a rigorous research investigation that would allow for further development via a focused research initiative.

I.B Significance

This project derives its uniqueness from its target population, curricular focus, and interdisciplinary project personnel.

Target Population Rationale: Serving the Blind and Visually Impaired

The Individuals with Disabilities Education Act (IDEA, 1997) mandates that all children receive appropriate educational services. The U.S. Department of Education (ED) reports[4] that blind students completing 12th grade took an average of two math units (one year) and received an average grade of "C." Additionally, ED reports that 72% of blind eighth graders receive a high school diploma and 70% of those high school graduates enroll in post-secondary education. Upon graduation, the unemployment rate for the blind is high; according to the American Foundation for the Blind[5], the incidence of unemployment among the blind ages 18–69 runs approximately 65%, reflecting a disproportionate difficulty in securing jobs, compared with their sighted peers.

Curricular Focus Rationale: Math 101

Math 101 was selected as the instructional focus of this project for four reasons. First, since the mathematics baseline for most blind students is high school arithmetic, the next logical progression would be an introductory algebra course, typically "Math 101" in most institutions of higher learning. Second, Math 101 is the "gateway" course for more advanced algebra, calculus, and differential equations, courses essential to most STEM programs. Third, the target audience for this project is high school students, most of whom will already have had at least the essential prerequisites to Math 101. Fourth, selection of a higher level math course, say, Calculus, would result in a much smaller pool of students.

Interdisciplinary Project Personnel: 125 Years of Cumulative Experience

The key project personnel represent a unique blend of interdisciplinary interests including biomedical engineering, mathematics, education of the blind, adaptive technology, instructional technology, and mathematics education. Their 125 years of cumulative experience makes them uniquely postured to address a significant problem that transcends traditional academic boundaries.

I.C. Relation to Longer-Term Goals of PI's Project

Five experienced professionals constitute the key project personnel. Full biosketches are found in the appendices.

The final sentence in this section foreshadows that if the demonstration project is successful, the grant leader will apply to the sponsor again in a future cycle for a focused-research initiative grant, which is typically three years in duration. This demonstrates the grant leader's long-term vision and plan.

Though the RFP guidelines ask only for a description of the "relation of the longer-term goals of the PI's project," the following five paragraphs identify all of the partners by name, institution, and their work. This added information conveys to reviewers that success of the initiative is founded in the shared long-term goals of all the collaborators, not just the grant leader.

Project Director: Dr. Stan Cronk. Dr. Cronk is Assistant Director for Education at the Center for Biomedical Engineering and Rehabilitation Science and an Assistant Professor of Biomedical Engineering at Louisiana Tech University. His overarching research thrust deals with the applications of ergonomics and human factors engineering to special populations. His specific research focus has been, and continues to be, on human computer access for people with disabilities, a central component of this proposal. Prior to joining the Louisiana Tech faculty, he was a Clinical Rehabilitation Engineer at the University of Tennessee Health Science Center in Memphis.

Project Co-Director: Dr. Ronald Ferguson. Dr. Ferguson is a Senior Research Fellow, Coordinator of the Orientation and Mobility Program, and Assistant Director of the Professional Development and Research Institute on Blindness at Louisiana Tech University. Long-term, his scholarly research concentrates on involvement of blind and visually impaired children in science, technology, education, and mathematics. His administrative and academic background makes him well postured to not only conduct this project but cast it in the larger context of educational policies designed to solve social problem. Dr. Ferguson is visually impaired.

Algebra Instructor: Dr. Charles Patterson. Dr. Patterson has 10 years of experience teaching high school math, including algebra and geometry. Additionally, Dr. Patterson has six years experience as a college instructor in the mathematics and statistics program at Louisiana Tech University. Holding undergraduate and graduate degrees in mathematics education, Dr. Patterson has trained public school math teachers in conjunction with a regional math and science center. Further, he has worked with secondary school curriculum redesign teams to align the content of mathematics courses to isomorphically match the National Council of Teachers of Mathematics Standards and the State of Louisiana Benchmarks. Finally, he received the Outstanding Teaching Award from the College of Engineering and Science, Louisiana Tech University, 2002.

Nonvisual Access Technology Consultant: Curtis Chong. Mr. Chong is an internationally recognized expert in the field of access technology for the blind. He presently serves as director of Project ASSIST (Accessible Step-by-Step Instructions for Speech Technology with Windows) for the Iowa Department of the Blind. He has over a quarter century of experience in commercial Information Technology and twenty years of experience in nonvisual access technology. Prior to working for the Iowa Department of the Blind, he was Director of Technology, National Federation of the Blind, where he directed their national technology programs. Mr. Chong has served as a member of the Electronic Information and Technology Access Advisory Committee of the architectural and Transportation Barriers Compliance Board. Mr. Chong is blind.

The grant leader possesses leadership characteristics related to goal sharing, including adaptability and flexibility of approach; capacity to manage, decide, and set priorities; intelligence and judgment in action; and task competence. The grant leader also possesses characteristics related to interaction, including capacity to motivate; outward display of trust; skill in dealing with people; and understanding of constituents and their needs.

Collaborators are fueled by passion and energy, not just money; they have lived with disabilities and are dedicated to improving the quality of life for others. The grant leader's talent for defining precise roles for collaborators and keeping them motivated fosters inclusive participation and engagement.

Collaborators discussed the use of the word "isomorphically" in the fourth sentence of the paragraph. While it is familiar to mathematicians, it may be unfamiliar to other grant reviewers. Because this is a math project, they ultimately agreed to risk using this word and to remain optimistic that others could derive its meaning by knowing that an "isosceles" triangle has two equal sides.

Math Education Consultant: Susan Osterhaus. Ms. Osterhaus has been teaching secondary mathematics for 25 years at the Texas School for the Blind and Visually Impaired in Austin, Texas. She has a bachelor's degree in Mathematics, a master's degree in Mathematics Education, and certifications in Secondary Math, English, and Teaching the Visually Impaired from the University of Texas at Austin. In addition to her teaching duties, she has served on the Texas Assessment of Academic Skills (TAAS) committee, which developed guidelines for adapting and transcribing TAAS math and science questions for Braille readers. She also served as an expert on a three-year national research project, which produced the Computerized Nemeth Tutor. She has beta-tested three Nemeth Code translation and two voice recognition software packages, a talking scientific calculator, and an accessible graphing calculator.

I.D Relation to Present State of Knowledge in Field

Much current interest focuses on screen access technology and its blending with voice recognition systems.

Screen Access Technology. A 2004 report by Walker and Stageberg[6] summarizes current developments in screen access technology. Screen access programs, also called screen readers, most commonly provide information through synthesized speech. The information provided by screen access programs can also be shown on a refreshable Braille display. The Braille support offered in the two most popular screen access programs, *JAWS for Windows*[7] and *Window-Eyes*[8].

JAWS for Windows provides three Braille "modes" that determine how information sent to the Braille display is presented, what commands are available, and how Braille-related commands function. This allows a great degree of flexibility, but adds complexity that makes this program more difficult to learn and use for a Braille-only user. Since much of the spoken information is not displayed in the default Braille mode, the process of switching modes, reviewing this spoken information, and then switching back to the default display mode is unnecessarily complex. Further, it only reads equations formatted in MathML, which is essentially a special form of HTML that facilitates the static display of equations in web page format but doesn't provide the blind user with an interactive experience.

In *Window-Eyes,* information displayed in Braille corresponds to spoken information. Three options exist to display text: (1) from the line at the insertion point in a document, (2) the selected item in a menu, or (3) the line of text at the location of the mouse pointer. Commands to provide spoken information that are not displayed on the computer screen also display the information in Braille for a specified period of time. Nevertheless, no

This collaboration exhibits dynamic factors relating to goal sharing, including commitment, goal orientation, motivation to pursue goal, persistence, priorities, and risk tolerance. All partners have a long history of instructing people with disabilities; their careers are marked by taking risks to bring incremental improvements to educational settings.

This collaboration also exhibits dynamic factors relating to interaction, including change orientation, communication, and trust. Some partners had prior histories of working together, and all shared the long-term goal of advancing the interests of blind people, so high levels of trust existed. They willingly shared resources and communicated with each other, providing access to assistive technologies and exchanging nearly 700 e-mails during the development of this proposal.

This literature review section establishes the credibility of the grant leader and the project as well as justifies the sharing of technology resources among partners.

indication is given regarding which of the three display options is being presented.

Combining Voice Recognition with Screen Readers. McCall[9] recently described a client-based approach to using voice recognition with screen readers. Combining technologies affords the visually impaired blended solutions for computer competency. Examples of blended solutions include combining *WindowEyes* by GW Micro with *Dragon NaturallySpeaking,*[10] *JAWS for Windows* from Freedom Scientific with *JawBone*[11] from Next Generation Technology, or *Dragon NaturallySpeaking* with IBM *ViaVoice.*[12] McCall recommends matching students with existing technologies to ensure the blind make good use of a computer, a screen reader and voice recognition technology.

MathTalk. Gray[13] is developing an approach called MathTalk for the Visually Impaired.[14] The program, which works with speech recognition, a screen reader, and a Nemeth converter software, is designed to allow the user to dictate work done in Nemeth Braille[15] into the computer so it can be converted into a print format and printed for the course instructor. While MathTalk provides a method for a blind user to solve math problems and create graphs using speech recognition, Braille is an output but not an input option, thereby limiting its use by the blind, especially for visualizing graphs.

I.E Relation to Work in Progress by Key Project Personnel under Other Support

Dr. Cronk is currently Project Director (15% FTE) on an assistive technology grant funded by the Rehabilitation Services Administration, Office of Special Education and Rehabilitative Services, U.S. Department of Education (Award No.: H129E980000; $500,000, 9/01/1998 to 8/31/2004). The purpose of this project was to develop a set of distance learning courses in assistive technology for professionals with a wide variety of backgrounds, including engineering and vocational counseling. Upon successful completion of the year-long, 15 semester hour program, each student is well prepared to take the Assistive Technology Practitioner (ATP) professional certification exam offered by RESNA.

Dr. Ferguson is currently Project Director (5% FTE) on a STEM project that examines the involvement of blind and visually impaired children in math and science education. The project is funded by the Rehabilitation Services Administration, Office of Special Education and Rehabilitative Services, U.S. Department of Education (Award No.: H235J030017; $49,675, 07/01/03 to 06/30/04). Briefly, this project investigates the reasons why blind and visually impaired children drop out of the STEM track so early in their educational pathways and identifies ways to

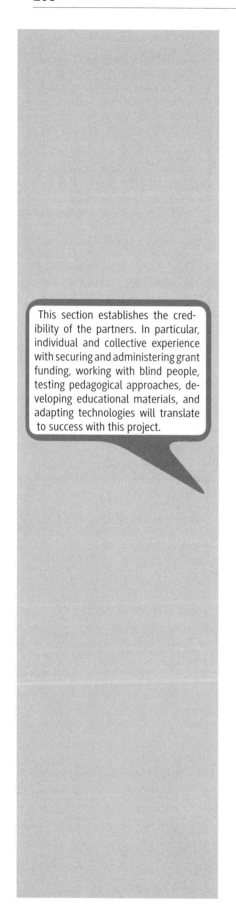

This section establishes the credibility of the partners. In particular, individual and collective experience with securing and administering grant funding, working with blind people, testing pedagogical approaches, developing educational materials, and adapting technologies will translate to success with this project.

avoid this aspect of "brain drain" which can hopefully be turned into a "brain gain."

Dr. Charles Patterson. As a math educator, Dr. Patterson regularly serves as a math content expert seeking to increase mathematics content knowledge and pedagogical content knowledge. He is presently working with a Louisiana Board of Regents grant entitled *Making Mathematics Meaningful (M³) for Elementary Teachers,* a three-year partnership among Louisiana Tech University and elementary schools in North Louisiana. He is also a math faculty member on an NSF grant, *Building Bridges and Leadership Capacity in Middle Grades Mathematics and Science,* which is currently under review. This grant would seek to develop a Math/Science Partnership among Louisiana Tech and middle school teachers in Louisiana and the surrounding region.

Mr. Curtis Chong leads the Iowa Department for the Blind's work on project ASSIST, launched in 1997, (Accessible Step-by-Step Instructions for Speech Technology with Windows). The purpose of Project ASSIST is to develop and distribute computer training materials to blind and visually impaired individuals. In 2002, Project ASSIST received a grant from the National Institute on Disability and Rehabilitation Research (NIDRR) to expand its training efforts. The goal of this new project is to create a comprehensive array of computer training materials tailored to the needs of deaf-blind individuals.

Ms. Susan Osterhaus is presently developing math guidelines for the new Texas Assessment of Knowledge and Skills (TAKS). She continues to serve on the Texas Braille Textbook Review Panel to assure the quality of math Braille books, with particular emphasis on the Nemeth Code and tactile graphics. Through her efforts, the American Printing House for the Blind now produces an affordable Braille/Print Protractor, which allows blind and visually impaired students to measure and construct angles independently.

I.F Relation to Work in Progress Elsewhere

Related work clusters mainly into applications of adaptive devices or development of new languages.

Digital Talking Books for Math. Schleppenbach[16] recently summarized research currently underway to develop a standard for the production of Digital Talking Book[17] versions of Math and Science Books (using MathSpeak), and a software player (the gh PLAYER™)[18] module that can properly render math aurally and visually. Specifically, several mathematics textbooks, one science textbook, and a standardized test involving math and science have been prepared in this format by gh and tested among

During the development of this proposal, collaborators shared information about available technologies that might be adapted to teach algebra to blind students. Some collaborators already owned and had experience working with a few of these devices, so they shared these resources with the other partners.

print disabled students in a variety of settings ... is an extension of the basic MathSpeak™[19] grammar and lexico... y developed by Dr. Nemeth for use by a human reader.

Introductory Calculus for the Visually Impaired. With funding from NSF (Award # 9450166), Kress and colleagues[20] at CUNY Staten Island are developing and testing instructional materials usable by these visually impaired students taking beginning calculus. It will use the most effective current audio and tactile technology to provide access to graphical information. In the proposed three year project, the investigators will develop courseware for teaching the calculus to first year college students. For the basic course content, the investigators will use a successful self paced mastery course in calculus developed for STEM students at Carnegie Mellon University.

Mathematics Accessible to Visually Impaired Students (MAVIS). (MAVIS) is an NSF funded (Award # 9800209) access project dedicated to ensuring that communication between mathematics faculty and their blind students is clear and meaningful. Gillan[21] and his New Mexico State University colleagues note two major problems exist when attempting to establish this communication. The MAVIS project attempts to identify intuitive tools that give blind students quality materials and produce quality standard print technical documents for their instructors

Math Translation Software. Gurari[22] and his Ohio State University colleagues, with current NSF support (Award # 0312487) are developing transcribing software to make scientific and technical literature freely and almost instantaneously available to Braille readers through fully-automated translation of both MathML and LaTeX to Nemeth Braille. The resulting software will be the first Braille transcribing utility capable of simultaneous and automated processing of mathematical formulas, scientific text, spatial arrangements and XML-described formats.

Speech Assisted Learning. Mangold[23] and her colleagues received a NSF SBIR Phase I Award (# 19760018) to create unique speech-assisted Braille mathematics in the form of a stand-alone self-study system. Their Speech Assisted Learning (SAL) system utilizes synthesized speech for tutorials, verification of Braille symbols, and feedback. No keyboarding skills are required. The overall objective is to determine whether visually impaired individuals can augment Braille math instruction via the SAL.

Nemeth Braille Code. Recent research by DeMario[24] found that teachers are not adequately trained at the university level to transcribe materials using the Nemeth code and recommends that it should be taught in a separate teacher training course, not the same course as literary Braille. However, even training does not ensure classroom competency. Kapperman and Stricken[25] surveyed teachers who have been trained in the use

> By citing four projects in a row that were funded by the sponsor, the collaborators attempt to situate this initiative into the pipeline of activity. Simply put, funding this project is a means for the sponsor to leverage its own funds to achieve even greater results.

of Nemeth code and found that only a small proportion of the 34 teachers sampled could provide the dot configures for five basic symbols of the Nemeth code. Conclusion: training does not ensure retention and application.

Eight Dot Braille Notation. Several investigators are exploring the use of an eight dot Braille code as opposed to the standard six dot form. For instance, Durre and Durre[26] examined the instant print-Braille compatibility with COBRA, an eight dot computer Braille notation system, which achieves immediate print-Braille compatibility through one-to-one representation of letters and others character. The Braille-print compatibility affords ease of use for classroom teachers who are unskilled in writing Braille. Another eight-dot Braille notation has been advanced by Gardner,[27] his DotsPlus system also uses raised-line graphical systems instead of Braille symbols. Once mathematical symbols are translated into Braille notation, they are enlarged 2.5 times and printed out on a machine that sets type in raised wax, an approach that is not cost effective.

Scientific Notebook. Osterhaus[28] and colleagues have developed Scientific Notebook, a print math editing program that scripts mathematics in a clear, unambiguous way that is ideal for transcription into Nemeth Code. It has a number of automatic formatting controls for text elements, such as headers, displayed equations, and bulleted or numbered lists. Although these features make mathematics look pretty on print paper, the ability to detect and eliminate these additional structures is crucial to getting correctly formatted Braille out on a Nemeth Code converter. In addition, Scientific Notebook includes a built-in scientific graphic calculator, which has a view screen that can be enlarged to 400%, used with a computer program that enlarges texts, or used independently by a student with low vision to complete homework assignments.

II. Outline of General Work Plan

Although the 1997 federal Individuals with Disabilities Education Act (IDEA) requires public schools to provide equal and appropriate education for all students, school personnel are not fully trained to consider all possible career options for the blind. In particular, blind students may be steered away from highly technical careers with the possibility of high salaries because of their difficulty interpreting visual materials such as graphs and charts. Even commonly taught mathematical equations such as the solution to the quadratic equation,

$$x = \frac{-b \pm \sqrt{b^2 - 4ac}}{2a}$$

are difficult to read unless provided in character format without graphic enhancements. The following discussion explains, step-by-step, how we

This transitional paragraph reminds reviewers of the significance of the problem for blind students, punctuated by presenting the quadratic equation as an expression rather than simply in words, then outlines that this project will develop, implement, evaluate and disseminate a new Math 101 model.

will develop, field test, evaluate, and disseminate an evidence-based approach to teaching Math 101 to the blind.

II.A Broad Design of Activities to be Undertaken

Overview of Activities. Classroom experience demonstrates that assistive technologies help blind students learn. Accordingly, this technology focused project represents a blend of activities for Phase One (Curriculum Development), Phase Two (Curriculum Implementation) and Phase Three (Curriculum Evaluation and Dissemination) that will occur during the 12 month project period. The research subjects will consist of ten junior and senior high school or college students (all legally blind: ≤20/200 visual acuity and visual field of 20 degrees or less) who will be recruited nationwide to participate in a six week summer algebra workshop. The key project staff will technologically adapt a conventional introductory algebra course for use with blind students. Sample lessons will be available for distribution on CD-ROMS. Formative and summative evaluations will assess project progress and outcomes. Project outcomes will be disseminated using a range of active/passive, visual/verbal dissemination strategies.

II.B Project VROOM Methods and Procedures

The methods and procedures cluster into the three project phases and grow organically from the measurable objectives, repeated below in bold text, followed by the resulting action items.

Phase One: Curriculum Development

1. **Between November, 2004 and December, 2004, the five key project personnel will synthesize existing literature review and anecdotal information regarding Math 101 learning barriers** by listing and prioritizing the frequently reported Math 101 barriers, e.g., inadequate teacher training, technology limitations, and student perceptions. Focus group meetings with math educators, blind professionals with knowledge of advanced math, and upper level blind students will pinpoint ways to improve the teaching/learning process. The resulting analysis will yield a Math 101 Barrier Matrix that serves as the starting point to adapt appropriate technologies.

2. **Between January, 2005 and April, 2005 the key project personnel will develop technologically appropriate pedagogies for Math 101** by reviewing existing technologies in light of Barrier Matrix findings and identifying potential low-cost, widely applicable solutions. More precisely, Dr. Patterson will work closely with Mr. Chong and other math educators to develop technological approaches to algebra instruction. The outcome of this step will be a corpus of technologically appropriate pedagogies that could be potentially integrated into the Math 101 curriculum.

This paragraph touches on all program specific hot buttons—"demonstration," "enrichment," "information dissemination," and "evaluation"—and both distinctive features—"best practices" and "assistive technology."

The entire Work Plan specifies which partners will collaborate on what activities and when. Given the complexity of the project, collaborators shared their combined resources—assistive and instructional technologies, educational materials, access to blind students, and specialties in content and pedagogy—to deliver the stated objectives.

The grant leader planned to conduct round-robin focus groups with students and instructors on a few of the more promising approaches to teaching algebra to the blind. Engaging students and instructors in the planning stage increases the likelihood of their participation in the implementation stage.

3. **Between April 2005 and May, 2005, the key project personnel will compile and critique the draft Math 101 curriculum** by matching the technological solutions with Barrier Matrix problem identified. Specifically, all key project personnel will work together to develop teaching strategies and to integrate high and low tech technologies to teach Math 101. Once the tentative technological barriers have been addressed, then the proposed solutions will be critiqued via a Focus Group procedure by our Math Advisory Board (MAB), which consists of six blind math educators with a minimum of 10 years of experience.

4. **Between May 2005 and June, 2005, revise Math 101 curriculum** by implementing recommendations from the Math Advisory Board. Specifically, the revised Math 101 curriculum will be pilot tested with three students at the Louisiana Center for the Blind, adjacent to the Louisiana Tech campus.

As a result of the following these procedures and developing these systems, the Math 101 curriculum is ready for field testing.

More broadly, the key project personnel will identify the basic content that should be included in an introductory algebra course, such as

• Rational Numbers	• Area of Polygons
• Equations with Rational Numbers	• Congruent Polygons
• Using Reciprocals to Solve Equations	• Similar Polygons
• Ratio, Proportions, & Percents	• Square Roots
• Percents	• Pythagorean Theorem
• Perimeters & Circumferences	• Frequency Tables

Pre- and post-test questions will be administered to the blind students, sampling knowledge in each of these areas, determining baseline behavior, and quantifying subsequent learning. A representative pool of test questions is found in Appendix One.

Once the essential course content has been identified, the key project staff will concentrate on presenting traditional visual, two-dimensional and nonlinear mathematical information in a meaningful technology form for blind students. The recent work of Cahill[29] provides important adaptation guidelines. She reports that the blind and partially sighted students find their greatest challenges in handling the mechanical aspects of mathematics. More precisely, when solving algebraic expressions, in comparison to a control group of sighted students, the blind and partially sighted reported significant difficulty with accuracy and speed of manipulation and memory overload. Teachers' interviews complemented the results of these findings.

Course Adaptations

Nov 2004– Mar 2005	Recruit instructional staff and mentors	Drs. Cronk, Ferguson & Patterson
Dec 2005	Survey algebra course syllabi	Dr. Patterson, Ms. Osterhaus
Jan 2005	Focus group survey of six blind math teachers	Drs. Cronk, Ferguson, Patterson, Ms. Osterhaus, Mr. Chong
Feb 2005	Identify major instructional barriers	Drs. Cronk, Ferguson, Patterson, Ms. Osterhaus, Mr. Chong
Mar 2005	Strategize non-technology adaptations needed	Drs. Cronk, Ferguson, Patterson, Ms. Osterhaus
Apr 2005	Finalize algebra course syllabus	Dr. Cronk, Dr. Patterson, Ms. Osterhaus
May 2005	Review syllabus with instructional staff and mentors	Dr. Cronk, Dr. Patterson, Ms. Osterhaus
May 2005	Conduct in-service workshop for STEM faculty at Louisiana Tech	Drs. Cronk & Patterson

Technology Adaptations

Nov 2004– Jan 2005	Review existing hardware	Dr. Cronk, Dr. Patterson, Mr. Chong, Ms. Osterhaus
Nov 2004– Jan 2005	Review existing software technologies	Dr. Cronk, Dr. Patterson, Mr. Chong, Ms. Osterhaus
Feb–Mar 2005	Adapt assistive technologies for blind	Dr. Cronk, Dr. Patterson, Mr. Chong, Ms. Osterhaus
Apr 2005	Field test with local LCB students	Drs. Cronk & Paterson
May 2005	Revise adaptations	Dr. Cronk, Dr. Patterson, Mr. Chong, Ms. Osterhaus

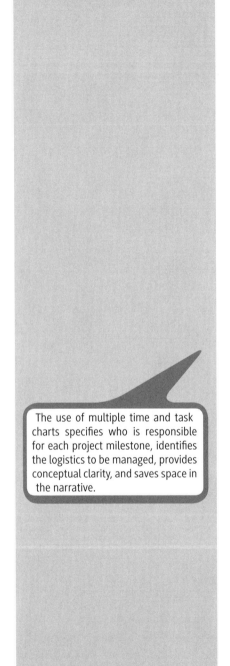

The use of multiple time and task charts specifies who is responsible for each project milestone, identifies the logistics to be managed, provides conceptual clarity, and saves space in the narrative.

The timeline for making appropriate course and technology adaptations is as follows. It indicates the dates, tasks, and responsible persons.

Phase Two: Curriculum Implementation

The locus of activity during Phase Two centers on the summer workshop (June 13, 2005 through July 22, 2005).

Recruitment. To ensure the broadest possible project impact, blind students will be selected from throughout the nation. Specifically, program announcements will be sent to the presidents of the state affiliates of the National Federation of the Blind for distribution at state conventions, which holds special sessions for parents and teachers of blind children. The National Federal of the Blind (NFB), the nation's largest and most influential membership organization of blind persons. Additionally, program announcements will be sent to state conventions of parent/teacher organizations, math teachers at state schools for the blind and visually impaired, state directors of special education programs, and directors of the 35 university programs that offer training in orientation and mobility, rehabilitation teaching, rehabilitation counseling, or teaching of visually impaired children. Finally, program announcements will be distributed to university mathematics department chairs throughout the country, and through the listserv of the American Mathematical Society, and the National Council of Teachers of Mathematics.

Selection. Successful applicants will have completed at least one year of high school mathematics and have an ACT score greater than 22, which suggests, based on past experience, a capacity for handling the intellectual rigors of algebra. Additionally, the students must have an endorsement letter from an appropriate school official. Beyond these academic criteria and recommendation letters, the applicants must fill out an application form.

A timeline for recruiting and selecting blind students appears on the following page.

The proposed summer workshop will provide six weeks of algebra-related instruction. Mornings will be devoted to formal classroom instruction via lectures, discussions, and question and answer sessions. Afternoons will be spent in the Math Technology Laboratory and devoted to student mentoring activities, primarily reinforcing classroom presentations, solving daily homework problems, review of note taking skills, and preparation for tests.

Once students complete their daily academic work, they will be given multiple opportunities for participation in social activities with peers at the nationally-renowned Louisiana Center for the Blind (LCB), located within one mile of the campus of Louisiana Tech University; LCB students will share weekend social activities, including but not limited to visiting Six Flags in Dallas, a minor league baseball game in Shreveport, and a cook out at the beach.

Specific activities for students, teachers, and mentors follow on the next pages.

In problem-solving investigations, students demonstrate an understanding of concepts and processes that allow them to analyze, represent,

Collaborators are so passionate and committed to advancing their shared goal of improving the quality of life for blind students that they willingly provide unlimited access to their professional and personal networks. In this case, the partners' contributions constitute a whole that is greater than the sum of its individual parts.

Student Recruitment and Selection		
Nov 2004	Distribute Program Announcement to NFB	Dr. Ferguson
Nov 2004	Contact State PTOs	Dr. Ferguson
Nov 2004	Contact State Schools for B&VI	Dr. Ferguson
Nov 2004	Contact State Directors of Spec. Ed.	Dr. Ferguson
Nov 2004	Contact University training programs	Dr. Ferguson
Nov 2004	Contact American Mathematics Society and National Council of Teachers of Mathematics	Dr. Ferguson
Nov 2004	Establish Web Presence	Dr. Cronk
Nov 2004–Jun 2005	Respond to potential applicant questions	Dr. Ferguson
Nov 2004–Mar 2005	Collect applications and review for completeness	Drs. Cronk and Ferguson
Mar 2005	Convene Advisory Panel to review applicants and select participants, including alternates	Drs. Cronk and Ferguson
Mar 2005	Notify applicants	Dr. Ferguson
Mar–Apr 2005	Finalize local arrangements	Drs. Cronk and Ferguson

and describe relationships among variable quantities and apply algebraic methods to real-world situations. Specifically, workshop participants will use manipulatives, models, graphs, tables, technology, number sense, and estimation as they extend their investigations of problems involving the concepts and application of algebra. As a result, the participants will be able to do the following:

- demonstrate the ability to translate real-world situations (e.g., distance versus time relationships, population growth, growth functions for diseases, growth of minimum wage, auto insurance tables) into algebraic expressions, equations, and inequalities and vice versa;
- recognize the relationship between operations involving real numbers and operations involving algebraic expressions;
- use tables and graphs as tools to interpret algebraic expressions, equations, and inequalities;
- solve algebraic equations and inequalities using a variety of techniques with the appropriate tools (e.g., hand-held manipulatives, graphing calculator, symbolic manipulator, adaptive computers, or stylus).

This bulleted list of student learning outcomes addresses the program-specific hot button of "evaluation." Collaborators know exactly what changes in knowledge and behaviors they expect from project participants.

Workshop Teacher Objectives

May 2005	Adapt Math 101 instructional materials for use with blind students	Dr. Patterson, Dr. Cronk, Mr. Chong, Ms. Osterhaus
Jun–Jul 2005	Teach Math 101 to 10 project participants using newly adapted instructional materials	Dr. Patterson
Jun–Jul 2005	Provide Instructional Support in Math Technology Lab	Dr. Cronk
Jul–Aug 2005	Evaluate effectiveness of Math 101 instruction: Pre-Post Test, Attitude Survey, Weekly Focus Groups, Exit Interviews	Drs. Cronk, Patterson, Ferguson

Student Participant Objectives

Jul 1–Aug 15 2005	Complete Math 101 at LTU with passing grade: Attend classes regularly, Complete homework daily, Communicate with mentors daily	Student Participants
Jul 1–Aug 15 2005	Master 10 homework problem completion strategies: Maintain math journal notebook, Describe helpful and unhelpful techniques	Student Participants
Jul 1–Aug 15 2005	Share Math 101 learning experiences with peers: Suggest one new idea at each days-end wrap-up session. Critique technology tools used daily	Student Participants

Workshop Mentor Objectives

Jul 1–Aug 15 2005	Attend 90% of Math 101 Classes	Workshop Mentors
Jul 1–Aug 15 2005	Be on-site for homework tutoring at least two hours daily	Workshop Mentors
Jul 1–Aug 15 2005	Maintain log of student question and successful response strategies; follow mentoring guidelines, Appendix Two	Workshop Mentors

The time and task charts validate the authenticity of the collaboration, clearly illustrating roles and responsibilities of each project partner. The time interval for most activities is 4–6 weeks, which provides a level of detail to show that the logistics of the project have been carefully considered.

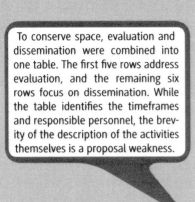

To conserve space, evaluation and dissemination were combined into one table. The first five rows address evaluation, and the remaining six rows focus on dissemination. While the table identifies the timeframes and responsible personnel, the brevity of the description of the activities themselves is a proposal weakness.

II.C Phase Three: Plans for Evaluating and Sharing Curriculum Materials

Time	Task	Responsibility
Jul–Aug 2005	Conduct summative evaluation	Drs. Cronk, Patterson, Ferguson
Aug 2005	Conduct exit interviews with blind students	Dr. Ferguson
Aug 2005	Analyze student, teacher, and mentor logs	Drs. Cronk, Patterson
Aug 2005	Compare pre- and post-test scores	Dr. Cronk
Sep–Oct 2005	Conduct formative evaluation	Drs. Cronk and Ferguson
Nov 2004– Oct 2005	Post project details on Web site	Dr. Cronk
Sep 2005	Submit article for publication	Drs. Cronk, Ferguson, Patterson
Sep 2005	Submit papers for presentation at professional society meetings	Drs. Cronk, Ferguson, Patterson
Sep 2005	Web Cast	Drs. Cronk, Ferguson, Patterson
Sep 2005	Executive Summaries	Drs. Cronk, Ferguson
Oct 2005	Instructional Materials	Drs. Cronk, Ferguson, Patterson

See Section D 4 below for further discussion of dissemination approaches.

II.D Broader Impact Results from Proposed Activities

Five broad outcomes will result from the completion of this project.

1. Integration of Research and Education

One core element in the current NSF Strategic Plan is advancing discovery and understanding while promoting teaching and learning. This proposal uses a knowledge-based approach to designing new strategies that reduce substantial mathematical learning barriers for the visually impaired. More precisely, it integrates research activities into the teaching of math for upper division high school and lower division college students. It will develop research-based educational materials. It creates special mentoring programs for project participants, high school students, and undergraduates. It involves graduate students in undergraduate teaching activities. Most important, it develops, adapts, and disseminates disseminate effective models and pedagogic approaches to mathematics teaching.

2. Broadened Participation of Underrepresented Groups

A second NSF priority is to broaden participation and enhance diversity in NSF programs. Clearly, the blind and visually impaired are underrepresented minorities and their strength is not being fully captured. One hundred percent (100%) of the student participants in this project will come from the underrepresented minority category of blind and visually handicapped. The locus of project activities will occur at an EPSCoR institution. Early career students will be mentored (not just tutored) with caring guides, also from underrepresented groups. The underrepresented population will live temporarily in an academic community and capture the flavor of scholarly accomplishments. Selecting student participants from throughout the country increases the likelihood of broad scale informal educational collaborations. The participants will be active participants in developing new approaches to learning algebra, particularly as regards the role of information technology.

3. Enhanced Infrastructure for Research and Education

A third NSF focus is to foster and support the development and use of computer and other scientific and engineering methods and technologies, primarily for research and education in the sciences and engineering. This project directly involves the acquisition of new computer technology knowledge (research) and the application of existing knowledge (education). It forges crucial interdisciplinary and inter-institutional collaborations. It stimulates the development of next-generation instrumentation and shared educational platforms. It upgrades the informational tools available to overcoming the visual constraints of algebra instruction.

4. Broad Project Dissemination

A fourth main concern of NSF regards the criticality of open scientific communication. Significant findings will be promptly submitted for publication. Instructional tools and products, including software and CD-ROMs will be shared with the scholarly community in a timely manner on a cost recovery basis. Specifically, six different dissemination strategies will be used. They are listed below and elaborated upon in Appendix Three. (1) Project details will be posted on a Web site; (2) Articles will be submitted for publication; (3) Papers will be presented at society conventions, (4) Two Web casts will be presented; (5) Executive summaries will be distributed, and (6) Instructional materials will be distributed.

5. Potential Benefits to Society

A fifth NSF commitment fosters connections between discoveries and their use in service to society. The knowledge provided by NSF-funded projects

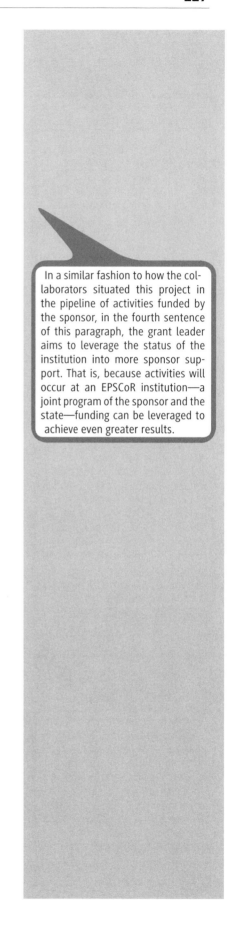

In a similar fashion to how the collaborators situated this project in the pipeline of activities funded by the sponsor, in the fourth sentence of this paragraph, the grant leader aims to leverage the status of the institution into more sponsor support. That is, because activities will occur at an EPSCoR institution—a joint program of the sponsor and the state—funding can be leveraged to achieve even greater results.

offers a rich foundation for its broad and useful application. This project directly contributes to understanding of adaptive technologies, public policy/diversity relationships, and an appreciation of individual differences. In a broad sense, this project demonstrates the linkage between discovery and societal benefit by providing specific examples and explanations regarding the potential application of research and education results to an underutilized population. Further, it partners with academic scientists and State government specialists to integrate research into broader programs and activities of national interest. It analyzes, interprets, and synthesizes research and education results in formats understandable and useful for non-scientists. Finally, it provides information for policy formulation by Federal, State and local agencies.

REVIEWER COMMENTS

Reviewer # 1

PROPOSAL NO.: *0435684*

INSTITUTION: *Louisiana Tech University*

NSF PROGRAM: *RES IN DISABILITIES ED*

PRINCIPAL INVESTIGATOR: *Cronk, Stanley R*

TITLE: VROOM: *Visualizing the Real Operations Of Mathematics*

RATING: *Excellent*

REVIEW:

What is the intellectual merit of the proposed activity?

I have the utmost confidence in Ms. Osterhaus and Mr. Chong to support the activities of this LTU-based team. I would be more ecstatic to know that Ms. Osterhaus was present during the summer session to give on-the-spot advice for problems that will inevitably arise. The LTU members seem to have lots of successful grant experience, especially demonstrated by the well-detailed work and evaluation plan. The resources described should be quite adequate for achieving success. (I will be interested in finding out how well Equation 3.0 works for them)

What are the broader impacts of the proposed activity?

The tools to successfully teach algebra to blind students continue to evolve and emerge. The proposers recount the latest developments quite nicely, including recent presentations within the past three months. This proposed work addresses a problem of national relevance for blind students. The proposers point out the dwindling supply of qualified teachers.

As spelled out in the RFP guidelines, the proposal was 15 single-spaced pages long. In addition, the application contained four appendices: (1) Math 101 Test Questions—66 examples of algebraic operations that students will learn; (2) Mentoring Guidelines—an operational definition and specific guidelines adapted from a publication produced by the sponsor; (3) Dissemination Strategies—six detailed approaches that expanded on the information presented in the proposal for reaching a wide audience; and (4) References—29 citations that demonstrated the grant leader's knowledge of best practices published in journals, Web sites, and grant awards.

The sponsor had three grant reviewers critique the proposal independently and give the application one of five ratings: "excellent," "very good," "good," "fair," or "poor." Reviewers addressed the primary evaluation criteria on the evaluation form—intellectual merit and broader impacts—as well as provided an overall summary statement. Reviewer 1 scored this proposal as "excellent."

Reviewer 1 accepts the grant leader, co-investigators, and consultants as an established collaboration with a history of success. This reviewer's approval of the work and evaluation plans is also an open acknowledgement that the hot buttons of "information dissemination" and "evaluation" were addressed.

If techniques utilizing state-of-the-art assistive technologies can leap that hurtle, the STEM career fields will be more available. The dissemination strategies and plan for recruiting students seem on track to me.

Summary Statement

I would publish results in education and math discipline specific journals. I am not certain that ASEE or AERA fit the broadest dissemination possible with a limited budget. AHED would be a great place to publish and/or distribute literature. I did not have the time to look at all the references, but I did not find the American Psychological Association one listed. This proposal meets a critical need for blind students even outside STEM activities; I mentor a student who nearly failed/quit his college career because of difficulty in algebra.

Reviewer # 2

PROPOSAL NO.: *0435684*

INSTITUTION: *Louisiana Tech University*

NSF PROGRAM: *RES IN DISABILITIES ED*

PRINCIPAL INVESTIGATOR: *Cronk, Stanley R*

TITLE: VROOM: *Visualizing the Real Operations Of Mathematics*

RATING: *Excellent*

REVIEW:

What is the intellectual merit of the proposed activity?

Potentially great merit in the development of methods for teaching fundamental entry level math for STEM. Since the methods are to be explored or developed in the course of the project, this should be thought of as an open-ended program. Personnel are definitely qualified.

What are the broader impacts of the proposed activity?

If successful, the project will promote access to higher education and careers in STEM. Problems of dissemination of instructional materials are not treated in sufficiently adequate detail to gauge likely impact.

Summary Statement

A very worthwhile undertaking. The tentative nature of the development is intrinsic to the approach and should not count against the proposal.

> Reviewer 1 was pleased with the timely literature review, which demonstrated state-of-the-art knowledge of the field. The reviewer's comments also touch on the distinctive features of "best practices" and "assistive technology."

> Although Reviewer 1 noted in the "broader impact" section that the dissemination strategies were "on track," alternative journals in which to publish project outcomes were offered. The reviewer's final comments of "this proposal meets a critical need" and "I mentor a student" are recognition of the hot buttons of "demonstration" and "enrichment," respectively.

> "VROOM: Visualizing the Real Operations of Mathematics" is a catchy project title, one that would appeal to teenagers. Reviewer 2 scored this proposal as "excellent."

> Reviewer 2 provides very brief comments but does affirm that the proposal is methodologically sound and that collaborative partners have the credentials and experience to be successful.

> This reviewer grants that the proposed project has the potential to promote participation and achievement in STEM, representing the hot button of "demonstration," yet questions the approach to sharing project results, representing the hot button of "information dissemination."

> Reviewer 2 maintains that the project's potential for success overall outweigh shortcomings in the description of the dissemination plan.

Reviewer # 3

PROPOSAL NO.: *0435684*

INSTITUTION: *Louisiana Tech University*

NSF PROGRAM: *RES IN DISABILITIES ED*

PRINCIPAL INVESTIGATOR: *Cronk, Stanley R*

TITLE: *VROOM: Visualizing the Real Operations Of Mathematics*

RATING: *Fair*

REVIEW:

What is the intellectual merit of the proposed activity?

The intellectual merit of this proposal is rather low. The proposers understand that there is a problem, but they demonstrate no new insights into solutions. The proposal is essentially to convene study groups to quantify the difficulties, quantify the possible technologies that can be applied, then to match the latter to the former and somehow magically emerge with solutions that have eluded competent researchers forever. The proposal seems extremely naive.

What are the broader impacts of the proposed activity?

The broader impacts of this research, even if the project is far more successful than this referee anticipates, would be limited. The result would be an introductory algebra curriculum tailored specifically for blind students. The curriculum is not likely to be useful except possibly within some schools for the blind. Unfortunately, most US blind students capable of doing algebra do not receive their math instruction in schools for the blind. They are mainstreamed. Consequently the impact of the project would be very narrow at best.

Summary Statement

The proposal lists the following steps:

1. Develop a "barrier matrix,"
2. Develop a "corpus of technologically appropriate pedagogies,"
3. Match "the technological solutions with Barrier Matrix,"
4. "revise Math 101 curriculum by implementing recommendations from the Math Advisory Board,"
5. Field test in summer workshop.

The "barriers" are well-known and the most important could be ticked off extemporaneously by Ms. Osterhaus and Mr. Chong (whose letter of

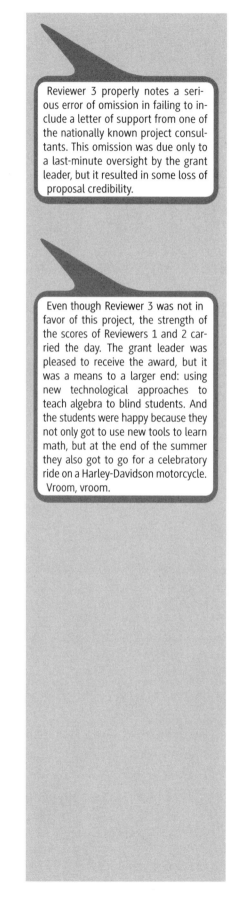

support was not included). These two consultants could also supply a nearly complete list of technologies useful for math education.

This reviewer believes that the proposers will learn very little additional useful information after completing steps 1 and 2. Certainly they will find no "magic bullet" unless a major new technology, presently unanticipated, is introduced in the meantime. This reviewer seriously doubts that this group is likely to find a match that is significantly better than the one Ms. Osterhaus has already developed at the Texas School for the Blind and Visually Impaired. This referee has searched in vain for any hint whatsoever that these proposers have any bright new idea that may have escaped others who have taught math to blind students. Most experts in the field would claim that it is essentially impossible to develop a Math 101 curriculum that will satisfy the needs of blind students in general with today's technology. Some blind students know Nemeth Braille well, and some do not. Some blind students have enough vision to be useful, and some do not. Some have good hearing, and some do not. Some can comprehend tactile graphics easily, and some cannot. What works for one student will not work for another. The problems are well understood, and yet another study group isn't likely to do anything other than add to the list. Mr. Chong is one of the best-informed persons in the US on current educational technologies for teaching math to the blind. This referee is very disappointed to see no support letter from Mr. Chong that might clarify what might possibly produce something new in step 3 above.

Reviewer 3 properly notes a serious error of omission in failing to include a letter of support from one of the nationally known project consultants. This omission was due only to a last-minute oversight by the grant leader, but it resulted in some loss of proposal credibility.

Even though Reviewer 3 was not in favor of this project, the strength of the scores of Reviewers 1 and 2 carried the day. The grant leader was pleased to receive the award, but it was a means to a larger end: using new technological approaches to teach algebra to blind students. And the students were happy because they not only got to use new tools to learn math, but at the end of the summer they also got to go for a celebratory ride on a Harley-Davidson motorcycle. Vroom, vroom.

CHAPTER 8

Coalition Collaboration: Substance Abuse and Mental Health Services Administration Conference Grants

"Building resilience and facilitating recovery" is the mission of the Substance Abuse and Mental Health Services Administration (SAMHSA). Through three Centers and supporting Offices, SAMHSA directs attention and funding to programs that improve the quality of life for people with or at risk for mental health issues, substance abuse, or co-occurring disorders.

With a $3.4 billion annual budget (FY2010), this federal government agency administers a variety of competitive, formula, and block grants that invest in organizations, communities, and states. By focusing on the priority areas of the Center for Mental Health Services, Center for Substance Abuse Prevention, and Center for Substance Abuse Treatment, SAMHSA aims to realize its vision of "a life in the community for everyone."

The SAMHSA Web site (http://www.samhsa.gov) is rich with information about its mission, budget, strategic plan, data strategy, matrix of priorities, programs, funding opportunities, past grantees, online application process, publications, applied statistics, and staff biographies.

In this chapter we examine a successful proposal to the Conference Grants program within SAMHSA's Center for Mental Health Services. The purpose of the program is to disseminate knowledge about practices within the mental health services and substance abuse and prevention and treatment fields and to integrate that knowledge into real-world practice as effectively and efficiently as possible. Grants provide support for up to 75 percent of the total direct costs of planned meetings and conferences. Applicants are urged to apply for funds one year in advance of the event. Awards range from $25,000 to $50,000 for a project period of one year.

While collaboration is not an eligibility requirement per se, it is expected. The RFP guidelines identify one of SAMHSA's priority principles as "collaboration with public and private partners" and describe the Center for Mental Health Services as "an agent of change in the field of mental health, working in partnership with other Federal agencies, State and local mental health authorities, service providers, consumers of services, and their families." And, the proposal must "describe the collaboration in the planning,

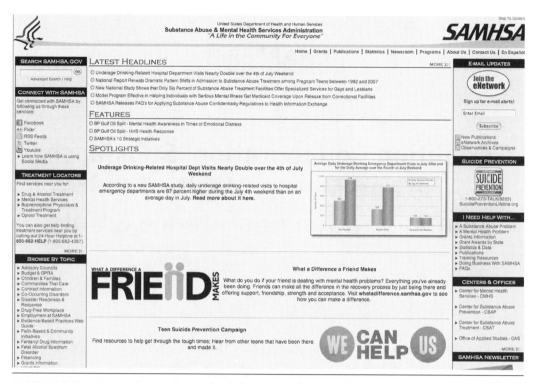

FIGURE 8.1   Screen image from the Substance Abuse and Mental Health Services Administration home page used with permission (www.samhsa.gov).

implementation, and evaluation of the conference among all of the following constituencies: consumers, advocates, researchers, and providers."

A nuanced analysis of the RFP guidelines revealed three hot buttons and one distinctive feature. The hot buttons, listed here, were given importance over other criteria because of their repetition throughout the RFP.

- **Cultural Competence:** key phrases included "cultural competency"; culturally appropriate"; "cultural awareness"; "consideration for the culture, values and traditions of the individuals and communities being served"; "awareness, acceptance, and respect for differences"; "diverse populations"; and "competence in culture, language, and gender issues."

- **Family and Consumer Involvement:** key phrases included "customer driven (family and consumer)"; "community-based"; "broad constituency"; "general public"; and "describe the collaboration in the planning, implementation, and evaluation of the conference among all of the following constituencies: consumers, advocates, researchers, and providers."

- **Evidence-Based Practice:** key phrases included "data and evidence-based outcomes"; "research-based treatments and support services"; "literature citations"; "integrate that knowledge into real-world practice as effectively and efficiently as possible"; and "bringing new science-based knowledge to community-based prevention."

A distinctive feature that stands out in the RFP guidelines is *GPRA* (the Government Performance and Results Act). This act is one way Congress helps to ensure accountability. Grantees are expected to collect baseline data on the number of attendees, achievement of conference goals, and satisfaction with the conference by using a specific form provided by the sponsor. The guidelines also state that the proposal must "discuss how you will comply with the GPRA requirements, including a 30-day follow up with a minimum of 80% of all baseline participants." More broadly, although addressing this distinctive feature may not be enough to win the grant, failing to address it may provide sufficient justification for reviewers to reject the application.

The purpose of this coalition collaboration, represented in exhibit 8.1, was to address a widespread but silent chronic disease: perinatal and postpartum depression. Many of the collaborators had worked together on three earlier phases of this long-term mental health initiative, thus a pattern of interaction and goal sharing already existed. In their ongoing discussions, they recognized the need to get perinatal and postpartum depression information out to more health providers. They concluded that holding regional conferences would be an effective means to heighten awareness of this form of depression that reaches clinical significance more often than many people realize, especially among select cultural groups.

The proposal is presented next, in its entirety. Note that bibliographic citation numbers were retained in the proposal to remain true to the original document, although the references themselves and other appendixes are not included. More significantly, key dimensions of the collaboration, leadership, and proposal are highlighted in the call-out thought bubbles. Following the proposal is the actual feedback from external reviewers. Our reactions to the reviewer evaluation form are also noted in call-out thought bubbles.

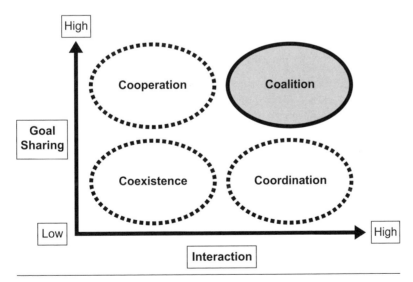

EXHIBIT 8.1   Coalition Collaboration

The RFP guidelines limited the abstract to 35 lines, or approximately 425 words. The opening paragraph represents a condensed summary of the entire project that can be used by the sponsor in publications, press releases, and reporting to Congress.

This paragraph makes an initial signal of the three hot buttons that will be woven throughout the proposal narrative: "cultural competence," "family and consumer involvement," and "evidence-based practice." Equally significant, it confirms that the grant leader understands the logical and psychological needs of the sponsor.

The final sentence of this paragraph addresses the distinctive feature of "GPRA." It acknowledges specifically that collaborators are prepared to comply with federal expectations for accountability.

SUBSTANCE ABUSE AND MENTAL HEALTH SERVICES ADMINISTRATION CONFERENCE GRANTS

Abstract

Overview. The perinatal period, pregnancy through early life, is a developmental epoch that is critical to maternal and infant mental health. The Perinatal Foundation will host seven regional conferences throughout Wisconsin to bridge the gap between knowledge and practice regarding prenatal and postpartum depression—a clinically significant diagnosis affecting more than 10,000 Wisconsin women annually, especially those representing culturally diverse backgrounds.

Problem. Depression during the prenatal and postpartum period is a major public health problem affecting 15% of all women and up to 30% of women living in poverty. Depression does not often resolve without treatment, yet many practitioners are untrained or inexperienced in identifying depression, or may lack referral sources for effective treatment. Of approximately 70,000 Wisconsin births last year, more than 10,000 mothers experienced clinically significant yet treatable depression that often remained undiagnosed. The consequences not only affect the mother-baby dyad but usually the entire family unit as well.

Solution. Prenatal and postpartum depression is identifiable and treatable. Early identification and treatment by primary care providers or mental health specialists is crucial. The goal of this proposal is to disseminate and integrate knowledge about prenatal and postpartum depression into the practice of providers throughout the state. Since research shows that best practices are more likely to be adopted when providers participate in face-to-face interactions, a series of seven regional conferences will be held. Given the ethnic and cultural diversity that exists within Wisconsin, improving cultural competence is a major thematic focus of the seven regional conferences that will reach 350 participants. The outcomes will produce nine different conference products that will be distributed verbally and visually, actively and passively to appropriate culturally diverse audiences.

Evaluation. Since the four project objectives are expressed in measurable terms, an external evaluation consultant will evaluate each one. Culturally and linguistically appropriate evaluation tools will collect participant feedback at the end of the conferences and again 30 days later with a minimum of an 80% response rate among regional conference participants.

Long-Term. The Perinatal Foundation has made a long-term commitment to reducing the knowledge-practice gap regarding prenatal and postpartum depression. The proposed regional conferences represent Phase IV in a series of initiatives to achieve this goal. Earlier activities have included public awareness campaigns (Phase I), a best practices symposium (Phase II), and a blueprint for action initiative (Phase III). The proposed Phase IV regional conferences represent a systematic continuation of prior events on this topic of prenatal and postpartum depression, which has enormous human and economic consequences for women, their families, and the health care system.

SECTION A: POTENTIAL SIGNIFICANCE OF THE PROPOSED PROJECT

A.1: Brief Literature Review

Participants in our proposed regional conferences will consider a significant and growing body of knowledge about depression, especially regarding prenatal and postpartum depression. This review examines a sampling of the depression literature during pregnancy and after delivery.

Prevalence

Prenatal. The research literature suggests that the prevalence of clinically significant prenatal depression is about the same as for postpartum depression: about 15%.[1] However, for certain groups, the prevalence of depression during pregnancy doubles: impoverished, inner-city pregnant women, including teens,[2] those who lack a cohabitating partner,[3] and women who experience difficult pregnancies.[4] Some authors[5,6] conclude that depression is at least as common, and perhaps more so, during pregnancy as it is during the postpartum period.

Postpartum. Psychiatric disorders associated with child bearing are traditionally divided into three categories that reflect severity: postpartum blues, postpartum depression, and postpartum psychosis.[7] Clinical estimates suggest that while more than 80% of women may experience some fluctuations in mood in either during pregnancy or after delivery, some 15% may meet the American Psychiatric Association DSM-IV criteria[8,9] for major depression and 0.1–0.2% will show signs of psychosis, although the prevalence is higher for some cultural groups.[10] The symptoms are the same as generalized depression but always affect at least the mother-baby dyad and in most case the entire family unit. Of these three categories, depression during pregnancy and after delivery is our primary focus since it is the largest category of clinical significance and often goes untreated.

Depression: Definition and Description

Depression is a serious and common medical condition that affects the physical health, mood, and thoughts of approximately 19 million American adults annually.[11] While most people experience depressive symptoms at

---

As a whole, the final paragraph is a first signal that this knowledge dissemination project represents a longer-term commitment by collaborators toward dealing with a significant mental health issue. Partners have worked together on three prior phases, reflecting a history of goal sharing and interaction, and they have a solid platform upon which to build.

Even though this opening paragraph is only two sentences long, it foreshadows how the hot buttons of "evidence-based practice" and "family and consumer involvement" will be met. Namely, regional conferences around the state will allow a broad constituency to learn the latest strategies for addressing an important mental health issue.

To facilitate proposal reading, four levels of headings were used. The Level 1 heading, "Section A," and the Level 2 heading, "A.1: Brief Literature Review," followed the organization of the reviewer's evaluation form. The Level 3 heading, "Prevalence," and the Level 4 heading, "Prenatal," were specific to the organization of the proposal. The headings, set off with a combination of text formatting and emphasis, revealed the main ideas of the proposal at a glance to reviewers. Proposals with too many heading levels, however, may become difficult to track.

some point in their lives, including sadness, grief and sleep disturbances, clinical depression may manifest anhedonia, hopelessness, and loss of mood reactivity. Suicidal thoughts and psychotic symptoms such as delusions or hallucinations virtually always signify a pathological state.

Psychosocial Dimensions of Perinatal Depression

The range of psychosocial risk factors of postpartum depression include previous episodes of depression: significant life stress in the last year, an unplanned/unwanted pregnancy, miscarriage, unexpected birth outcomes, child care stress, marital conflict, low social support, fatigue, genetic predisposition, and an infant with health problems.[12,13] Depending upon the population group, prenatal depression may lead to postnatal depression between 18% and 75% of the time.[14] The impact of perinatal depression is not limited to mothers; it can also have long-lasting effects on the cognitive, emotional, behavioral, and social development of children.[15]

Assessment of Perinatal Depression

Need for Screening. The American College of Obstetrics and Gynecology (ACOG) advises that all women should be considered at risk for postpartum depression and therefore all postpartum women should be screened.[16] Screening is necessary to ensure that such programs affect rates of diagnosis rather than merely rates of referral.[17] Pregnant women need to be screened for signs and symptoms of depression during and after pregnancy so early identification and prompt intervention can be offered.[18] [19]Women with a previous history of depression have a 50% greater risk of developing postpartum depression.[20] Further, these women should be counseled before conception that they are at-risk for recurrent depression during pregnancy and the postpartum period.[21] Medical specialists[22] recommend that all women presenting with prenatal and postpartum depression should be screened for physical illness, psychiatric history, and life circumstances. Among the many assessment tools available, the Edinburgh Postnatal Depression Scale (EDPS) is the most commonly used screening tool for postpartum depression. It consists of ten statements relating to mood[23] and has been validated,[24] computerized,[25] used as a telephone screen,[26] introduced into clinical trials,[27] and translated into at least a dozen languages around the world.[28]

Prenatal Assessment. Orr[29] and her colleagues found that a group of depressed African-American women had a significantly higher incidence of spontaneous preterm births than their nondepressed peers. Fairman *et. al*[30] observed that close monitoring during the prenatal period aids in the management of depression in women who present prenatally with no current mood disorder yet are deemed to be at risk for developing a postpartum depression due to a family history of depression. Treatment

The RFP guidelines called for a "brief" literature review, so the superscript numbers refer to the citations included at the end of the proposal. Citing more than 70 references is hardly brief, but because the grant leader had never before received a grant from the sponsor, a thorough review afforded a first opportunity to establish credibility by demonstrating a comprehensive understanding of a multifaceted problem.

recommendations include staying in the hospital for up to five days in the postpartum period—an unlikely occurrence given the current state of managed care. Rest and medications are also appropriate.

Postnatal Assessment. It is axiomatic that early mother-infant relations are crucial for positive subsequent child development. Postpartum depression interferes with a woman's ability to engage in behavioral and emotional interchange with her baby—a necessary condition for successful mother-infant interaction. In this context, Beck[31] reported at the 2001 Marcé Conference on the results of effective screening and cognitive-behavioral treatment for improving maternal depression. An experimental group improved their control of depression and anxiety in comparison with a control group. More importantly, the improvements remained at the 12-month follow-up and resulted in improved ability to relate to child, family and community.

Treatment in Perinatal Depression

Effectiveness. Treatment effectiveness for depression varies with the type of depression as well as sensitivity to cultural and language differences.[32] Treatment is, of course, a personal choice that involves risk/benefit decisions that are complicated by pregnancy and lactation considerations. Treatment options include medication, psychotherapy, or a combination of both during the prenatal and postpartum periods. Women with mild to moderate symptoms can often be treated effectively with interpersonal psychotherapy, couples counseling, and group therapy. Women who are unresponsive to various forms of psychotherapy can often be treated effectively with pharmacological interventions. Often, depressed women don't seek early medical or psychological treatment for depression. A long-running study on medical and psychotherapy treatment presented at the 2002 annual meeting of the American Psychiatric Association[33] challenged conventional thinking about depression treatment. It concluded that cognitive behavioral therapy is just as effective as medication for severe depression, although it worked more slowly and was not as effective in chronic cases.

Barriers. Bumagin and Cohen[34] surveyed current practices in the treatment of depression among all types of patients in primary care settings and found four significant barriers.

- **Stigma:** Some 20–50% of primary care patients who are referred to mental health specialists will not comply with the referral
- **Access:** Some 72% of primary care physicians say they cannot always obtain high quality outpatient mental health services for their patients
- **Reimbursement:** Reimbursement systems do not usually provide incentives for primary care providers to adequately address mental

> Even the literature citations were selected carefully to suggest a collaborative nature. That is, this knowledge dissemination project takes the results of research and interprets it for practitioners, which requires substantial interaction between groups of health care professionals.

health issues, especially in light of insurance caps on mental health treatments

- **Competing priorities:** The fast-moving pace of practice, especially in managed care systems, allows less time for attention to depressive symptoms in favor of physical or new complaints

National Initiatives. Approaches to treatment have attracted the attention of several major national organizations. For instance, Rand Health[35] launched a *Partners in Care* program that integrates the use of medications and psychotherapy to improve quality of depression treatment. In like manner, the John and Catherine MacArthur Foundation[36] started a 1997 research initiative on depression and primary care with emphasis on improving current practices. That initiative is ongoing. The commitments of these major organizations underscore the criticality of finding effective approaches to the treatment of depression—a silent national problem.

Psychopharmacology

Treatment of depression involves medication, psychotherapy, or some combination thereof. In some environments, psychotherapy may not be accessible; psychopharmacological approaches may be the only practical intervention regimen. Steiner[37] reviewed the evidence on the biological bases of postpartum depression and offers recommendations for the use of medications, including circumstances in which mothers are breastfeeding.

Economics of Depression

On average, depressed people use two to four times more health care than people without a mental illness.[38] Total corporate medical expenditures for people with common mental disorders, including depression, were four and one-half times greater than expenditures for people without mental illness.[39] Depression is a common disability that accounts for about half of all psychiatric disability claims and has the longest average length of disability and holds the highest probability of recidivism.[40] Depression's greatest costs are not for health care services. Rather, they are the indirect costs associated with disability and lost productivity when depression is unrecognized or poorly treated. Authors of a 1993 study[41] analyzed expenditures for the treatment of depression in 1990 concluded that poor recognition and treatment of depression exposes employers to avoidable loses of time and productivity. Each $1 spent on effective treatment reduced as much as $2 of productivity losses. The authors concluded that poor recognition and treatment of depression exposes employers to avoidable disability and productivity-related costs. More recently, Vastig[42] and Zuvekas[43] issued a call for mental health parity, one that has implications for managed health care, namely, that it may be more expensive not to provide treatment than to do so.

Conclusions

The current research literature warrants the following conclusions:

Depression Generally

- Affects 19 million Americans annually
- Impacts one in six during a lifetime
- Is a major cause of workplace disability
- Costs industry billions of dollars in health care expenditures
- Affects women more so than men
- Often co-occurs with other symptoms

Prenatal and Postpartum Depression

- Seriously affects 15% of women but may double in select populations
- Can be identified with screening tools
- Significantly impacts mother-infant relationships
- Influences child growth and development
- Can impinge on families and communities
- Can be effectively treated

Conference Relationship to Knowledge in Field

The proposed regional conferences will help close the growing gap between knowledge about perinatal depression and its effective treatment in a clinical setting. More broadly, this gap is widely evident in the whole field of depression. For instance, it has captured the interest of the Robert Wood Johnson Foundation[44] (RWJ), the world's largest private foundation supporter of health-related projects, who recently issued a five-year, $5 million call for proposals to increase the use of effective depression treatments in primary care settings. In issuing this call, they noted that people with depression who seek medical treatment most likely do so in a primary care setting. The proposed regional conferences are consonant with the three RWJ themes, namely, (1) depression is a serious and prevalent chronic disease that should be conceptualized in a parallel way to other chronic conditions, e.g., asthma, or diabetes; (2) longitudinal chronic illness care approaches to depression are effective but not currently implemented by health systems and practitioners; and (3) multilevel clinical and systemic strategies are needed to overcome barriers among target groups and implement chronic illness care models for depression in primary care. These three themes form the basis for our bridge building from research to practice.

A.2 Value of Regional Conferences

Perinatal depression is a major public health problem affecting 15% of all women and even more in certain cultural groups;[45] [46]early identification

While the RFP guidelines limit the total length of the proposal to 20 pages, no specifications are provided for the length of each section. Simple math would suggest dedicating five pages to each of the four required sections. In this case, a total of seven pages were dedicated to Section A, three pages of which document that a significant need exists to address prenatal and postpartum depression. This table summarizes in concise form major points from the literature review.

This paragraph takes a unique approach to creating urgency for conducting this project right now. In particular, the timely release of an RFP to increase the use of effective depression treatments from the largest private funder of health and health care in the country helps justify the need for bridging the gap between knowledge and practice without further delay.

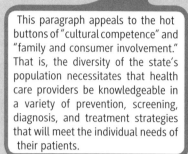

This paragraph appeals to the hot buttons of "cultural competence" and "family and consumer involvement." That is, the diversity of the state's population necessitates that health care providers be knowledgeable in a variety of prevention, screening, diagnosis, and treatment strategies that will meet the individual needs of their patients.

This paragraph is a testimonial to credibility. In the vernacular, the proposed project is not about chasing grant dollars. Rather, it is the next logical step in a long-term commitment the grant leader and collaborators have made toward addressing the mental health issue of depression. In addition, the third sentence describes how internal dollars were leveraged to secure external funds from the largest public sponsor of medical and behavioral research in the country; by inference, the results of this project, too, will have an impact well beyond the end of the granting period.

and treatment by primary care providers or mental health specialists are crucial. The proposed regional conferences will communicate culturally relevant best practices to 350 providers and consumers throughout the state of Wisconsin. Collectively, the conferences will advance the field of mental health services (prevention, screening, diagnosis, and treatment), especially for the ethnically and racially diverse populations in Wisconsin (see section C.4: Cultural Competence). The regional conferences represent Phase IV of a five-phased long-term approach to dealing with prenatal and postpartum depression among culturally diverse groups. (Section B.1 describes all five phases) Furthermore, the value of this project includes, but is not limited to, six value-added factors discussed below.

1. Raise provider awareness about prenatal and postpartum depression

Motherhood should be a life highlight. While pregnancy and new parenthood can be filled with wonderment, hope, and anticipation, these are also times when women are susceptible to depression. In the best of circumstances, the childbearing period from conception through the first year of life (prenatal through postpartum) is fraught with ups and downs. When the downs are a depression, the mother needs treatment. However, a woman may not know that she is experiencing depression and providers may not think to ask about the mother's mood. In addition, if the onset of depression occurs after the only postpartum visit to the provider at six weeks, the depression cannot be recognized. By mobilizing all systems of care—obstetrical, pediatric, family practice, public health, and mental health—women with depression will be recognized.

2. Extend systematically the work of the Perinatal Foundation in disseminating and integrating information about depression

The Perinatal Foundation has made a long-term commitment to prenatal and postpartum depression because of its current clinical neglect, high impact, and favorable prognosis. Accordingly, the Perinatal Foundation has systematically provided pilot support for research and training about postpartum depression. For instance, seed funding from the Perinatal Foundation allowed Clark to examine the role of dyadic therapy in the treatment of depression and resulted in an NIMH grant to study individual versus group psychotherapy treatment effectiveness; findings have been translated for lay audiences.[47] The focus of Perinatal Foundation efforts is that postpartum depression is identifiable and treatable, and that women do not have to suffer needlessly. The Perinatal Foundation has seen a steadily increasing demand for detailed information, evidence-based practice guidelines, and public policies that reduce barriers to treatment.

3. Promote routine screening of women for prenatal and postpartum depression as a "best practice"

Routine screening is one of the most promising practices to identify women experiencing early and secure necessary treatment for their clinically significant prenatal and/or postpartum depression. Prenatally, Zlotnick[48] administered psychotherapy to pregnant women who were at risk of postpartum depression and found that interpersonal therapy was successful in preventing the occurrence of a major postpartum depression for a group of financially disadvantaged women. Implication: early screening can lead to early intervention. From the postpartum perspective, recent studies have demonstrated that the incidence of postpartum depression identified through use of a valid screening tool was significantly higher than the incidence detected by routine clinical evaluation alone.[49] Screening is recommended for high-risk groups, which includes pregnant and postpartum women.[50] A prior history of depression, anxiety, or other mental illness, especially during a previous pregnancy or postpartum, and a family history of mood or anxiety disorders are risk factors in the prenatal and postpartum period. There are social risks as well: poverty, unemployment, child-care stress, and lack of support from a partner.[51]

4. Promote referral and treatment among appropriate physical and mental health professionals

Health outcomes for women, their infants and families can be greatly improved through various pathways of early screening, effective referral systems, and treatment options. Communities need evidence-based systems to screen, refer, and treat perinatal depression. Presently, different healthcare providers are developing such guidelines. For instance, the Scottish Intercollegiate Guidelines Network (SIGN) recently published postnatal depression guidelines[52] and called for cultural changes to destigmatize depression. Frequently, identifying a problem will increase both the number of people served and the demand for more service providers. This increase puts an unexpected clinical load on providers and systems that are already under-equipped to handle the customary caseloads. In the case of prenatal and postpartum depression, the load increase is magnified by an inadequate infrastructure presently in place. As a result, an ever-widening gap is projected between service demands and service providers.

5. Foster collaboration across agencies who value early identification and intervention for women with postpartum depression

Wisconsin agencies—governmental, nonprofit organizations, educational institutions, and research centers—generally recognize the importance of mental health services. In fact, Wisconsin is one of the very few states that includes mental health in its state health plan. Specifically, the Wisconsin State Health Plan for the year 2010 addresses 11 health priorities; one of them is mental health. Among other things, the Plan advocates screening for depression across all systems. Members of the group that developed the mental health portion of the state health plan will participate in this proposed project. As a result, the proposed project grows organically out of a statewide priority. Appendix Four lists 18 specific state agencies and health-related organizations that will be invited to take active roles as conference participants and presenters. Perhaps a major benefit of the regional conferences is the opportunity for diverse health professionals to come together, network, exchange ideas, plan future clinical and research collaborations, and share best practices.

6. Disseminate regional perinatal depression information among ethnically and racially diverse populations

Wisconsin is a multiethnic state, as noted in the following Section A.3. Culturally diverse adaptations of best practices will better serve all residents. The literature on the complex relationship between culture and mental health is voluminous and growing rapidly. Each regional conference will emphasize cultural competence as it is disseminated and integrated in clinical practice and to what extent it varies among cultural groups. The overall five-phase program design capitalizes on the educational multiplier effect of regional outreach. The method of approach in Phase IV will provide the full picture of prenatal and postpartum depression: magnitude, consequences, neurobiology, screening, research, and intervention strategies among culturally diverse groups.

A.3 Relevance to SAMHSA Priorities

The proposed project is consistent with SAMHSA support for conferences that address the following priorities, for which the workshop presenters at the symposium (Phase II) have been directed to include in their presentations. The Phase III outcomes serve as the knowledge basis for disseminating and integrating information in the Phase IV regional confe
The seven priorities are as follows.

1. **Data and evidence-based outcomes.** The current health care demands that best practices demonstrate the value of evidenced-based outcomes in identifying, screening, treating and preventing perinatal depression. Implementation requires an ambitious collaboration among researchers, clinical partners and health care facilities. Evidence must back up claims, information and guidelines. Phase III provides the empirical basis for the data and evidence-based outcomes to be cited in the Phase IV regional conferences.

2. **Collaboration with public and private partners.** Collaboration is a principle inherent in every aspect of this program designed to foster partnerships among and between agencies (c.f. Appendix Four)

This paragraph stresses the value of collaboration. The state health plan provided motivation for collaboration among 18 different health-related organizations. The grant leader felt it essential to keep all organizations current on project development and progress. The challenge was to supply enough information without overwhelming them with details. A combination of periodic e-mail summaries, a quarterly newsletter, and an annual conference presentation were used to provide updates.

When viewed collectively, these six conference benefits specify the key dimensions of postpartum depression that will be addressed: prevention, identification, diagnosis, and treatment. Collaborators share a common goal of providing excellent health care to women and infants and will interact through the conference to communicate their health information.

This paragraph addresses the hot button of "evidence-based practice." Conference presenters will draw on best practices from data-driven outcomes research and validated methods, not intuitive knowledge and long-standing but untested techniques.

and individuals interested in early identification and intervention for women with prenatal and postpartum depression, such as state of Wisconsin agencies, other non-profit agencies, educational and research institutions, health care providers, consumers, and advocates. The collaborations are not new; this proposal represents a systematic continuation of prior partnerships with agencies and individuals sharing these values.

3. **Recovery/reducing stigma and barriers to services.** Funding this proposal will systematically extend the work of the Perinatal Foundation in promoting early identification and intervention for women with prenatal and postpartum depression and their families. In particular, the regular promotion of routine screening of women for prenatal and postpartum depression as a "best practice" will help reduce the stigma associated with admitting the need for help.

4. **Financing strategies and cost-effectiveness.** The Perinatal Foundation's commitment to a five-phase program design more than multiplies the effect of any single dissemination strategy alone. It builds and maintains momentum with on-going collaborative activities supported by Phase V funds set aside by the Perinatal Foundation.

5. **Rural and other specific settings.** Wisconsin has a larger population of rural residents (34.3%) compared with the nation as a whole (24.8%). Because of its rural setting and its cultural diversity, Wisconsin is an ideal state to develop best practices that could apply to many situations.

6. **Workforce development.** Training local healthcare providers to sensitively implement best practices will both raise and address the need for cultural competence in workforce development. To accomplish this, providers will participate in the seven regional conferences. Implementing best practices will address the need for local training that is culturally relevant. Local training about implementing best practices will include cultural competence considerations.

7. **Cultural competency/eliminating disparities.** Successfully raising awareness about prenatal and postpartum depression requires "buy-in" by local constituencies. The program design expressly and financially supports the development of new research, education, and model program activity. The diversity present within seven regions of Wisconsin allows practitioners to examine identification, referral, and treatment practices in very different populations. They include White, Hispanic, African American, American Indian, and Asian individuals in targeted settings.

The final sentence of this paragraph provides reassurance that partners have a long history of working together. Said differently, this collaboration is not a knee-jerk response to a grant opportunity. Rather, partners have invested considerable time, energy, and resources prior to developing this request and will work together afterward to improve health for women and infants.

This paragraph confirms explicitly that the impacts of this project will continue beyond the granting period. Namely, as part of a long-term commitment to addressing prenatal and postpartum depression, internal funds have been budgeted to support a few field-research projects that will inevitably emerge as a result of the regional conferences.

This paragraph touches on the hot buttons of "cultural competence" and "family and consumer involvement." To secure buy-in from a broad base of constituents, they must be involved in the planning, implementation, and evaluation processes. What's more, diverse participation ensures that best practices are sensitive to individual needs.

These opening three paragraphs in Section B of the narrative overview that the project plan will address the hot buttons of "cultural competence," "family and consumer involvement," and "evidence-based practice." That is to say, they summarize *what* the project will do, *how* activities will be accomplished, and *why* this specific approach was selected.

SECTION B: MERIT AND APPROPRIATENESS OF PROJECT PLAN

Rationale for Approach

Three major factors drive the methodological approach in this proposal. First, while depression is a serious problem affecting many, research demonstrates[53] that chronicity, rather than severity of depression, has a more deleterious effect on infants and children. Further, while some women experience an onset of symptoms during pregnancy, those with a history of depressive symptoms are at increased risk.[54]

Second, the need for culturally sensitive identification and treatment practices increases as our population grows. Many practitioners who are caught in the vortex of changing administrative priorities need straightforward access to significant bodies of scholarly research if they are to effectively address increases in demand.

Third, regional conferences are a cost-effective way to disseminate knowledge and influence the behavior of those who are most likely to integrate best practices. Disseminating knowledge about clinical effectiveness and outcomes research is a necessary step in improving quality of care. The techniques that improve the chance for success, according to the Rand Corporation,[55] include face-to-face interactions with health providers, promoting the active involvement of the learner, repeating the message, making recommendations explicit and relevant to clinical practice, and making use of opinion leaders and peer influence. The proposed project, described below, incorporates these principles of effective dissemination.

B.1: Goals, Objectives, Approach

Rationale. Often, health care providers fail to perceive prenatal and postpartum depression as a noteworthy problem because it is viewed as a "low tech" illness not warranting serious attention. Either they are unaware of the consequences of perinatal depression, or they are reluctant to become involved without adequate identification and treatment resources. Perinatal depression has a negative impact on mothers, children, families and communities. Research shows that young children exposed to maternal depression in infancy are at higher risk for behavior problems,[56] (e.g., hyperactivity, aggression), social adjustment difficulties,[57] poor performance on academic and intellectual measures,[58] and difficulty bonding and forming healthy interactions.[59] In essence, prenatal and postpartum depression is a phenomenon that takes a cumulative toll not only on the mother but also on those who interact regularly with her. Ironically, depression is a treatable problem; the prognosis for recovery is high with appropriate medical and/or behavior therapies.

Goal Setting Context. The Perinatal Foundation, in conjunction with the Wisconsin Association for Perinatal Care (WAPC), has developed a two-year, five-phased approach to knowledge dissemination and integration regarding prenatal and postpartum depression. The five sequential phases of this comprehensive approach are designed to ensure that women with prenatal and postpartum depression will be identified and treated more effectively. All five phases primarily target health and allied health care providers who stand at the fulcrum of potentially influencing positive systemic changes in an imperfect system. While all five phases are summarized below, Phase IV, Regional Conferences, for which funding is being requested in this proposal, is presented in fuller detail. In fact, outcomes from Phases I-III feed into Phase IV which is designed to have a major impact on Wisconsin Women.

Impact of Regional Conferences on Wisconsin Women. This project will impact over 10,000 Wisconsin women annually with clinically significant prenatal and postpartum depression, based on analysis of demographic data from the U.S. Census Bureau[60] for the year 2000. Over 7% of these women are nonnative English speakers, primarily Spanish; over three thousand report they do not speak English "very well." More than 20% of the families with a female householder and no husband present had incomes below the poverty level; these two thousand women are at twice the risk for depression than their peers in high socioeconomic levels. Further, one-third were from unmarried women (widowed, divorced, and never married), again representing a higher at-risk segment of the population. Finally, the regional conferences will have a positive impact on minority women[61] and stepfathers[62] who may be unsupportive of mental health treatment, either because they perceive it as a reflection on them as providers or they are so threatened that they would be left to care for children already at home. Deep concerns exist over the inadequacy of social support systems.

Phase I: Public Awareness

In October 2002, the Perinatal Foundation invested over $10,000 in a public awareness campaign directed at consumers and providers regarding prenatal and postpartum depression. The campaign includes two post-cards, each sent to 15,000 people. The message of the first postcard is *"You Can't Tell by Looking"* that a woman is depressed. Providers need to ask women about their mood and consumers need to tell their providers how they are feeling. The second postcard, to be sent in January 2003 will promote routine screening for prenatal and postpartum depression.

Phase II: Best Practices Symposium

On June 10, 2003, the Perinatal Foundation and the Wisconsin Association for Perinatal Care will hold a symposium on the topic: *Prenatal and*

> In order for the collaborators to sustain a multi-phased effort, certain behaviors and attitudes were crucial. They demonstrated dynamic factors relating to goal sharing, including accountability, commitment, effort, persistence, and priorities. This collaboration also exhibited dynamic factors relating to interaction, including communication, conflict management, diplomacy, time management, and trust.

Phase	Purpose	Duration
I. Public Awareness	• Raise awareness of the gravity of prenatal and postpartum mood disorders • Conference registration invitation to 15,000 regional and national constituents	Fall 2002 though Winter 2003
II. Best Practices Symposium	• Disseminate research • Identify best practices • Set priorities for future research • Form Partnerships	June 10, 2003
III. Blueprint for Action	• Prepare dissemination products • Outline strategies for implementation	Summer 2003
IV. Regional Conferences (detailed below)*	• Disseminate best practices to constituents • Integrate best practices into prenatal and postpartum health care systems	September 2003 through August 2004
V. Field Research	• Call for fundable research proposals that address the effectiveness of culturally-relevant, strategic dissemination and system implementations	August 2004-05

> This table places the proposed project in the context of the collaboration's longer-term commitment to reducing the incidence of perinatal depression. That is, partners share common goals and have interacted in the past on similar activities. The current Phase IV knowledge dissemination project merely represents a continuation of prior efforts.

Postpartum Mood Disorders—You Can't Tell By Looking. Nationally and internationally known researchers and clinicians will convene to define the parameters for early identification and intervention practices, effective screening tools, psychotherapeutic and pharmacological treatment options, and referral resources required to effectively address the impact of prenatal and postpartum depression, c.f. Appendix Nine.

Phase III: Agenda Setting—A Blueprint for Action

A panel of constituents that includes consumers, providers, policy makers, and media representatives will convene immediately following the Phase II Symposium to thoroughly review symposium documents and identify a set of priorities to implement best practices. Critical research findings and emerging issues identified during the symposium will comprise a *Blueprint for Action* that proactively addresses the critical need to better identify and treat prenatal and postpartum depression.

Phase IV: Regional Conferences (Proposal Request)

The proposed project incorporates these principles of effective dissemination: the concept of diffusion of knowledge and information as well as the acceptance, inculcation, and utilization of dissemination information.[63] Practically speaking, this proposal identifies two major goals and subsequent measurable objectives to be addressed: *dissemination* and *integration.*

Goal #1: To *disseminate* best practices to constituents

- **Objective 1.1: By March 2004, develop an information architecture for disseminating best practices**
- **Approach for Objective 1.1**

In order to disseminate best practices an information architecture must exist to provide the key intellectual content and delivery systems for transferring research knowledge to practitioners. Information architecture, in this case, represents the knowledge base generated from the Symposium Proceedings (Phase II) and the Blueprint for Action (Phase III). In essence, the approach of choice establishes the communication infrastructure for disseminating knowledge. To accomplish this, one specific approach will be implemented. Specifically, the knowledge base for the information architecture will come from Phase II, the Best Practices Conference and Phase III, the Blueprint for Action. Electronic (Web-based) proceedings will be hosted on the Perinatal Foundation Web site. The deliverable for this objective is to collate, print and bind the Blueprint for Action that will be distributed to an estimated 300 symposium attendees in advance of the regional conferences.

> For the purposes of Goal 1, "dissemination" is another way of saying there will be interaction among collaborators and constituents with the aim to enhance goal sharing.

- **Objective 1.2: By June 2004, disseminate select prenatal and postpartum depression information throughout seven state regions**
- **Approach for Objective 1.2**

Once the information architecture is built, the host information will be widely disseminated to targeted consumers and prenatal and postpartum practitioners throughout the state using two different approaches. First, the Phase I mailing campaign identified 15,000 prenatal and postpartum health care providers who will be notified by a third postcard (earlier ones sent on November 2002 and January 2003) about access to an electronic version of Symposium Proceedings/ Blueprint for Action (15,000 distribution). Second, beyond the symposium participants, electronic (Web-based) and bound printed Symposium Proceedings and a Blueprint for Action will be distributed to an estimated 350 conference professionals who will participate in the regional conferences, described below.

> For the purposes of Goal 2, "integration" is another way of saying there will be a blend of goal sharing and interaction among collaborators and constituents.

Goal #2: To *integrate* best practices among constituents

- **Objective 2.1 By August 2004, conduct seven regional conferences: Integrating Best Practices**
- **Approach to Objective 2.1**

Seven regional constituent-based conferences will be convened to encourage and support the exchange of effective implementation strategies; Appendix Six contains a map of regions and possible site locations. The regional conferences will identify culturally sensitive topics, define best practice models relevant to each region, present an overview of Symposium Proceedings and a Blueprint for Action, define cultural and/or systemic barriers that hinder integration into clinical practice, identify criteria for regional customization, and generate customized regional integration strategies.

- **Objective 2.2 By August 2004, promote partnerships that will stimulate the integration of best practices**
- **Approach to Objective 2.2**

The following actions will promote the development of new strategic partnerships. (1) Expert clinicians, as conference presenters, will establish communications with regional leaders at the seven regional conferences. (2) Practitioners at the local level will identify clinical and systems opportunities of mutual interest as a result of networking. (3) Strategic partners will identify interventions and topics for multi-regional clinical research through networking.

Phase V: Field Research

Phases I through IV will provide an agenda for research, education, and model project grants designed to measure and compare the efficacy of the implementation in seven distributed regions. As a follow-up to the symposium and regional conferences, the Perinatal Foundation has committed $30,000 in Phase V for regional implementation grants to be awarded on a competitive basis to organizations that participated in the conference. Specifically, conference and symposium participants will receive preferred status for funding of appropriate and culturally sensitive proposals that extend the value of these dissemination and integration priorities. Participants in the symposium (Phase II) and regional conferences (Phase IV) will receive preferred status in seeking Phase V funding. Prior participation will be a substantial incentive to encourage active involvement on the part of those capable submitting vital and relevant proposals for continuing clinical research, dissemination strategy development, and systems integration initiatives.

B.2 Feasibility of the Conference Agenda

The Perinatal Foundation, through its collaboration with the Wisconsin Association for Perinatal Care, has been in the conference "business" for over three decades. Early on, it learned that any conference must be conceptually sound, administratively efficient, and pedagogically effective. The conceptual-administrative-pedagogical triad ensures a feasible conference agenda, as explained below.

Conceptual Soundness

The conference topic and agenda are conceptually sound for five reasons.

1. The problem clinically affects approximately 15% of childbearing women.
2. The problem exists across cultures.
3. It has been the focus of a substantial body of research literature.
4. It is a long-term priority for the Perinatal Foundation.
5. The two overarching conference goals—dissemination and integration—are supported by four specific, immediate, measurable, practical, logical, and evaluable objectives.

Administrative Efficiency

An administrative efficiency empowers the agenda. The Perinatal Foundation has an established track record of effectively administering conferences. (See C.1: Prior Conference Experience.) Specifically, a decade of conferences brings invaluable experience that transfers directly to this proposal. This includes, but is not limited to the following:

• Planning	• Instructional Technology
• Evaluation Forms	• Contract Signing
• Publicity	• Food Service
• Local Arrangements	• Recording
• Registration	• Confirmations
• Budgeting	• Transportation
• Committees	• Parking
• Guest Presenters	

> This table calls attention to the myriad details that must be addressed in order to ensure overall conference success. It also helps to establish the credibility of collaborators by showing that they have thought through the project down to minute levels.

Pedagogical Effectiveness

The conference agenda is pedagogically effective. Clinicians, researchers and consumers from culturally diverse backgrounds will help plan the regional conferences. Both the format and length of the workshop agenda take advantage of the principles of adult learning: practical information presented in an interesting and interactive format to give solid clinical best practices that one can use now. Practitioners who participate in these regional conferences will be able to (1) describe the value of early detection and intervention for a woman suffering from prenatal and/or postpartum depression; (2) implement screening into a busy practice; (3) identify effective referral and treatment strategies; (4) implement policies and practices to reduce outcome barriers; and (5) help local constituents establish relationships with experts in the field.

B.3 Collaborative Efforts

For more than a decade, the Perinatal Foundation, with support from the Wisconsin Association of Perinatal Care, has held regional conferences

> This paragraph appeals to all three hot buttons—"cultural competence," "family and consumer involvement," and "evidence-based practice." Namely, encouraging inclusive participation from clinicians, researchers, and consumers from culturally diverse backgrounds will ensure the appropriateness of the conference content, and using pedagogically sound principles will ensure that participants reach the five targeted learning outcomes.

This paragraph emphasizes the level, extent, and duration of collaborative efforts. Partners represent public and private organizations, health care and academia, grantmakers and grantseekers, physical and mental health professionals, providers and consumers. They have addressed diverse topics affecting the health of women and infants, and they've been doing it together for more than a decade. In other words, this project is not an attempt to chase grant dollars because they exist; rather, it's a systematic extension of prior activities.

(c.f. C.1) on topics ranging from prenatal care coordination, public policies, breastfeeding, fetal monitoring, HIV counseling, newborn hearing screening to postpartum depression. The resulting networks and partnerships carry over into strategic planning for this proposal; collaborative efforts included consumers and health care professionals from multiple disciplines, private non-profit organizations, academic centers, prenatal and postpartum centers, state maternal and child health and mental health agencies, foundations, and clinical settings. Collectively, these individuals and agencies will reflect the needs of rural and urban women in various cultures with prenatal and postpartum depression. From the multiple perspectives represented in the planning, implementation, and evaluation phases of this project, all will profit from the cross-pollination of ideas. Indeed, multiple viewpoints are needed to traverse the milieu of prenatal and postpartum depression.

B.4 Cultural Awareness

To effectively identify, diagnose, and treat prenatal and postpartum depression, health professionals must go beyond cultural knowledge,[64] cultural awareness,[65] and cultural sensitivity[66] to manifest cultural competence. Cultural competence requires a set of congruent behaviors, attitudes, and policies among professionals if it is to work effectively in cross-cultural situations.[67] Operationally defined, cultural competence is the integration and transformation of knowledge about individuals and groups of people into specific standards, policies, practices, and attitudes. Used in appropriate cultural settings, cultural competence increases the quality of health care, thereby producing better health outcomes.[68] Cultural competency emphasizes the idea of effectively operating in different cultural contexts.

Achieving Cultural Competence among Attendees

Cultural competence among attendees will be achieved in two different ways: through participant selection and through information dissemination. First, invitations will be specifically extended to healthcare providers who serve predominant diversity groups in each of the seven regions. To maximize conference attendance, representatives in the region that are known to the service providers will extend personal invitations. Second, the conference participants will be given a list of suggestions to improve cultural competence among the providers in their clinical settings. Participants are then free to select the options that are most appropriate to their situations.

Sample Suggestions [69]for Achieving Cultural Competence

- Provide cultural sensitivity training to service providers
- Hold "Open Houses" to information communities about available mental health services

- Develop information brochures in different languages about services
- Have a formalized, written cultural competency plan
- Form advisory boards with diverse membership, reflective of the cultures being served
- Develop and implement standards for recruiting and hiring culturally competent providers
- Direct consumers to treatment modalities that are culturally acceptable to them

B.5 Conference Plans for Speakers

Plans for Speakers

The Phase II Symposium will include keynote speakers and major presenters. In contrast, Phase IV focus is different. It will concentrates on engaging practitioners and promoting partnerships for disseminating and integrating best practices at the regional level. Because the seven regional conferences are designed to engage and network among practitioners and consumers, it is intentional that no "keynote" speakers will be used. With adult learners, integration occurs best through dialog and information sharing, not famous lectures.

Plans for Presenters

Appendix Eight contains a tentative agenda for the regional conferences. These presenters will follow a standard but flexible format that explains how best practices can be adopted within each region. At least two of the presenters will include a primary care provider and a mental health provider. A prerequisite to be a presenter at the regional conferences will be participation in the June 10th symposium (Phase II). Among the best practices to be discussed: screening approaches for primary care providers, intervention strategies, and regional resources.

Plans for Participants

We will notify a broad audience about the regional conferences through printed and electronic media. A typical mailing list for regional conferences is about 5000. However, for this project, the expanded mailing list of 15,000 will include a variety of mental health providers, academic centers, cultural groups, and those from specialty prenatal and postpartum service programs such as prenatal care coordination and teen pregnancy services.

B.6 Disseminating Conference Products

Dissemination of Phase IV knowledge and products is essential because education has a multiplier effect. Project dissemination offers many

> These two paragraphs appeal primarily to the hot button of "cultural competence" and secondarily to the hot button of "evidence-based practice." In particular, six literature citations document that the grant leaders are knowledgeable in the theory and practice of culturally competent care.

advantages, including increasing public awareness, soliciting additional support, locating more clients, alerting others to new ideas, and adding to the stockpile of knowledge. Effective dissemination requires the use of multiple strategies. Conference products will be distributed verbally and visually, actively and passively, as appropriate, to target audiences. Collectively the comprehensive approaches tabled below allow learners to choose the dissemination approach of greatest value to their learning styles.

The table below highlights details regarding each of the nine product dissemination strategies.

Format	Distribution Points	Quantity	Distribution	Recipients	Cost to Recipients
Regional Conferences	Regional Sites	Seven	Regional	Participants	Nominal
Blueprint Document	Regional Conferences	1000	Unlimited	Unlimited	Included
Instructional Materials	Regional Conferences	350	Statewide	Participants	Included
E-Transcripts	Internet	Unlimited	Unlimited	Unlimited	Free
Web Sites	Internet	Unlimited	International	Unlimited	None
Press Releases	Mass Media	Unlimited	Unlimited	Unlimited	N/A
Postcards	USPS	15,000	Statewide	Constituents	Free
Awareness Posters	Regional Conferences	500	Statewide	Participants	Free
Awareness Reminders	All Symposia	750	Statewide	Participants	Included

In this table, the grant leader seized an opportunity to provide substantial detail about planned dissemination strategies in a compressed space. Whereas the table took up about half a page of the proposal, conveying this same information in narrative form would have taken up at least three-fourths of a page. Equally important, the table is easy to read and comprehend.

SECTION C: MANAGEMENT PLAN, STAFFING, PROJECT ORGANIZATION, AND RESOURCES

C.1 Prior Conference Experience

Wisconsin Association for Perinatal Care, with the support of the Perinatal Foundation, has over 30 years of experience hosting annual statewide conferences and meetings. The goal of the annual statewide conference is to provide leadership and education for improved prenatal and postpartum health outcomes of women, infants, and their families. These annual meetings are the premier events for the Foundation, bringing together approximately **300 people** for the purposes of addressing maternal and fetal care, infant and family issues, and public health and other health care systems. The annual meetings are intended for physicians and nurses, public health personnel, social workers, nutritionists, therapists, mental health professionals, consumers, administrators, and educators.

The 2003 Annual Meeting will convene April 13–15 at the Marriott West in Madison. Confirmed plenary speakers include Cheryl Tatano Beck, PhD, CNM, FAAN, and George Little, MD. In addition, 13 of the 16 small group session presenters have been identified and confirmed.

During the past five years, the Perinatal Foundation and WAPC hosted the following annual meetings at regionally diverse locations.

April 21–23, 2002, Olympia Resort, Oconomowoc

April 22–24, 2001, LaCrosse Center and Radisson Hotel, LaCrosse

April 9–11, 2000, Park Plaza Paper Valley Hotel, Appleton

April 18–20, 1999, Monona Terrace Convention Center and Inn on the Park Hotel, Madison

April 19–21, 1998, Olympia Resort, Oconomowoc

> In Section C of the narrative, once again, there is an emphasis on the lengthy history collaborative partners have in working with each other and the specific outcomes they have achieved. The fact that collaborators have organized conferences across the state in each of the past five years, drawn significant and diverse audiences, and produced tangible products establishes their credibility to successfully do it again.

The Perinatal Foundation and WAPC also sponsored a major conference in 1997 to address the care of infants and families who have experienced the neonatal intensive care unit, as they are discharged to the home and community. The conference took two years to plan. Approximately 200 people participated. Two major products grew out of the conference, a manual for providers and one for families. The provider manual, *NICU Babies in the Communities: A Continuum of Care* was published in April, 2000 and distributed to providers. It is referenced as the standard of care in Wisconsin. The second product, *Baby Steps,* was published for parents. It is a three ring binder that provides resources but also engages parents in the care of their infants. *Baby Steps* is available in Spanish, *Pasitos de Bebè.*

C.2 Administrative and Organizational Structure

The shared staff of the Perinatal Foundation and Wisconsin Association for Perinatal Care will pool their human resources, expertise, and prior experience to organize and manage the regional conferences to disseminate and integrate the goals, objectives and approaches. The staff is a seasoned team with a cumulative 85 years of experience in conference management, generally, and specifically dealing with the topic of prenatal and postpartum depression. In fact, there is currently no other nonprofit group

> The last sentence of this paragraph is a powerful statement of credibility: no other organization in the state has more experience with prenatal and postpartum depression than this collaboration.

> Successful collaborations are led by individuals who inspire confidence that mutual goals will be achieved. The grant leader created a positive emotional climate of high expectations through abundant formal and informal communications, thorough preparations, knowledge of the strengths of all partners, and a desire to work together.

> The grant leader possesses leadership characteristics related to goal sharing, including responsibility; capacity to manage, decide, and set priorities; courage, resoluteness, and steadiness; intelligence and judgment in action; and need to achieve. In practical terms, the grant leader has the ability to see and communicate to collaborative partners the relationship between the "big picture" vision and day-to-day project activities.
> The grant leader also possesses leadership characteristics related to interaction, including capacity to motivate; confidence; outward display of trust; skill in dealing with people; and understanding of constituents and their needs. A grassroots approach persuaded people, even some skeptics, that collaborating was a practical way to get bigger wins for women's health.

in the state of Wisconsin that has had more experience with conferences and perinatal issues than the applicant.

Working closely with the project staff will be members of the Phase II Planning Committee—18 professionals with multidisciplinary perspectives in health and psychology—consumers, and select representatives from each of the seven different regions in the state.

The Executive Director of the Perinatal Foundation and WAPC will serve as Project Director, overseeing planning, execution, and evaluation of the conference presentations. The Project Director will advise on conference content and coordinate speakers, sites, and resources. Additionally, the Development Director's role will maximize public relations opportunities. Support staff will assist with logistics and material preparation.

C.3 Capability and Experience

The key project personnel include the conference director, program director, evaluation consultant, cultural competency consultant, and media director. Abridged résumés are found in Section G.

The Project Director, **Ann Conway,** has over 30 years of professional experience in the healthcare field with a special emphasis on perinatal health. Her dual role as Executive Director of the Perinatal Foundation and the Wisconsin Association for Perinatal Care makes her uniquely suited to coordinate conference activities. In her present position, she has access to experienced support staff that are essential to managing conference logistics. Her primary conference responsibilities are to oversee all aspects: from process to products.

The Program Director, **Dr. Rana Limbo,** is Program Director for the Wisconsin Association for Perinatal Care. Working closely with the project director, her primary conference responsibilities are to serve as a resource guide for the collection and distribution of best practices while, at the same time, assist presenters in meeting conference goals.

The Evaluation Consultant, **Dr. Russell Kirby,** Professor of Public Health at the University of Alabama at Birmingham, has conducted numerous evaluation studies for public health programs and projects, and has designed and conducted many evaluations for continuing education programs. A specialist in perinatal epidemiology, Dr. Kirby spent two decades in Wisconsin prior to moving to Alabama in 2002. He will be responsible for data collection, analysis, and interpretation.

The Media Director, **Kristen Forman,** is Development Director for the Perinatal Foundation. Her primary conference responsibilities include media awareness of prenatal and postpartum depression as a "silent" health concern. Further, she will help ensure that diversity is reflected in all promotional materials publicizing the regional conferences and resulting conference products.

The Cultural Competency Consultant, **Professor Mary Jo Baisch,** is interim director of the Institute for Urban Health Partnerships at the University of Wisconsin—Milwaukee. Her primary conference responsibilities include ensuring principles and practices of diversity are fully reflected in the conference process, products and evaluation findings.

C.4 Cultural Competence

Demographics of Diversity in Wisconsin

The value of diversity is no longer merely a social goal. Health professionals now realize the need to acquire new techniques and skills if they are to understand, motivate, and empower all patients regardless of race, gender, religion, or creed. The future of health care in the state depends on our ability to effectively talk with one another, to reach mutual understanding, and to realize that in diversity there is strength. Therefore, it is crucial that practitioners recognize the rich diversity in Wisconsin.

Wisconsin demographics demand special sensitivity to cultural competency issues. A multi-ethnic state with rich German heritage dating back more than a century, Wisconsin has progressively increased its diversity. According to the 2000 report from the U.S. Census Bureau, of Wisconsin's 5.4 million residents, the predominant non-white ethnic groups in Wisconsin are Hispanics, African-Americans, American Indians, and Asians. Salient Census Bureau statistics for each group are summarized below. (Appendix Six contains a map of Wisconsin.)

Hispanics

From 1990 to 2000, the Hispanic population in Wisconsin more than doubled. This 107% change represented the largest increase of any racial or ethnic group in the state and twice the national average for that group. Four counties have more than 10,000 Hispanic persons, located primarily in southeastern Wisconsin: Milwaukee (82,406), Racine (14,900), Dane (14,387) and Kenosha (10,757). The statistical changes are especially dramatic when viewed on a county-by-county basis. For example, Brown County's Hispanic population more than quadrupled (470%) between 1990 and 2000, from 1,525 to 8,698 persons, the largest increase of any Wisconsin county.

African Americans

Wisconsin's African American population increased 24.5% from 1990 to 2000. African Americans are the second largest racial group in Wisconsin

While the RFP guidelines do not require projects to have a cultural competency consultant, the grant leader recognized that including one as a key member of the staffing plan would significantly enhance the credibility of the project as well as appeal directly to the hot button of "cultural competence."

and are 5.7% of the state's total population. The African American population is mostly concentrated in southeastern and south central Wisconsin. The five counties with the largest African American population are Milwaukee (231,157), Racine (19,777), Dane (17,067), Kenosha (7,600), and Rock (7,048).

American Indians

The number of people of American Indian origin increased 19.9% from 1990 to 2000 in Wisconsin. Although the number of American Indians represent a small (0.9%) percentage of the state's overall population, they cluster into four northern counties where they comprise more than 10% of county populations: Menominee (87.3%), Sawyer (16.1%), Forest (11.3%) and Ashland (10.3%). According to the U.S. Census Bureau, there are 29 different tribes in Wisconsin scattered throughout the state; approximately 10% of the American Indians live on reservations; most are concentrated in the greater Milwaukee area.

Asians

Asians are the third largest racial group in the state of Wisconsin with 88,763 persons. The Asian population clusters primarily in the eastern portion of the State. The counties with the five largest Asian populations are: Milwaukee (24,145), Dane (14,735), Marathon (5,715), Waukesha (5,381) and Brown (4,935).

The largest subgroup among Asians in Wisconsin is the Hmong population. In fact, Wisconsin has a higher relative percentage of persons of Hmong origin compared to the United States population as a whole: nationally = 0.06% of total; Wisconsin = 0.33%. In Wisconsin, Hmongs represent roughly one-third of the state's total Asian population of more than 100,000. Seven counties in Wisconsin have more than 2,000 persons of Hmong origin: Milwaukee (7,883), Marathon (4,453), Brown (2,957), Sheboygan (2,706), Outagamie (2,504), La Crosse (2,282), and Dane (2,235).

Project Implications

Two major conclusions can be drawn from the demographic information presented above.

1. The ethnic and racial diversity of Wisconsin is accelerating at a rate exceeding the national average.
2. Cultural diversity is not confined to major metropolitan areas but is manifest throughout the state of Wisconsin.

Accordingly, it is essential that outreach efforts extend to all regions in Wisconsin, which covers over 56,000 square miles. Therefore, regional conferences target health care providers who encounter prenatal and postpartum depression in seven different locations.

Cultural Competence in Staffing

The staff will demonstrate cultural competence in two major ways. First, the conference presenters will be members of diverse communities, thereby ensuring regionally appropriate cultural perspectives in their presentations. Second, the Cultural Competency Consultant, through her statewide networks, will help ensure diversity at host sites and among presenters.

Cultural Competence in Perinatal Foundation

From academic training, clinical experience, and field feedback, the Perinatal Foundation recognizes that cultural competence is an unmet need. The Foundation considers cultural competence as a key factor in making grant awards. For instance, the Perinatal Foundation funded a pilot project to increase the ability of health care providers to deliver culturally competent care for depressed Hmong women.[70] Among the many findings in the project report, one was particularly noteworthy: the Hmong language has no word for the concept of "depression" nor does it recognize the phenomenon of postpartum depression. As another example, the Foundation funded a recent conference (aka "The Gathering") addressing ethnic disparities in maternal and child health; among other things, the 350 Gathering attendees emphasized the great need for culturally sensitive and respectful medical services.

Cultural Competence in Conference Products

Cultural competence becomes a thematic focus of all conference products. For example, the Web site will host a special cultural competence section. Printed materials will include pictures of people from diverse cultural backgrounds. Distribution of conference products will be specifically targeted to culturally diverse groups, e.g., Black Health Coalition and the Great Lakes Intertribal Council. Prior products include a bilingual publication dealing with hearing loss in infancy, becoming a parent, and parenting an infant who has been in the neonatal intensive care unit. The Cultural Competency Consultant will assure that diverse perspectives are mirrored in conference products.

SECTION D. APPROPRIATENESS OF EVALUATION PLAN

D.1: Evaluation Plan

Summative Evaluation: The Perinatal Foundation will collect data necessary to judge the ultimate success of the regional conferences. The goal is to document the extent to which the conference objectives were

> In addition to addressing the hot button of "cultural competence" throughout the narrative, two solid pages are dedicated to describing the demographics of diversity in the state and the cultural competence of the staff, organization, and conference products. The narrative does not rely on vague promises of "being sensitive to the needs of diverse peoples"; multiple concrete examples illustrate, repeatedly, partners' attention to culture, language, and gender issues.

> The fourth sentence of this paragraph provides a forceful example of the collaborative partners' cultural awareness. Organizations and staff only casually aware of cultural differences would not know that the Hmong people of southeast Asia have no word for "depression" nor recognize the phenomenon of postpartum depression. Or, said differently, this deep knowledge and familiarity helps to establish the credibility of collaborators.

achieved; that is, to what extent did the proposal do what it was designed to do? Each proposal objective was written in concrete, measurable terms, thereby simplifying the summative evaluation process.

Goal #1: To *disseminate* best practices to constituents

- **Evaluation Plan for Objective 1.1: To develop an information architecture for disseminating best practices**

From the knowledge base in Phase II, the Best Practices Symposium and Phase III, the Blueprint for Action, the information architecture must be established. To evaluate this objective, the key questions to answer are as follows: By October 2003, has the following been accomplished: Phase II Symposium held? Audio cassettes analyzed? Phase III analysis written? Web site hosting symposium deliverables?

- **Evaluation Plan for Objective 1.2: To disseminate select prenatal and postpartum depression information throughout the state**

Once the information architecture is built, the host information will be widely disseminated to targeted prenatal and postpartum practitioners throughout the state using print and electronic means. By June 2004 did the following occur: Mail 15,000 postcards to perinatal health care providers regarding access to an electronic (web-based) version of Symposium Proceedings/Blueprint for Action (Phase III)?

Goal #2: To *integrate* the prenatal and postpartum depression Best Practices

- **Evaluation Plan for Objective 2.1: To conduct seven regional conferences**

By August 2004, were the seven regional workshops held? Did presentation topics include an overview of prior project phases, discussions of cultural competence, barriers to clinical integration, regional approaches to best practices, and networking opportunities? To what extent did initial and follow-up surveys indicate participant satisfaction?

- **Evaluation Plan for Objective 2.2 To promote partnerships that will stimulate the integration of best practices**

By August 30, 2004, have (1) conference presenters established communications with regional leaders at the seven regional conferences; (2) practitioners at the local level identified strategies for effectively integrating best practices; (3) practitioners and presenters identified additional opportunities for model program education and research; and (4) a minimum of 80% of the conference participants responded to the follow-up survey?

In Section D of the narrative, the goals and objectives are repeated from Section B as a way to set the stage for the specific questions that will be able to be answered as a result of the evaluation. The evaluation plans for each objective indicate the quantitative and qualitative data that will be gathered to assess project results and effectiveness.

Item 4 in the evaluation plan for Objective 2.2 touches on the distinctive feature of "GPRA." The evaluation plan does not focus exclusively on achieving an 80% response rate—nor should it—but this item confirms for the sponsor an awareness of and attention to meeting federal reporting requirements.

D.2 Culturally and Linguistically Appropriate Tools

Cultural Context for Tool Selection

The ultimate purpose of this proposal is to disseminate and integrate culturally useful information that either leads to changes in current practice or confirms it. Experience shows that possession of information does not mean it will be used.[71] To avoid bias or inaccuracies in interpretation, members of diverse communities will be included in the tool selection and evaluation phases of this project, as recommended by Duarte & Rice.[72]

Selection of Culturally Appropriate Tools

Methodologically, the regional conferences are both interdisciplinary and multi-cultural. To stress the cultural dimension, attendees will receive a confirmation notice that refers them to the Perinatal Foundation Web site, which contains a bibliography of approximately 200 literature references germane to the conference. While the two survey instruments are not culturally dependent, the demographic information will allow a cross-tab analysis to probe for cultural differences in participant responses. Moreover, the Cultural Diversity Consultant and Evaluation Consultant will take lead roles in avoiding cultural biases in data interpretation.

> This paragraph explicitly confirms that the Cultural Diversity Consultant and the Evaluation Consultant will work together to ensure that data is interpreted accurately, including when it's viewed through a cultural lens. Put differently, even the external consultants recognize the value of interacting with each other to achieve their overlapping goals.

The goal of all dissemination should be utilization. Utilization may mean different things to different members of a culturally diverse audience; in some cases, it may mean rejection of a product or so-called best practice. The critical element of utilization is that the best practice must be critically and thoroughly digested, and clinicians must fit the new information with their prior understandings and experience. One of the most effective ways to increase utilization and to improve the quality and relevance of best practices is to involve potential users in planning and implementing the regional conferences. The follow-up survey will help pinpoint the extent to which culturally appropriate information is being integrated.

D.3 Compliance with GPRA Reporting

The Perinatal Foundation agrees to comply fully and unconditionally in a timely manner with the GPRA reporting requirements, including (1) number of events, (2) satisfaction with the events, and (3) utilization of materials and information to make a change in their practice as a result of the event. More precisely, we will collect baseline GPRA data at the end of the regional conference on all participants. In addition, we will conduct a 30-day follow up of at least 80% of the regional conference participants. Response rates to the last three Perinatal Foundation post-conference surveys have been 68%. With the added incentive of improved eligibility for Phase V funding, an 80% response rate is certainly realistic. The Perinatal Foundation is accustomed to complying with GPRA-like reporting requirements, which are very similar to the Wisconsin Maternal and Child Health

> This final paragraph of the proposal addresses the distinctive feature of "GPRA." Because the grant leader did not have a history of receiving funding support from the sponsor, rather than writing a generic sentence that said, "we agree to comply with GPRA," she went into greater detail. In particular, seven sentences are used to confirm explicitly that the three reporting requirements will be met and to justify, based on prior experience, the feasibility of achieving an 80% follow-up participant response rate.

Data System reporting requirements. Our systems and procedures are organized to collect such information.

REVIEWER COMMENTS

Proposal Section	Evaluation Criteria	Assigned Grade
A. Potential Significance of the Proposed Project		
	Present a brief literature review on the topic area and describe how your conference represents knowledge in the field(s)	A
	Describe the value of the conference to advance the field of substance abuse and/or mental prevention, treatment, and rehabilitative services, particularly in reference to culturally and racially diverse populations	A
	Describe the relevance of the proposed project to the SAMHSA Priorities and Principles found in the Program Overview section of this announcement	A
B. Merit and Appropriateness of the Project ⌐		
	Identify and justify overall goals, ⸳s, and approach of the conference.	B
	Discuss the feasibility of the confe⸳ ⸳e agenda	C
	Describe the collaboration in the planning, implementation, and evaluation of the conference among all the following constituencies: consumers, advocates, researchers, and providers. Attach letters of support and/or agreement to participate in the conference in Appendix 1.	C
	Explain how your conference will address, develop, and/or improve the cultural awareness and/or competence of attendees	B
	List plans for speakers, presenters, and participants. Attach letters of collaboration, support, and/or agreement to participate in the conference in Appendix 1.	B
	Describe plans for development and dissemination of conference product(s) (e.g., publications, reports)	B

The sponsor uses a two-tier proposal review process. First, applications are reviewed by an Internal Review Group (IRG), which consists of experts who examine the project narrative and budget. Once they rate a proposal, it is forwarded on to a second level of review conducted by the appropriate Center's National Advisory Council (NAC). While the IRG evaluates the scientific merit of an application, the NAC focuses more broadly on how the proposed project fits within the sponsor's overall mission. The resulting IRG score, accepted by the NAC, was 94 out of 100 points, which was high enough to get funded.

Proposal Section	Evaluation Criteria	Assigned Grade
C. Management Plan, Staffing, Project Organization and Resources		
	List any previous conferences you have conducted or coordinated, include dates, topics, attendance, and products. Also indicate if you have not conducted or coordinated conferences before	A
	Describe the administrative and organizational structure that will facilitate goals, objectives, and approach of the conference	A
	Briefly describe capability/experience of the proposed conference director and other key personnel. Attach their résumés in Section G–Biographical Sketches and Job Descriptions	A
D. Appropriateness of the Evaluation Plan		
	Describe your plan for evaluation of conference planning, content, and outcome	A
	Describe how the proposed evaluation (for instance, the methods and instruments used) is appropriate to the culture and values of the attendees and that the interpretation of findings will be accurate.	B
	State your agreement to comply with the GPRA reporting requirements to be provided in the terms and conditions of the grant awards from CMHS and CSAP. If applying for a conference grant from CSAT, discuss how you will comply with the GRPA requirements (including a 30-day follow up with a minimum of 80% of all baseline participants followed up) specified in Appendix A of this document)	A

Overall, the proposal received high marks. Unfortunately, the reviewer's evaluation form did not provide specific written feedback regarding the four major proposal sections. The letter grades give some indication of perceived strengths and weaknesses, but there are no real clues as to why reviewers reacted so favorably to all three items in Section A, "Potential Significance of the Proposed Project," and severely downgraded two items in Section B, "Merit and Appropriateness of the Project Plan."

PART III

EVALUATION STRATEGIES FOR COLLABORATIVE GRANTSEEKING

In part III, we focus on evaluating the effectiveness of collaborations and on one of the grant leader's most challenging responsibilities—namely, handling difficult people and situations. Different types of evaluations can be used for assessment purposes during, at the conclusion of, and beyond the granting period. In chapter 9 we outline three methodological approaches and a handful of qualitative and quantitative strategies frequently used to document the present status of the project and collaborators. What's more, to measure the attitudes and satisfaction of collaborative partners, we arm you with a pool of 180 sample questionnaire items that examine attributes related to goal sharing and interaction and from which you can generate a customized measurement tool that fits your specific situation and needs.

Grant leaders exert their leadership skills in a manner that ensures an environment of equality. In addition to influencing, motivating, and enabling others to contribute toward a common cause, you must foster respect, trust, inclusiveness and openness; combine the perspectives, resources, and skills of partners; and resolve conflict among collaborators. Left unattended, challenging episodes can compromise the ultimate success of a collaborative grant project. That's why in chapter 10 we present scenarios for five commonly encountered difficulties that occur during the conduct of collaborative grants. For each scenario, we offer a situational analysis, annotated dialogue scripts, and reflections on the psychological strategies used to smooth the road to success. You too can use these strategies to redirect unacceptable behavior toward the positive.

CHAPTER 9

Evaluation in Collaborative Grantseeking

True genius resides in the capacity for evaluation of uncertain,
hazardous, and conflicting information.

—Winston Churchill

Accountability. More and more, sponsors are demanding it, to make certain their funds are being spent wisely. At the same time, grantseekers require it, to ensure their programs are functioning properly and goals and objectives are being met. To satisfy the multiple needs of sponsors and grantseekers, evaluations are essential.

While detailed guidance on conducting broad-scale evaluations of projects is widely available, less has been written about assessing the effectiveness of collaborations. Accordingly, this chapter reviews the central elements of evaluations—types of evaluations, qualitative and quantitative methods, evaluation steps, and choosing an evaluator—and places a special emphasis on assessing collaborators' satisfaction and performance.

CHOOSING AN EVALUATOR

Who should evaluate your project and collaboration? You have three choices. First, grant leaders can do it internally with program staff. They have great knowledge of inner project workings and relationships, though they may lack expertise in research design and statistical analysis. Second, external experts with appropriate training and experience may be hired to evaluate your project and collaboration. The consultants may need some time to learn subtle nuances of the project's details, which will increase evaluation costs. Third, a combination of approaches can be used, employing both internal and external evaluators to conduct a comprehensive, multidimensional assessment.

Internal Evaluators

In some collaborative endeavors, internal expertise exists to devise evaluation questions and methods, collect and analyze data, and disseminate results. This may be the responsibility of the grant leader or a designee. The evaluation process may solicit feedback from a variety of individuals. For example, one person may be responsible for the production of print materials used in the project and have oversight responsibility for all the people involved. Others might be responsible for coordinating meeting space, equipment, participants, focus groups—all of the myriad logistical and programmatic components needed to run the project smoothly. Their evaluative input can be critical to the assessment of project operations and outcomes.

Using internal evaluators has the advantage of looking in fine detail at as many components of the project and collaboration as is desirable. What's more, evaluations usually cost less when conducted in-house. Because internal evaluators are knowledgeable about project specifics, weak and strong areas can be identified rapidly, allowing changes to be made in midstream rather than waiting until the project is completed. The major disadvantage is a possible lack of objectivity and reliability. In problem areas, people may be reluctant to respond candidly; participants may fear loss of services and staff may fear retribution. Everyone wants to look good, so assessments can be biased to give a favorable view of the work done. However, that is a risk worth taking and the degree of risk is significantly reduced when there has been ongoing communication with the partners throughout the project.

External Evaluators

In other collaborative initiatives, external evaluators are used, usually because insufficient internal expertise is available, because sponsors demand it, or because a strong desire exists for "objective" findings. External evaluators are typically hired from nearby universities or nonprofit organizations and have established track records of evaluating similar projects. Hopefully, they helped craft your objectives, which determine precisely *what* will be evaluated. In larger collaborative projects, an Evaluation Steering Committee is often formed to oversee the evaluation process and reports directly to an Advisory Board.

External evaluators usually offer objective and reliable findings; they have no axe to grind nor obligations to do anything other than assess your project and collaboration and report the results. On the other hand, external evaluators can only see select individuals and components firsthand; they must trust in the second and thirdhand information provided to them. External evaluators will depend heavily on the clarity of the goals and objectives presented in the project plan and the measurement methods used to assess their completion. The external evaluator's "arm's length" relationship is designed to promote objectivity and to flesh out the most meaningful aspects of a project's operations and outcomes, both good and not-so-good. This greatly enhances the validity of future decision making by the project staff and collaborators.

Combined Evaluators

In the best of all worlds, using a combination of internal and external evaluators would yield the most meaningful assessment of project operations and outcomes. In fact, a few sponsors explicitly require that both internal and external evaluations be conducted. The primary advantage, of course, is that the results from the two groups can be compared. The extent to which internal versus external evaluation results agree is an important yardstick in determining the overall validity of the evaluation results.

Internal and external evaluators may ask the same questions. Both agreement and discrepancies should exist between the two assessments, because the two groups have different perspectives. The internal evaluators are stakeholders in the project, and the external evaluators have no vested interest. Whether the external evaluators' results are positive or negative, it is of little importance to them. In contrast, stakeholders, especially the collaborators, and their future project efforts may be directly affected.

If the project ends with poor results and dissatisfaction, the consequences may include the following.

- The likelihood of future funding may be jeopardized.
- Some staff may suffer loss of employment.
- Needs not satisfied by the project may remain unmet.
- Constituents who stood to benefit from the project may be shortchanged.
- Professional reputations may be adversely affected.
- Present collaborators may not be interested in participating on future projects.
- New collaborators may be difficult to attract.

Conversely, good or outstanding results can produce positive aftereffects.

- Projects may continue and expand.
- The likelihood of future funding may increase.
- Additional staff may be needed.
- Old project needs are met.
- New needs can be addressed.
- Present collaborators remain on board.
- New collaborators may be attracted.

The process of selecting an individual to evaluate your project and collaboration may well be determined by the some of the time, cost, and quality factors in exhibit 9.1. Ultimately, you will choose the best combination that suits your needs. Some sponsors retain lists of evaluators with whom they have worked successfully in the past. Contact your targeted sponsor or a nearby University Grants Office for names of possible evaluators.

TYPES OF EVALUATIONS

You may engage in different types of evaluations to assess the effectiveness of your project and collaboration during, at the conclusion of, and beyond the granting period. Three types of evaluations include process, outcome, and impact. Public and private sponsors

- ability to collect and analyze information
- accountability for use of funds
- availability
- cost
- credibility
- dissemination of results
- ethical issues
- experience with institution
- experience with target population
- knowledge of context

- knowledge of program and operations
- name recognition
- organizational investment
- real and perceived objectivity
- reasonableness of fees
- references from colleagues
- scheduling
- specialist skills and expertise
- use of evaluation results
- willingness to criticize

EXHIBIT 9.1   Factors to Consider When Choosing an Evaluator

During the grant period	*Conclusion* of grant period	*Beyond* the grant period
process	outcome	impact
• structure	• outputs	
• process	• outcomes	
formative	summative	impact
immediate outcomes	short-term outcomes	long-term outcomes
initial outcomes	intermediate outcomes	end outcomes

EXHIBIT 9.2   Evaluation Terminology at Different Grant Time Periods

sometimes use different terms to describe the same types of evaluations. For instance, the U.S. Department of Education uses the terms formative and summative evaluations, whereas the W. K. Kellogg Foundation uses the terms process and outcome evaluations; they are synonyms. Exhibit 9.2 lists some of the common evaluation terms used during different grant periods.

Note that some evaluation terms overlap; that is, one term can have more than one meaning. For instance, "process" is the umbrella name given to evaluation conducted during a grant; it is also the name of one facet of the evaluation, along with "structure." The semantics of evaluation terminology are not consistent among sponsors; the following discussion attempts to defuzzify the various evaluation terms.

Process Evaluations

Process evaluations generate information that will improve the effectiveness of the project and collaboration during the granting period. They systematically examine internal and external characteristics associated with the delivery and receipt of services. They may include evaluating structure, and the environment and settings in which services occur. Understanding the strengths and weaknesses of your organization and partners, the target population and their community environment, and the procedures your organization is using to interact with the community will provide immediate feedback to help you in the process of meeting project objectives.

Evaluation indicators are specific characteristics that you will track and measure to gauge project success. Process-level indicators may examine features such as the intensity of the intervention, the quality of service provided, and the cultural competence of the intervention. Structure-level indicators may assess elements such as who provided the intervention, what type of intervention was used, where the intervention occurred, when and how long the intervention took place, and the length of participant involvement.

Outcome Evaluations

Outcome evaluations examine the end result of an intervention. The goal here is to document how well the project did what it was designed to do. Outcomes are the benefits, changes, or effects that occur to the target population due to participation in your project. Outcomes are generally expressed in humanistic terms—for instance, improved health status, increased knowledge of parenting skills, and decreased youth violence. Some sponsors may also ask you to identify outputs, products generated as a result of your program activities—for example, a curriculum to teach oral health to middle school students, the number of conflict resolution classes taught, the number of volunteers recruited.

The core of outcome evaluations is measurement: collect data to document the extent to which project objectives were accomplished. Outcome indicators—specific characteristics selected for measurement—must best describe an associated end result. Three common types of outcome indicators are functional status, humanistic, and economic. Keep in mind that "ideal" outcomes can vary with perspective, and collecting data to evaluate all aspects of each type of outcome indicator would be extremely difficult and prohibitively expensive. Instead, do like successful grantseekers do: identify a few outcome indicators that will demonstrate meaningful end results to your organization and partners, the target population, and the sponsor.

Impact Evaluations

Impact evaluations generate information to measure the overall worth and utility of the project and collaboration beyond the granting period, whether six months, one year, or three years. An impact evaluation goes beyond assessing whether goals and objectives were achieved and focuses on an even bigger picture: the long-term, fundamental changes in participants' knowledge, attitudes, or behaviors. That is, improving outcomes at the program level may effect change over time at the community level. By their nature, many outcomes are delayed, occurring beyond the granting period. Impact evaluations attempt to attribute outcomes exclusively to an intervention, although data may be difficult to obtain over the long term.

You can demonstrate impact at several levels: the target population, the community at large, and beyond. Lasting changes in the target population demonstrate the overall value of the project and collaboration. Inclusive participation by the community may contribute to long-term project sustainability. Regional and national buy-in for targeted interventions and outcomes can promote large-scale project replication. Collectively, conducting process, outcome, and impact evaluations increases accountability. While sponsors routinely allow grant funds to be spent on process and outcome evaluations, they rarely support impact evaluations. Instead of planning to conduct an impact evaluation, then, your organization and collaborators may embed assessment methods into activities on an ongoing basis with the aim to use feedback to guide continual improvement.

EVALUATION METHODS

There are three evaluation approaches typically used to document the present status of the project and collaborators: qualitative methods, quantitative methods, and mixed methods, which involve a combination of the two. Your choice of methods will depend on your answers to these basic questions.

1. "What do I want to know?"

2. "How rigorous do I need to be?"

3. "What decisions will I make based on the evaluation results?"

4. "Who will be affected by the accuracy or the level of measurement used?"

5. "What are the risks involved in using inadequate measures?"

6. "Were specific types of measurements stipulated in the RFP guidelines?"

Experienced evaluators know that qualitative and quantitative methods each have different advantages and drawbacks that must be weighed carefully. The choice of methods is often influenced by three opposing forces: time, cost, and quality. Time is the available window of opportunity to conduct the assessment. Cost represents the financial resources on hand to support the assessment. Quality denotes the desired level of breadth, depth, and precision in collecting, analyzing, and reporting assessment data. In many cases, one of these forces is fixed and the other two vary in proportion to each other. For instance, when the price is fixed, the quality of the evaluation will be influenced by the time available.

In actual practice, many project evaluations constitute roughly 10 percent of the total grant budget, but may range from 5 to 20 percent. Qualitative evaluations and quantitative evaluations often distribute budget dollars differently, though one approach is not necessarily cheaper or more cost-effective than the other. For instance, whereas quantitative evaluations may have modest personnel costs for database development and data entry and have modest non-personnel costs associated with purchasing and distributing survey instruments, qualitative evaluations may have high personnel costs due to the labor-intensive nature of data collection and have low non-personnel costs. One common budget mistake is failing to include sufficient resources relative to the magnitude and complexity of the evaluation plan. Itemize and justify each budget item.

Qualitative Methods

Qualitative methods record descriptions in order to understand people's perceptions of reality. Their judgments are usually placed somewhere on a continuum between just about any set of polar opposites you might generate, such as good–bad, satisfactory–unsatisfactory, preferred–not preferred, highest–lowest, largest–smallest, youngest–oldest, fastest–slowest, friendly–hostile, easy–difficult, liberal–conservative, and innovative–commonplace. Because a qualitative analysis occurs in a natural setting, a context is provided for people's feelings toward the project, the collaboration, and resulting outcomes. Qualitative data are often rich in contextual detail and, as a result, have limited generalizability to other situations and environments. In some cases, grant leaders can use anecdotal feedback to make process improvements during the project period.

Quantitative Methods

Quan͟ ͟tive evaluations focus on numeric information as a way to classify and explain phe͟ ͟o͟ ͟a. For example, projects may measure the number of first-generation minority ͟ ͟͟ts who earn college degrees, the percentage of adults who abuse prescription mec͟a͟cions, and the availability in the community of dental services for children with disabilities. In other words, numeric values are established and then subjected to statistical analysis and interpretation. Statistical analysis allows you to determine whether the results, hypothetically, are attributable to the project or to random chance. Though quantitative methods may miss contextual details, because of their precise measurement and objectivity, they are sometimes regarded as being more "powerful" than qualitative methods.

Mixed Methods

Qualitative and quantitative methods each have their strengths and weaknesses, hence many project evaluations use both, for balance. Seldom do project participants live in controlled and restrictive environments. Employing mixed methods at different points in the evaluation process can reveal a more complete picture, clarifying exactly what is going on, why it's happening that way, and how participants feel about it. Mixed methods, whether applied concurrently or sequentially, allow grant leaders to triangulate feedback, which in turn increases the reliability, validity, and generalizability of evaluation data. That said, mixed methods have potential drawbacks: they take more time, increase costs, and require specialized knowledge.

EVALUATION STEPS

Regardless of methodology (qualitative, quantitative, or mixed), evaluation consists of five steps: determining your evaluation priorities, formulating questions, defining measurable outcomes, describing your information collection plan, and specifying approaches to data interpretation and reporting. Each is discussed below.

Step One: Determine Your Evaluation Priorities

If you wrote measurable objectives for your proposal, you may already be finished with step one of your evaluation. Your objectives determined your evaluation priorities; they specified precisely *what* you wanted to change and the stakeholders who would be affected.

Suppose, for example, that you were conducting a collaborative project between Midwest University and a public school system to train mentors who would support newly certified teachers as they work in inner-city schools. One of your objectives might read as follows:

> **Objective:** By June 2015, a cadre of 25 mentors will be trained to support future teacher graduates.

Your project objectives describe the specific activities that, if achieved, will lead you to conclude that you did what you said you would do. (*How* the trainings will be conducted and the topics to be addressed are detailed in the methodology section of the proposal.) In this example, if we can document that 25 mentors have been trained to support new teachers, then we can say our objective has been met. The key stakeholders might include university professors in teacher education programs, school administrators, pre-service and in-service teachers, parents, children, and state departments of public instruction, among others. Each stakeholder can now take advantage of a valuable resource that was not available before the grant started.

Step Two: Formulate Your Evaluation Questions

In step two, you identify what formative and summative evaluation questions are of interest to selected stakeholders.

Continuing with the mentor training example above, your sample evaluation questions might include the following:

> **Formative (Process) Evaluation Questions:** Have program participants demonstrated success on key course assessments? What key course assessments need revision? At the end of each semester, are program participants making suitable progress?

> **Summative (Outcome) Evaluation Questions:** Have program participants completed all courses in the academic sequence? Have program participants maintained the required 2.5 GPA? Do program participants feel adequately prepared to enter the classroom?

In terms of time frames, the formative questions focus on activities *during* the project period, while the summative questions concentrate on the *end* of the project; both center on the mentors and mentees. If funds were available to support evaluations *after* the project were completed, then the questions would be broadened to include the impact on stakeholders—for instance, children who were in the classrooms of mentored teachers, parents, school administrators, and state departments of public instruction.

Step Three: Define Your Measurable Outcomes

In step three, you determine the criteria for success; that is to say, how much change is enough to declare the results important or valuable? Your options for deciding how much change is enough include the following.

- **Statistical Significance:** "A statistically significant change has occurred."
- **Prior History:** "Experience of others has shown that one can reasonably expect this much change."
- **Professional Judgment:** "The opinion of experts suggests that this much change can be expected."

Continuing with our mentoring example, your outcome criterion might be as follows:

> **Outcome Criterion:** The attrition rate of project participants will be less than 20 percent, based on the prior history of similar teacher training at other institutions of higher education.

To implement the outcome criterion (or criteria), three kinds of resources need to be considered: time, money, and staff capability. The extent to which these resources are available will influence your selection of outcome criteria.

Step Four: Describe Your Information Collection Plan

In step four, you identify the process used to collect project data and information against which the outcome criteria will ultimately be applied. A rigorous information collection plan describes the methods, strategies, and instruments to be used; the types of data that will be collected at which specific points in time; and the credentials and capabilities of the responsible personnel. Depending on the evaluation approach you select, your qualitative and/or quantitative data will reflect changes in participants' knowledge, attitudes, and behaviors.

Using the mentoring example, your information collection plan might read as follows:

> **Information Collection Plan:** The methods and instruments the Evaluation Team will use to collect project evaluation information include the following:
>
> - literature reviews of existing curricula
> - focus groups with mentees and mentors
> - academic records of mentees

- participant satisfaction surveys administered semi-annually
- interviews with mentees who failed to secure jobs

Use of these methods and instruments will generate the following types of data.

- course grades and cumulative GPAs
- participant satisfaction scores
- end of program evaluation reports
- focus group reports
- curriculum manuals

This step assembles pertinent data that becomes the "raw material" which is critically examined to determine whether sufficient change occurred to conclude that your objective has been met. It is imperative that data-collection protocols are accurate, consistent, and unbiased. Analysis of unreliable data leads to unreliable interpretation and conclusions.

Step Five: Specify Your Data Interpretation and Reporting Plan

In this final evaluation step, you analyze the data you collected in step four and then report your findings to project stakeholders. In essence, step five answers two related questions: "What does my collected evaluation information mean?" and "Who needs to know about it?"

The mentoring project responded as follows.

> **Interpretation and Reporting Plan:** The collected evaluation information and data for each project objective will be critically reviewed by the Project Director and the External Evaluation Committee. They will generate an External Evaluation Report that includes the summary project evaluation data and the interpretations placed on it. The evaluation findings will then be disseminated to appropriate stakeholders through the use of a Web site, www.midwest.edu/mentor, conference presentations, journal articles, and white papers to all directors of training programs and state educational agencies.

Your data interpretation is ultimately a matter of making your best professional judgment on the basis of the information collected. Usually, the analysis represents the collective conclusion of seasoned experts. Your data reporting section is often a freeze-dried restatement of your project dissemination plan and could include an appropriate mix of such active and passive dissemination strategies as conferences and workshops, demonstrations, site visits, webcasts, teleconferences, convention papers, staff presentations, poster sessions, Web postings, books and manuals, executive summaries, journal articles, newsletters, pamphlets, and press releases.

QUALITATIVE EVALUATION STRATEGIES

In this section, we describe six conventional qualitative strategies utilized in project evaluations. These include surveys, interviews, observations, focus groups, case studies, and document review. These qualitative strategies can be used during the granting period to assess project progress as well as at the conclusion of the granting period to assess ultimate success.

Surveys

Surveys contain two basic elements: questions and responses. Questions may be open-ended, such as "How well did this collaboration work out for you?" which allows the respondents to answer in a free-flowing narrative form. Or they may be closed-ended, such as "To what extent did this collaboration work out for you?" which requires the respondents to select from a predetermined range of answers—for example, a five-point rating scale spanning "quite a bit" to "not at all." The Collaboration Rating Form presented later in this chapter offers you a pool of 180 closed-ended survey items to choose from to probe different dimensions of a collaboration.

Surveys are especially useful when you are collecting the same structured information from large groups. Survey instruments can be used for both formative and summative purposes and can gather descriptive data on a wide range of topics. The surveys may be administered as traditional pencil-and-paper instruments or via Web-based technologies, such as Survey Monkey (www.surveymonkey.com) and Zoomerang (www.zoomerang.com). You may use standardized survey instruments or make up your own. Surveys are relatively inexpensive to use and can be analyzed using a variety of existing software, but they have limitations: chiefly, because they are self-reports, surveys reflect only what people *say* they think, feel, or do, not what they *actually* think, feel, or do.

Interviews

As opposed to surveys, interviews are a more personal way to gather rich data and gain new insights. Interviews can range in format from highly structured to unstructured. In structured interviews, the same questions are asked of all participants, thus ensuring a level of consistency in the data-collection process. This format, however, may not allow enough spontaneity to explore topics fully. In unstructured interviews, participants have the flexibility to address the issues that are of greatest concern to them. This format effectively prevents the interview from being biased with preconceived notions about the project or collaboration, yet it may also produce a considerable amount of unconnected information. The compromise is to conduct interviews in a moderately structured format.

Semistructured interviews balance the need for consistency and flexibility. In practical terms, a structured list of questions is used with all participants to establish a basis for comparing responses and then varied follow-up questions are used to probe for additional details. Interview questions may span a continuum of time, from past actions to future intentions.

Conducting interviews, whether in-person or via telephone, can be time-consuming and may require highly trained interviewers to obtain useful information. And in some cases, in an effort to please interviewers, participants may distort information. Nevertheless, this combination of fixed and flexible questioning is an effective way to obtain interview results that are valid and reliable.

Observations

Another way to gather firsthand data is through direct observation. By entering into the natural setting and monitoring individual and group behaviors, it is possible to gain a broader understanding of context, environment, and culture. Observations may uncover issues that participants, project staff, and collaborators are reluctant to discuss openly in an interview or focus group. For instance, direct observation often reveals a gap between official administrative policies and everyday operational practices.

Observations can be a powerful means for understanding the relationship between a part of the picture and the whole picture. That is to say, by standing back and taking a serious look at a sequence of events, individual activities in themselves may become more (or less!) significant than originally recognized. While observations can be an economical way to gather data, it is also possible that participants change their behavior under observation precisely because they know they are being watched, thus compromising the validity of the evaluation. Highly trained observers who are also content experts may be able to mitigate this situation as well as uncover unanticipated project outcomes.

Focus Groups

Focus groups assemble a small cluster of individuals—typically 8 to 20—to engage in a roundtable discussion of selected topics in an informal setting. This qualitative strategy combines elements of both interviews and observations. The synergy of group interactions often produces a wealth of valuable data, ranging from the actual opinions of the group to firsthand observations of individuals' verbal and nonverbal communications. Facial expressions, body language, and vocalization cues can complement, emphasize, or even contradict what is being said. Focus group feedback can be used in the formative evaluation stage to make mid-course corrections and in the summative evaluation stage to assess end results.

Chapter 4 provides details on two common focus group formats, namely, brainstorming and round-robin. The difference between the two formats is essentially breadth versus depth. Brainstorming allows for interaction among participants and covers a wider range of topics, while round-robins limit participant interaction and focus on a narrow range of topics. Focus groups have been used in collaborative grantseeking in the past for such purposes as generating new ideas, defining problems, exploring methodological approaches, identifying partners' strengths and weaknesses, interpreting quantitative findings, and understanding attitudes toward project outcomes.

Document Review

A common qualitative data-collection strategy is to "follow the paper trail." Most organizations and individuals engage in a variety of formal and informal documentation of events that can be reviewed to retrace their history and understand their culture and environment. For instance, institutions frequently produce annual reports, mission statements, organization charts, policy and procedure handbooks, and memorandums of understanding, while individuals maintain expenditure reports, meeting calendars, e-mail correspondence, photo collections, and shadow systems. These print and electronic materials are rarely created with evaluative purposes in mind and often contain incomplete references, but they are an unobtrusive source of contextually informative data.

In addition to the contents of the documents themselves, it is valuable to know who authored key documents and to understand the target audience of, the purpose for, and rationale of each piece. In a few cases it might be possible to go back to the author directly to ask questions; in other cases, the author's original sources of information may be revisited. The aim is to examine accuracy, establish authenticity, and tease out bias from existing documents. In this way, the evaluation report can systematically add to institutional and individual histories.

Case Studies

Case studies are a qualitative strategy for describing, understanding, and explaining a complex issue. Whether single or multiple cases are examined, these studies involve an in-depth exploration of an event in order to determine not only *what* happened and *how,* but also *why.* Case studies can be time-consuming and resource-intensive, often employing several other strategies to collect data, including surveys, interviews, observations, focus groups, and document reviews. The triangulation of data collection is a strength of this evaluation strategy.

Case studies offer the advantage of providing meaningful insights to issues in real-world settings. They can present contextual evidence to explain why activities worked exactly as planned or, conversely, to account for gaps between theory and practice. While these studies afford a holistic view, caution needs to be exercised so that the finding of an individual case is not overinterpreted or overgeneralized. However, a consistent finding repeated over multiple cases often lends credibility to the collective results.

QUANTITATIVE EVALUATION STRATEGIES

In this section, we describe the two key facets of quantitative strategies: research design and statistical analysis. Quantitative data can be collected, analyzed, and interpreted during the granting period, which allows for mid-course corrections to the project as appropriate, and at the conclusion of the granting period, which allows for evaluation of overall project success.

Research Design

There are two basic types of research design, both of which aim to determine cause and effect: experiments and quasi-experiments. Experimental designs attempt to control all of the major variables that might influence an outcome, thus causality may be examined closely. In true experiments, participants are randomly assigned to various investigational and control groups. On the other hand, randomization is not always possible because of, for example, the ethical considerations of withholding treatment to participants, and this results in the use of quasi-experimental designs. In quasi-experiments, statistical techniques are used to control for as many confounding variables as possible, thereby improving the accuracy of the findings.

Often, research designs are needed that look at changes in a group as opposed to individual behaviors. The pre-test versus post-test comparison represents one common application. There are many permutations that produce varying degrees of useful evaluation information. The simplest pre-test versus post-test design involves observations before and after an intervention, often symbolized as follows.

(Experimental Group)   **O   X   O**   (Design 1)

If post-test scores differ appreciably from pre-test scores in Design 1, at first blush it might seem that the intervention caused a change. In reality, however, it would be difficult to attribute the changes exclusively to the intervention. Scores may have changed positively or negatively due to other external events.

To isolate the cause of the change in pre- versus post-test scores, it is essential to add a control group, as noted in Design 2.

(Experimental Group)   **O   X   O**

(Control Group 1)   **O   O**   (Design 2)

If the pre-test scores were the same for both groups and the post-test scores differed significantly, again your first reaction might be to conclude that the differences were the result of the intervention. But that's not necessarily so. Other factors may still account for the post-test differences. For instance, it is well documented that the people's behavior changes when they receive added attention. In Design 2, the pre-test could have sensitized the experimental group to the target behaviors, and the change might result from the sensitization rather than the actual intervention.

A "cleaner" approach would be to adopt Design 3, which controls for this pre-test sensitization by adding a second control group that receives only the post-test evaluation.

(Experimental Group)   **O   X   O**

(Control Group 1)   **O   O**

(Control Group 2)   **O**   (Design 3)

Design 3 results in the following comparisons and idealized outcomes.

1. A comparison of pre-test and post-test scores for the Experimental Group would show a statistically significant difference in favor of the post-test scores.

2. A comparison of the pre-test scores for the Experimental Group and Control Group 1 would should no significant differences, meaning both groups were representative of the same population.

3. A comparison of the pre-test and post-test scores for Control Group 1 would show no statistically significant differences, meaning that without the experimental treatment, no behavioral changes occurred.

4. A comparison of post-test scores for Control Group 1 and Control Group 2 showed no statistically significant differences, meaning that no pre-test sensitization effects occurred.

This research design is only one of the many options available. Other versions usually involve multiple control groups or multiple measurements.

Statistical Analysis

Once the research design is determined, then appropriate statistical analyses must be selected to describe the target population or quantify the changes that might occur. *Descriptive statistics* are numerical summaries from the target population without any effort to test a particular hypothesis. These measures of central tendency or measures of variability are often illustrated with simple graphics. *Inferential statistics* are tests of significant difference or tests of relationships, which enable you to make best guesses about the hypotheses being tested; in practical terms, this means "Is your difference a real one or due to random chance?" Exhibit 9.3 lists some of the more common statistical evaluation tools.

Parametric statistics make certain assumptions about the parameters of the population from which the sample is taken; namely, that all observations are independent, that the data is normally distributed and that, where treatment groups are compared, they show the same variance. When these assumptions are met, parametric statistics are powerful tools that can detect small differences between groups, particularly with complex experimental research designs and large data sets. *Nonparametric statistics* make fewer assumptions about the parameters of the population, though independence of observation is assumed. Nonparametric statistics are, in general, simple to use and are appropriate with small data sets.

If you have a background in research design and statistical analysis, you will find these tools to be familiar. If you lack this type of background, then you will want to seek

Statistical Analysis Options		
	Descriptive Statistics	**Inferential Statistics**
Parametric Statistics	Mean	t test
	Median	Analysis of variance
	Mode	Analysis of co-variance
	Range	Pearson r
	Standard deviation	Linear regression
Non-Parametric Statistics	Rank	Chi-squared test
	Graphical illustrations, including:	Mann-Whitney U
		Spearman Rho
	area plots	Kendall's Coefficient of Concordance
	histograms	Sign Test
	line graphs	
	pie charts	

EXHIBIT 9.3. Common Statistical Evaluation Tools

the services of an evaluation specialist to help you select the appropriate quantitative methods and tools. The first question you will expect to hear is "What do you want to know?" and your answer should lead you back to your project objectives.

MEETING EVALUATION FORM

It goes without saying that meetings can turn people on, vitalize them, and convert energy into action. Conversely, meetings can turn people off, deflate their interest, and send them on a mental picnic. The Meeting Evaluation Form in exhibit 9.4 contains 15 items that collect attitudinal information from collaborators regarding just-completed meetings. You can use this form as many times as you wish throughout the project to monitor how well the collaboration is working. It takes only a minute to fill out. You want the immediate reaction from participants, not long-thought-out responses.

If you plan to use the Meeting Evaluation Form with a variety of committees and subcommittees, you may wish to add additional contextual information to the form, such as date, purpose or title of meeting, and respondent category (e.g., project staff member, graduate student, volunteer, community participant, agency 1 representative, agency 2 representative). These contextual details might help to reveal patterns of engagement by specific groups over time and topic.

Once you collect the forms from participants, calculate the average score for each of the 15 items. The lower the mean scale values, the more favorable were the responses. If you are statistically inclined, you may also wish to calculate the variability among collaborators by looking at the range of scores or the standard deviation. Computer spreadsheets can simplify the calculation process. Finally, be sure to preserve respondent confidentiality.

COLLABORATION RATING FORM

When it comes to doing an in-depth analysis of the factors influencing participants' attitudes toward the collaboration overall, no one measurement tool will suffice to cover all pertinent situational factors. Rather than give you a "cookie cutter" to encompass all the nuances inherent in the types of collaboration, we opt instead to arm you with a pool of survey items from which you can generate your own measurement tool that fits your situation. Using a Collaboration Rating Form involves three simple steps.

1. **Select questionnaire items.** To assess your collaborators' thoughts and feelings, you will need to construct an attitude measurement scale. Begin by reviewing the sample questionnaire items below, which cluster into five attributes for each of the two main dimensions of collaboration. In total, there are 180 items. Do you have to use them all? Absolutely not! Select the ones that are of greatest value to you and your situation. As a general guide, you may end up choosing 25–30 items, drawing from both goal sharing and interaction dimensions. Better yet, bring together a few of your collaborators and let them help you decide which specific attributes you want to measure.

Directions. You are our only source of information about your reactions to our meeting. Please circle the number that best reflects your feelings about the meeting that just concluded.

Thank you for completing the meeting evaluation form. Use the space on the bottom to tell us anything else that you think we need to know to improve meeting efficiency and effectiveness.

Item	Very Satisfied	Satisfied	Neutral	Dissatisfied	Very Dissatisfied	Not Applicable
1. Overall quality of meeting	1	2	3	4	5	NA
2. Started on time	1	2	3	4	5	NA
3. Followed the agenda	1	2	3	4	5	NA
4. Discussion remained focused	1	2	3	4	5	NA
5. All collaborators were prepared	1	2	3	4	5	NA
6. All collaborators participated	1	2	3	4	5	NA
7. Effectiveness of meeting leadership	1	2	3	4	5	NA
8. Quality of handouts	1	2	3	4	5	NA
9. Usefulness of information presented	1	2	3	4	5	NA
10. Meeting achieved stated purpose	1	2	3	4	5	NA
11. Return on time invested	1	2	3	4	5	NA
12. Flow of information	1	2	3	4	5	NA
13. Specific meeting outcomes	1	2	3	4	5	NA
14. Use of resources	1	2	3	4	5	NA
15. Synergy among collaborators	1	2	3	4	5	NA

EXHIBIT 9.4   Meeting Evaluation Form

2. **Administer the questionnaire.** Give your collaboration some time to get started before administering the questionnaire. Usually the first administration is given six months into the project. If you wish to get baseline information at the outset of the project, you may need to modify some of the items. Repeat the survey periodically throughout the granting period, perhaps two to four times a year. You may also wish to give your final questionnaire to your project staff as well and look at the amount of congruence between collaborator and staff perceptions about the effectiveness of the collaboration.

3. **Summarize the results.** Collect the questionnaires from participants and use a spreadsheet program to calculate the average score for each scale item. The lower the mean score, the more favorable the attitude on that item. These become the strengths upon which your collaboration is able to build. Further, you can look at the variability in responses by calculating the standard deviation. A standard deviation score greater than 1.5 on a five-point scale indicates that there are significantly divergent views on the collaboration among your respondents. Use these divergent scores to pinpoint opportunities for mid-course corrections that will foster greater collaborator consensus.

Sample Questionnaire Items

We end this chapter with a pool of 180 sample questionnaire items that examine aspects of the five attributes related to each of the collaboration elements of goal sharing and interaction. Select, add, delete, or modify the items so that they are most appropriate to assessing your collaboration. The stimulus questions are written in present-tense verb form, which can be used for formative evaluation purposes. You can change the verbs to the past tense when conducting summative evaluations. Exhibit 9.5 draws 30 questions out of this pool and is formatted as a ready-to-go Collaboration Rating Form for administration to collaborators, beginning with a "Dear Colleague" introduction.

Dear Colleague:

You are our only source of information about your thoughts. As a valued member of our collaboration, we want your feedback on how well the collaboration is working.

For purposes of this survey, we operationally define "collaboration" as an interaction between two or more persons or organizations directed toward a common goal that is mutually beneficial. This definition has two key concepts: interaction and goal sharing.

The aim of the survey is to identify what works and what doesn't work in our collaboration. From past experience, we know that some collaborations work well while others may struggle. Your feedback will help us to more effectively operate the collaboration and meet project goals.

In this survey, there are no right or wrong answers. Please respond to every question and circle the number that best represents your experience, where 1 = Extremely Well;

2 = Very Well; 3 = Somewhat Well; 4 = Not So Well; 5 = Not Well At All; and NA = Not Applicable.

Thank you for your cooperation and candid feedback. Your responses will be pooled with others and only aggregate data will be reported. All individual responses will remain confidential.

Feel free to use the space below to tell us anything else that you think would be helpful for improving the overall efficiency and effectiveness of the collaboration.

How well does collaboration leadership ...

1. Create a shared vision that is embraced by collaborators?   1 2 3 4 5 NA
2. Empower collaborators?   1 2 3 4 5 NA
3. Encourage openness among collaborators?   1 2 3 4 5 NA

How well does the collaboration ...

4. Develop goals that are widely understood and supported by collaborators?   1 2 3 4 5 NA
5. Keep collaborators up-to-date on project developments?   1 2 3 4 5 NA
6. Exhibit passion and energy?   1 2 3 4 5 NA

How well does the collaboration ...

7. Use effective decision-making processes?   1 2 3 4 5 NA
8. Consider the viewpoints of all collaborators before reaching a decision?   1 2 3 4 5 NA
9. Generate a range of options before selecting a course of action?   1 2 3 4 5 NA

How well does the collaboration ...

10. Use awarded grant dollars?   1 2 3 4 5 NA
11. Use data and information?   1 2 3 4 5 NA
12. Use volunteers?   1 2 3 4 5 NA

How well does the collaboration ...

13. Use internal evaluators?   1 2 3 4 5 NA
14. Use external evaluators?   1 2 3 4 5 NA
15. Indicate a data reporting plan?   1 2 3 4 5 NA

How well does the collaboration ...

16. Provide orientation to new members as they join the collaboration?   1 2 3 4 5 NA
17. Minimize barriers to participation in meetings and activities?   1 2 3 4 5 NA
18. Publish minutes that accurately reflect proceedings of meetings?   1 2 3 4 5 NA

(continued)

At your organization, how well does the collaboration . . .

19. Increase institutional prestige?	1	2	3	4	5	NA
20. Facilitate networking and linkages?	1	2	3	4	5	NA
21. Expand the delivery of services?	1	2	3	4	5	NA

How well does the collaboration . . .

22. Communicate the vision of the collaboration to key external audiences?	1	2	3	4	5	NA
23. Create an environment where differences of opinion can be voiced?	1	2	3	4	5	NA
24. Communicate in a timely manner?	1	2	3	4	5	NA

How well does the collaboration . . .

25. Expand your understanding about services, programs, or other people in the community?	1	2	3	4	5	NA
26. Create a greater impact than you could have achieved on your own?	1	2	3	4	5	NA
27. Recognize the contributions of collaborators?	1	2	3	4	5	NA

How satisfied are you with the way . . .

28. The collaboration operates?	1	2	3	4	5	NA
29. The collaboration formulates plans to reach its goals and objectives?	1	2	3	4	5	NA
30. Your role contributes to the collaboration?	1	2	3	4	5	NA

EXHIBIT 9.5.   Sample Collaboration Rating Form

Goal Sharing

1. **Leadership** is the ability to influence, motivate, and enable others to contribute toward the success of shared goals. How well does collaborative leadership:

   - Create a shared vision that is embraced by collaborators?
   - Take responsibility for the collaboration?
   - Inspire the collaborators?
   - Motivate the collaborators?
   - Empower the collaborators?
   - Promote respect among collaborators?
   - Establish trust among collaborators?
   - Foster inclusiveness among collaborators?
   - Encourage openness among collaborators?
   - Resolve conflict among collaborators?

- Combine the perspectives, resources, and skills of the collaborators?
- Cultivate creativity?
- Help the collaborators look at things differently?
- Remain task oriented?
- Lead its collaborators?
- Work together among collaborators?
- Help collaborators reach higher levels of achievement?
- Provide effective and timely feedback?
- Persist in the face of setbacks?
- Display the vitality needed to sustain effective collaborations?
- Demonstrate the intelligence and judgment-in-action to guide the collaboration?
- Exhibit a thorough grasp of collaboration goals and their impact on collaborators?
- Possess the flexibility to make changes as warranted?

2. **Commitment** reflects the combined action of collaborators to achieve something larger than individual accomplishments. How well does the collaboration:

- Identify new and creative ways to solve problems?
- Include the views and priorities of collaborators?
- Develop goals that are widely understood and supported among the collaborators?
- Define community services, programs, or research needs?
- Implement strategies that were most likely to be effective in completing the project?
- Obtain support from other individuals and organizations that could either block the partnership's plans or help them move forward?
- Carry out comprehensive activities that connect multiple services, programs, or systems?
- Commit to collaborative grantseeking?
- Forge a collaboration that sustained itself beyond the grant?
- Demonstrate high interest?
- Keep collaborators up-to-date on project developments?
- Help move the project toward its goals?
- Care about its future?
- Have a shared vision of what it wants to accomplish?
- Exhibit passion and energy?

3. **Decision making** involves a process of mutually identifying problems and implementing solutions through discussion, negotiation, and conflict resolution. How well does the collaboration:

- Use effective decision-making processes?

- Make quality decisions?

- Enable you to participate in the decision-making processes?

- Pursue grants in response to RFPs from sponsors?

- Pursue grants in response to the entrepreneurial drive of top administrators?

- Pursue grants that are driven by your personal commitment?

- Periodically review its goals, objectives, and activities?

- Permit you to influence its direction?

- Make timely decisions?

- Make decisions on the basis of neutral accountability tools such as data, details, measurements, analyses, and tests?

- Consider the viewpoints of all collaborators before decisions are reached?

- Separate people from problems?

- Generate a range of options before selecting a course of action?

- Disseminate its decisions in a timely manner?

4. **Resources** include the sharing of human, physical, and fiscal resources, goods and services essential for an effective collaboration. How well does the collaboration:

- Use awarded grant dollars?

- Use matching non-grant dollars?

- Use in-kind cost sharing?

- Use grant-funded supplies?

- Use collaborators' available space?

- Use collaborators' existing equipment?

- Use collaborators' technology?

- Use data and information?

- Use intellectual property?

- Use time from project collaborators?

- Use expertise among collaborators?

- Use project personnel?

- Use technical expertise?

- Use networks?

- Use project leadership?

- Use volunteers?

5. **Evaluation** means using sound measurement tools to determine progress toward goal achievement and making adjustments as necessary. How well does the collaboration:

    - Define measurable objectives?

    - Use appropriate qualitative evaluation methods?

    - Use appropriate quantitative evaluation methods?

    - Use a strategic mix of qualitative and quantitative evaluation methods?

    - Use internal evaluators?

    - Use external evaluators?

    - Use process (formative) evaluation measures?

    - Use outcome (summative) evaluation measures?

    - Use project results to determine the need for post-grant sustainability?

    - Determine its evaluation priorities?

    - Formulate evaluation questions?

    - Adopt a meaningful data-collection plan?

    - Specify a data-interpretation plan?

    - Indicate a data-reporting plan?

    - Budget for evaluation costs?

    - Disseminate evaluation results to all internal collaborators?

    - Disseminate evaluation results to key external audiences?

Interaction

1. **Administrative management** considers the collaboration's use of its resources. How well does the collaboration:

    - Foster organizational activities, including meetings and projects?

    - Apply for and manage grants and funds?

    - Prepare materials that inform collaborators and help them make timely decisions?

    - Establish policies that ensure resources are consistently treated in an equitable manner?

    - Perform secretarial duties?

    - Orient new members as they join the collaboration?

    - Evaluate the progress and impact of the collaboration?

- Minimize the barriers to participation in collaboration meetings and activities?
- Make time to participate in collaborative grants?
- Handle routine matters quickly and efficiently?
- Start and end meetings on time?
- Distribute a detailed meeting agenda?
- Prepare background materials in advance of meetings?
- Publish minutes that accurately reflect proceedings of meetings?
- Provide timely notification of meetings?
- Participate in meeting discussions?
- Run meetings smoothly?
- Communicate among themselves?
- Communicate with project staff?
- Provide you with useful information?
- Provide adequate information on important topics?
- Schedule meetings that work well with your schedule?
- Interact among each other?
- Adhere to the project time and task chart?

2. **Incentives** are the factors that motivate involvement in the collaboration. At your organization, how well does the collaboration:

- Increase institutional prestige?
- Strengthen institutional financial footing?
- Increase salaries?
- Enhance job security?
- Spawn professional publications?
- Provide support for the people your organization serves?
- Facilitate networking and linkages?
- Expand the delivery of services?
- Improve your recruitment potential?
- Generate better ideas?
- Enhance your market position?
- Generate better research results?
- Reduce duplicated effort?
- Lower operating costs?
- Raise your public profile?

3. **Communication** aims for clear, open, and frequent communication among project leaders and collaborators. How well does the collaboration:

- Communicate the vision of the collaboration to internal partners?
- Communicate the vision of the collaboration to key external audiences?
- Work to develop a common language within the collaboration?
- Create an environment where differences of opinion can be voiced?
- Encourage participation among all collaborators?
- Use an appropriate mix of formal and informal communications?
- Communicate via formal meetings?
- Communicate via focus group feedback?
- Communicate via electronic communications?
- Develop a strategic communication plan?
- Evaluate its communications?
- Communicate clearly?
- Communicate in a timely manner?
- Secure feedback on its communications?
- Focus on behaviors and situations, not people?
- Follow policies that support good communications?

4. **Value of participation** involves getting something of benefit from participating in the collaboration. How well does the collaboration:

- Enhance your ability to address an important issue?
- Develop new skills for you?
- Increase your expertise?
- Expand your understanding about services, programs, or other people in the community?
- Enhance your ability to affect public policy?
- Establish new relationships for you?
- Enhance your ability to better meet the needs of your constituency or clients?
- Have a greater impact than you could have on your own?
- Strengthen your contribution to the community?
- Generate new knowledge?
- Apply existing knowledge?
- Increase your job satisfaction?
- Clarify your role as a collaborator?
- Contribute sufficient time to the project?

- Contribute sufficient money to the project?
- Contribute sufficient in-kind resources to this project?
- Recognize the contributions of its collaborators?
- Help your organization get additional funding?
- Build your own collaborative skills?
- Fit into your overall work responsibilities?
- Match up with your own organizational goals?
- Expand your understanding of how effective collaborations work?
- Strengthen your organizational infrastructure?
- Facilitate your access to additional funding?
- Enhance your organizational market position?

5. **Satisfaction with participation** reflects the feeling of gratification that comes with participation in the collaboration. How satisfied are you with the way:

- People and their organizations work together?
- You are able to influence collaboration activities and directions?
- Your role contributes to the collaboration?
- The collaboration formulates plans to reach its goals and objectives?
- The collaboration implements its plans?
- The collaboration achieves its desired outcomes?
- The overall benefits of participation exceed collaboration drawbacks?
- Collaborators trust one another?
- The collaboration helps your organization build its capacity?
- The collaboration works smoothly for you?
- The collaboration operates?
- The collaboration accomplishes important things?
- The collaborators demonstrate their competence?
- You learn from this collaborative project?
- The collaboration evaluates its effectiveness?

As you consider which questionnaire items to include in your survey, pay attention to the overall length. The rate of survey completion increases when the measurement tool is short and has a clean layout. Organize the questions in a logical sequence and put the most important ones first. And finally, because the Collaboration Rating Form is designed to assess participants' attitudes, be explicit with collaborators about any changes that are made because of their feedback. This simple gesture closes the feedback loop and will encourage them to complete future surveys.

CHAPTER 10

Handling Difficult People and Situations

What we have to learn to do, we learn by doing.

—Aristotle

Whether they are visionaries, strategists, team builders, motivators, or a combination thereof, grant leaders have a deep passion for bringing their projects to successful fruition. They channel their powers of influence to motivate project partners to action. The process of enabling others, however, sometimes requires the handling of difficult people and situations. If problems such as poor planning, collaborator complaints, intimidating people, poor listening, and nonperformance are not addressed by leadership, they often get worse.

In this chapter, we present five scenarios that are commonly encountered in the course of planning and implementing collaborative grants. Each scenario includes a brief description of the situation, an annotated dialogue script, and reflections on the psychological strategies used to transform the potentially disruptive incident into a constructive one. Challenging episodes may reveal themselves formally, through Meeting Evaluation Forms and Collaboration Rating Forms; or informally, through organic discussions and exchanges. Regardless, reviewing these scenarios will help build your confidence and prepare you to manage difficult people and situations.

POOR PLANNERS

"Never leave a meeting without a making a plan." This admonition should be visibly displayed on the desk of everyone who has responsibility for the success of a project and guiding the people involved. The statement might be amended with "or a scheduled appointment to make one." Often, time constraints or the content of the meeting do not allow for detailed action planning—hence the need to schedule a time to do so right away.

For the overall good of the project, it is incumbent upon grant leaders to handle poor planners. Guiding faltering partners through the process of effective planning entails posing targeted questions, probing for specific answers, avoiding traps and pitfalls, maintaining a focus on details, and asking for an unqualified commitment to the plan. It may not be necessary to ask every question listed below—they are intended as a guide—but the more questions asked, the fewer loopholes there will be in the plan, and the greater the likelihood of success.

1. Specifically, what do you want to obtain or achieve?
2. What exactly are you doing presently to get what you want?
3. How is it working out?
4. If you aren't getting what you want now, what else could you do?
5. What, in specific detail, are you willing to do?
6. When will you do it?
7. Where will you do it?
8. How many times will you do it?
9. What resources and information do you need in order to do it, and when they will be available?
10. With whom will you do it?
11. How will you know when you've done it?
12. Who needs to know that you've done it?
13. How do you want this to come out?
14. Are you committed to this plan?

The eight annotated dialogues that follow illustrate ways you can work with project partners to plan for success, not failure; plan specifically and within reason; and plan cooperatively while allowing partners to make decisions. That is, offering collaborators guidance, support, and encouragement in the process, rather than developing the plan for them, ensures that they take ownership for their part of the plan and responsibility for the resulting outcomes. "I'll try" is not a statement of commitment, and you should never accept it as one from a poor planner. If this occurs, you can respond by saying, "I didn't ask you to try. I need to know if you're going to do it."

Scenario

A nonprofit organization whose primary interest is health education wants to apply for grant funding to develop materials about infant health as part of a public awareness campaign. The target audience will be people living below the poverty line who reside in the small and remote towns in Appalachia. To gather some baseline information for the proposal, the grant leader is partnering with a nurse educator, Lindy Ross, to organize several round-robin focus groups with representatives of this population and collect firsthand responses concerning the most commonly used child care practices.

Although the collaborators agreed six weeks ago to organize the focus groups as soon as possible, it hasn't happened. The application deadline is now rapidly approaching and the proposal won't be nearly as competitive without this baseline data. So the grant leader is meeting with Lindy to discuss the problem and develop a plan to jump-start this process.

Dialogue 1

To illustrate how meetings often end, consider this exchange in which the grant leader has just finished a meeting with Lindy Ross. The grant leader reviewed her responsibilities and the difficulties she is having in fulfilling them. All of the tasks have been identified and briefly discussed, and the grant leader is ready to end the meeting.

Grant Leader:	Well, that seems to cover everything. I think we both know what needs to be done, and it's good to review it. I hope this helps.
Lindy:	Yeah, this is pretty complicated, maybe even more than I remembered. I just know it's a lot to get done, and I can see that I'm already behind.
Grant Leader:	Don't worry about it.
	(Lindy was inadvertently just let off the hook. Why shouldn't she worry about it? It's her responsibility.)
Grant Leader:	If you just bear down a little harder and get organized a little better you'll do okay.
	(How would she go about doing that?)
Grant Leader:	Just remember—detail, detail, detail!
	(Lindy is already overwhelmed with details.)
Grant Leader:	Take care of the details and everything else will take care of itself. That's the way *I* work.
Lindy:	I think I see that. I really do need to get organized better. But it's hard to know where to start when there are so many pieces.
Grant Leader:	You're right on. "The devil is in the details," they say. So, let me know how you're getting on. My door is always open.
Lindy:	Thanks. I appreciate your help.

Reflections on Dialogue 1

What happened in this meeting? Essentially, nothing. But several things were taking place: expressions of frustration and fear, a plea for help, some essentially worthless advice and, overall, a missed opportunity. Lindy offered her thanks and appreciation but goes away empty-handed and even more heavily burdened. Reviewing the multitude of tasks with an already overwhelmed collaborator and dismissing her without a specific plan of action just left her hanging out to dry. The grant leader stirred the pot, but neither of them looked to see whether any one significant action item floated to the top.

Dialogue 2

To illustrate an effective process of planning, examine the following exchanges in which the grant leader guides Lindy Ross systematically through a series of strategic questions. This dialogue concentrates on the question: specifically what do you want to obtain or achieve?

Grant Leader: Thanks for coming in, Lindy. We need to talk about the focus groups that were to begin a month ago. To my knowledge, they haven't started.

Lindy: Yeah, I know we should have been on this by now, but it's just an involved undertaking.

Grant Leader: Let's break it down: what do you see that needs to be done, specifically?

Lindy: Well, obviously we need to identify the potential participants to be contacted and set some dates. I see that as the first step.

Grant Leader: Good. I would agree with that. Is that what you'd like to do now?

Lindy: Yeah. We'll have to find locations, too, and see when they're available.

Grant Leader: Okay, so you'd like to find the places and schedule them right away.

(Strategy: lead Lindy to clarify what she needs to do as a first step—rather than telling her what to do—and nudge her toward taking action "right away.")

Dialogue 3

In this dialogue, the grant leader takes the next step, probing for details with a focus on the question: what exactly are you doing to get this project started, and how is it working out? The grant leader also navigates carefully around the "blame game" trap.

Grant Leader: Please tell me what you've done up to this point.

Lindy: Well, we had one team meeting, but not everyone was there so we really couldn't formulate any plans. We tried to schedule another meeting, but it became a logistical nightmare.

Grant Leader:	So the point is, nothing has happened? Nothing is being done?
Lindy:	Yeah, but it's not anyone's fault.
Grant Leader:	What would seem to be important is that there is no plan to get going on this as soon as possible. Does that sound right to you?

(Strategy: avoid blaming and excuses, which focus on the past. Instead, direct energies toward the future.)

Lindy:	I guess so.
Grant Leader:	You seem to have some doubt about that. Is there a problem we don't know about or some change we need to make?

(Strategy: probe for potentially bigger issues that could lead to future excuses for nonperformance.)

Lindy:	Well, not really. We just need to get going.
Grant Leader:	So you need to make a plan, right?
Lindy:	Yes, we do.
Grant Leader:	Since this is your responsibility, I'd like it to be your plan.

(Strategy: clarify that before any first steps can be taken, Lindy— not the grant leader—needs to make an explicit plan.)

Dialogue 4

The grant leader presses on in this dialogue, raising the question: what else do you think you could do?

Grant Leader:	As I understand it, you tried to have one meeting, but that didn't work out. What else do you think would work?
Lindy:	I started an outline on my own of what we needed to do to get things rolling. I thought we'd talk about it at the meeting, but that didn't happen.
Grant Leader:	Do you see any way to use your outline now?
Lindy:	Sure, I could finish it up. It's an electronic file and I could e-mail it out to the team. They could make any changes and offer suggestions and then send it back to me. We could try to get another meeting after that to make assignments.
Grant Leader:	Let's see if we have this clear. You said you need to find locations and schedule them. But you need to have a meeting with the team

first, to make assignments to accomplish this. Is that what you understand?

(Strategy: clarify intent—using the phrase "you said" reinforces that it was Lindy who formulated the plan.)

Lindy: That's right. We have to meet first. One person can't do it all, so we need to make assignments.

Dialogue 5

The discussion between the grant leader and Lindy Ross is beginning to pick up momentum. This dialogue explores the question: when do you plan to do this?

Grant Leader: When do you plan to schedule the meeting?

Lindy: Just as soon as I can get to it.

Grant Leader: When do you think that will be—tomorrow, next week, exactly when?

Lindy: You mean you want to know exactly when?

Grant Leader: That's the idea.

(Strategy: insist on specifics.)

Lindy: Well, I have some free time tomorrow afternoon.

Grant Leader: What time tomorrow afternoon?

Lindy: From two o'clock on I don't have anything scheduled.

Grant Leader: So you could finish your outline and e-mail it out tomorrow afternoon. Is that what I understand?

(Strategy: clarify the specifics.)

Lindy: Yeah, that's doable.

Dialogue 6

The conversation has turned the corner: Lindy Ross recognizes that the grant leader is asking questions to be helpful, not micromanaging. This next dialogue centers on the question: what additional resources and information do you need to move forward?

Grant Leader: Do you have all the information you need to finish your outline?

Lindy: Yes, I started a folder some time back, and it's all in there.

Grant Leader: That was good planning on your part. You didn't know you were going to have to do this, but now you're ready. Good work.

(Strategy: show enthusiasm for this new effort and reinforce the idea that this is Lindy's plan, not the grant leader's. Compliment Lindy on previous good planning behavior; since she demonstrated good planning behavior in the past, she might just do it again!)

Dialogue 7

The discussion is winding down, and both the grant leader and Lindy Ross are feeling good about the progress they've made. The core question in this dialogue—who else needs to know about this?—begins to open up the plan to include other project partners.

Grant Leader: Besides me, who else needs to know what you're going to do tomorrow afternoon?

Lindy: Let's see. Sharon Ball is heading up the team to find locations for the focus groups. I should copy her on the e-mail and call her to see how she's doing. If my team can meet and agree on our assignments, we can be ready to go pretty soon.

Grant Leader: Good idea. It's important to keep the teams coordinated.

(Strategy: reinforce, once again, Lindy's past planning activity and clarify the current focus.)

Dialogue 8

This last dialogue is a final attempt at the question: what else? Once Lindy Ross has answered all of these questions, the grant leader pushes to get her to commit to her newly formulated plan.

Grant Leader: Is there anything you see that would interfere with what you plan to do?

Lindy: Not really.

Grant Leader: So, let me be clear about this. At two o'clock tomorrow afternoon you will work to finish your outline and then e-mail it to your team by the end of the day. Also, you're going to call Sharon to check on her progress.

(Strategy: clarify, clarify, clarify!)

Lindy: Right.

Grant Leader: When will you call Sharon?

Lindy: Well, I'll do that just as soon as I get back to my office. If she isn't there, I'll leave a message for her to call me. She needs to know what I'm doing, and if she's having a problem finding space, that could make a difference.

Grant Leader: If she's having a problem, what will you do about your plan?

(Strategy: continue to press for specifics on alternate actions. It is important to set Lindy up to succeed, not fail for lack of an alternative if things don't go as planned.)

Lindy: Oh, I'll go ahead with it, because we need to get our part organized and ready. She'll eventually find the space.

Grant Leader: You sound pretty confident about this step.

(Strategy: encourage Lindy to make an honest commitment to her plan.)

Lindy: I'm sure going to try.

Grant Leader: You know, I'm not just asking you to try. This really needs to be done now.

Lindy: Okay, I understand. You can count on me. I'll let you know when I'm finished.

Grant Leader: That works for me. Thanks again for coming in.

(Strategy: be supportive but not overly complimentary—Lindy hasn't carried out her plan yet.)

Reflections on Dialogues 2–8

This scenario may sound somewhat unnatural, but seasoned grant leaders will tell you it isn't. The importance of nailing down specifics in an effective plan should not be underestimated. While not every question or detail was included in this particular plan, they may be necessary in others. Here, Lindy made the plan and now owns it. She seems committed to it. Having success with this step will greatly increase the likelihood that she will continue to make more plans and the project will move forward. If it stalls out again, the grant leader can meet with her and make another, perhaps more in-depth, plan. Experienced grant leaders know that proper planning prevents poor performance.

COLLABORATOR COMPLAINTS

Grant leaders use their powers of influence to motivate others to action. But sometimes when one collaborator does not follow through on activities as promised, a chain reaction can occur. A hold-up on one part of the project can cause further delays down the line. The rumblings of discontent start small and then gain force. The following scenario offers tips for handling collaborator complaints. Seasoned grant leaders find ways to empower project partners so that problems and conflicts can be resolved at the most appropriate level.

Scenario

A grant leader in Midwestern University's School of Education recently received a grant to teach reading skills to area at-risk youth. The Community Outreach Coordinator, Roxie Neighborhood, comes in complaining that the classroom teachers won't cooperate getting the baseline testing promised in the proposal, which is necessary before the reading instruction program begins. Without baseline information, the grant leader and Roxie will not be able to evaluate program effectiveness during and at the end of the granting period.

Dialogue

Here is an example of a dialogue that might occur between the grant leader and Roxie Neighborhood in order to resolve the problem of uncooperative teachers not wanting to provide baseline information. We call this scenario "My Monkey or Your Monkey?" Read on and you'll see why we gave it that name.

Grant Leader: Good to see you, Roxie. What's happening?

(Strategy: keep the opening statement neutral; it's unclear yet whether good news or bad news is to follow.)

Roxie: We can't get the baseline testing done, and we're three weeks behind now! The teachers won't let us have access to the kids! You need to call someone!

(Roxie's goal is to get the monkey off her back and pass it to the grant leader.)

Grant Leader: Well, first let's look at the baseline testing procedures outlined in our proposal. I believe you wrote them and did a great job too. You outlined five steps. Which ones are working, at least to some extent?

(Strategy: help calm Roxie down and let her hold on to the monkey, it's still hers.)

Roxie: Well, the first three steps are done—the test materials are ready. But we can't do four and five. That's where we arrange the schedule and do the baseline testing. But the teachers won't cooperate! You need to call all the principals and tell them to remind those teachers they agreed to help out.

(Roxie again attempts to pass the monkey.)

Grant Leader: You seem to feel talking with the principals would help. Who else could you talk to—the teachers? Maybe they've forgotten about their agreement to cooperate.

(Strategy: stop here and wait for her to respond; allow Roxie to come up with the solution and keep the monkey.)

Roxie: I suppose I could talk to them.

Grant Leader: Good. Who's one teacher you know best?

Roxie: Mrs. Witt. We've worked together before on other projects.

Grant Leader: So you'd be comfortable calling her?

(Strategy: confirm intent.)

Roxie: Yeah, I could do that.

Grant Leader: Good. When would be a good time to reach her?

Roxie: I can call the office and find out when she has a free period.

Grant Leader: When do you think you'll call the office?

(Strategy: press for specifics.)

Roxie: Well, I could do it when I get back to my office after I leave here.

Grant Leader: That sounds like a plan. If Mrs. Witt cooperates, maybe the others will come around too.

Roxie: Maybe so, but I still think you ought to call the administration.

(Roxie makes one more attempt to pass the monkey—her first objective in seeing the grant leader.)

Grant Leader: I think you're handling this very well. Your procedures are very sound. How do you think this will work out?

Roxie: Well, it's a start, and Mrs. Witt is a good teacher. I think she understands the project and how important it is.

Grant Leader: Good. Let me know how it turns out, and thanks for coming in.

Reflections

Does this conversation sound familiar? Have you been on the sending or receiving end of similar monkey business? Where are the current monkeys in your situation? The psychological strategies used in this scenario illustrate how to keep a monkey off your back and, equally important, help collaborators be more effective in solving problems.

INTIMIDATING PEOPLE

This scenario offers tips for handling intimidating people, which can be challenging, especially when the problem can only be resolved by talking face-to-face. While you may need to talk it out, you may also prefer to dodge this discussion, particularly if you think it might lead to some type of confrontation. You now find yourself in a classic "approach-avoidance" conflict.

Approach-avoidance works this way. When faced with the prospect of needing to confront an intimidating person, you, like many people, first begin to set up the conflict mentally by considering a series of irrational "What if..." questions such as the following:

- "What if I don't explain the situation clearly?"
- "What if I can't get a meeting scheduled soon enough?"
- "What if I haven't looked into this enough?"
- "What if I'm asked questions that I can't answer on the spot?"
- "What if I'm turned down?"

And on it goes. Now the approach-avoidance behavior begins. The closer you come to scheduling a meeting with the intimidating person to address the problem, the stronger is the tendency to avoid it. Pulling back and avoiding the contact only results in an increased need to approach and make the contact. So you end up swinging back and forth with rising anxiety for both approaching and avoiding.

Scenario

The grant leader at a social services agency is obliged to talk to Cory Crabface, the institution's business manager, in order to make some changes in the project's budget. Specifically, travel costs have escalated and there is now a shortage of travel funds. Although, theoretically, phone, e-mail, or other communications could be used instead of actual travel, for this project there is no real substitute for face-to-face meetings with participants. To cover the travel budget shortfall, the grant leader wants to shift some excess supply funds to the travel account.

Institutional policy requires that Cory approve the rebudgeting, but he has a history of being adamant about "budget tinkering" and would rather fault poor planning and lack of foresight instead of simply approving the change, even though the sponsor's guidelines allow for this transfer of funds. The grant leader knows this change is needed but is reluctant to face Cory and take the inevitable heat.

Dialogue

To resolve this conflict, the grant leader must consider one important question: what's the worst thing that can happen? In this mental dialogue, there may be rational or irrational responses to this key question. We call this scenario "My Worst Nightmare." Read on and you'll see why we gave it that name.

Irrational Response: If we don't make this change, it will just kill us!

Rational Response: Big deal, you're going to die some day anyway, so what's the *worst* thing that could happen?

Irrational Response: This is the biggest project of my life and I'm going to lose it.

Rational Response: You haven't lived your whole life yet, and what's the likelihood there will be other projects that are even bigger and better?

Irrational Response: People will think I can't do the job.

Rational Response: Who's just itching to trade places with you?

Irrational Response: Cory will really hate me now.

Rational Response: Cory has a reputation for attacking people rather than problems, it's true. However, you are not responsible for his misbehavior.

Irrational Response: If Cory turns me down, I guess I'll have to resign.

Rational Response: Cory hasn't turned you down yet. Besides, how would resigning help?

Reflections

Worst nightmares seldom come true. Exploring and analyzing what the worst consequence could be often results in the realization that the worst thing that can happen is the changes are approved and you now have to go and implement them. Or, your request is turned down and the problem has to be re-examined; the result may be a better solution or one that doesn't involve intimidating people at all. You end up gaining confidence in your judgments and reduce the likelihood of future communication conflict.

RELUCTANT LISTENERS

The following scenario offers tips on how to deal with someone who is "hard of listening." It's a real challenge to communicate effectively with someone who hears but just doesn't listen. Effective communication is a two-way street and occasionally you meet a one-way driver. This scenario is similar to the one for handling intimidating people, but it has more detail. The key to managing this form of difficult conversation is to not allow it to become personal and confrontational.

Scenario

The grant leader at a nonprofit organization needs to talk to the business manager, Pat Pennypincher, about some changes that must be made in the grant budget in order to maintain continuity of communications with project partners. The grant leader researched the sponsor's policies on rebudgeting grant funds and discovered that the proposed changes are within acceptable limits and do not require prior approval from the program officer. Nevertheless, Pat is risk-adverse and can be a tough one to handle. Before going to talk with Pat, the grant leader puts on a mental flak jacket and a plastic smile and then opens the office door.

Dialogue

We call this scenario "Can You Hear Me Now?" It is a conversation between the grant leader and Pat Pennypincher, the business manager, who is known for having a miserly attitude. Read on and you'll see why we gave it that name.

Grant Leader: Thanks for meeting with me. There's a very real need to approve our budget changes. The costs of gasoline and airfare have skyrocketed, and there isn't enough money to make the site visits to our project partners. After careful study, we think the problem can be resolved by moving the money in our travel line to the services lines. The money will be used to increase telephone and other electronic means of communication, specifically video conferencing. This will allow us to engage directly with our partners, and the information that would have been exchanged onsite will be obtained using a virtual face-to-face approach. It has worked well in other situations.

Pat: You know how I hate to start tinkering with budgets. You people think it's simple, but you should have thought of this from the beginning.

Grant Leader: These cost increases have happened since the budget was created, and they make it necessary to revise approaches.

(Strategy: repeat the key facts.)

Pat: I don't know why people don't anticipate the worst when they make up a budget. You always know there are going to be problems, and no one ever gets ready for it in advance. These problems could be avoided with a little bit of clear thinking.

Grant Leader: *(Silent.)*

(Strategy: let the ranting exhaust itself. Pat has lost focus on the budget problem at hand and is lecturing about people's incompetence. No response is required.)

Pat: Give me just one good reason why I should approve this change, since you don't know how to adequately budget for the future.

Grant Leader: Rising costs of gasoline and airfare preclude travel, but an effective alternative strategy is available in the form of electronic communications.

(Strategy: stay on message.)

Pat: How do I know you won't be back here next week asking to make another change because of another oversight on your part?

Grant Leader: A thorough review of the budget has been made, and no other changes will be necessary.

Pat: You seem pretty sure of yourself.

Grant Leader: The facts speak for themselves, and the budget is sound.

Pat: This is the last time I'm going to approve changes in your budget for the duration of this project. I hope that's clear.

Grant Leader: *(Silent.)*

(Strategy: remain silent. The best argument possible has been made and there's no point in defending against an unpredictable future.)

Pat: Well, when are you going to start talking to these partners?

Grant Leader: With your approval, everything can be put in place within a week.

Pat: That quick, huh?

Grant Leader: Quick action is very important. Approval will make it possible. The budget adjustment will make everything work quickly and efficiently.

(Strategy: the responsibility for this outcome has been strategically shifted to Pat without referring to this fact directly or using the pronoun "you." It is, nonetheless, clear that Pat has to make the decision.)

Pat: Well, okay, but this is the last time.

Grant Leader: Thanks. Your interest and concern are appreciated.

(Strategy: direct reference to Pat as a person is now appropriate, as in "your interest and concern." It speaks to Pat's self esteem and position of power. Even difficult people like to be stroked.)

Reflections

This conversation is designed to stay focused on the problem and not on the people. With reluctant listeners, you can do this by avoiding the use of personal pronouns—I, we, our, and you—until you've achieved your goal; using silence strategically and suppressing the urge to respond to everything being said; reflecting on their comments rather than challenging or responding defensively; and not getting sidetracked with other topics. In essence, these psychological strategies help separate people from problems, thus you can deflect personal attacks and resolve the problem more effectively.

NONPERFORMERS

There will come a time during a collaborative initiative when grant leaders must talk with a few partners who are not performing the tasks they accepted when the project was formed. In some instances, nonperformance occurs because the tasks are simply beyond someone's current abilities. Connecting them with training programs, linking them with coaches and mentors, and providing regular feedback may solve the problem. In other cases, nonperformers do not demonstrate the level or extent of goal sharing as was anticipated when they were invited to participate in the collaborative endeavor. This scenario offers tips for handling nonperformers, both removing them from and bringing them into the fold.

Scenario

The grant leader is meeting with Larry Lazie and two of his staff, Michael Molasses and Nick Naught. In this situation, they had agreed to develop drafts of training manuals and procedures for using new laboratory equipment in experimental studies of communicable diseases. Larry has past experience and is presently engaged in short-term, intensive training in other topic areas. He was a "natural" as a collaborator and presented a positive image in the pre-collaboration assessment (see chapter 3). Six months have gone by, and Larry has not filed the formative evaluation reports nor has he given any evidence that assigned tasks are being carried out. The grant leader now must decide whether to keep or dismiss Larry. His nonperformance is affecting other collaborators, which can jeopardize the ultimate success of the project.

Dialogue

Here is an example dialogue between the grant leader, whose principal task is to keep all collaborators on schedule according to the established Time and Task Chart, and the three nonperformers. We call this scenario "Tough Love, Collaboration Style." Read on and you'll see why we gave it that name.

Grant Leader: Thanks for coming over, and it will be helpful to have all three of you here. We can use input from everyone.

(Strategy: set the stage for inviting feedback from everyone, even though only Larry was expected at the meeting, not Michael and Nick. Larry has brought them along for a reason that will reveal itself.)

Larry: Well, I like to have my people involved, especially since I'm not sure what we're meeting about. You said you wanted to talk about our work on the project.

(This is Larry's not-so-veiled attempt to put the responsibility for the meeting on the grant leader and have some back-up available to support whatever position he may find himself in.)

Grant Leader: That's right. But before we start, may I offer you something to drink—water or coffee, perhaps?

(Strategy: establish a friendly but businesslike atmosphere.)

Larry: I'm okay. Do you guys want something?

Michael: I'm okay.

Nick: Me, too.

Grant Leader: In that case, let's get to the business at hand. This is a copy of the Time and Task Chart that was developed for the project and the list of assignments we all accepted at that point. Basically, there are two concerns. First, the initial formative evaluation reports haven't been sent in. It was agreed these reports would be filed quarterly. This information is very useful to be sure the project is on track, that each collaborator has what they need and to iron out any issues before they become problems. Secondly, according to the Time and Task Chart, the drafts of the training manuals were due three months ago.

(Strategy: identify the specific reason for meeting. Once the problems have been identified in concrete terms, stop talking. The pronoun "you," meaning Larry, has deliberately been avoided, and no accusatory remarks have been made. For that matter, only one "we" has been used. It's fair to assume Larry already knows what the problems are in spite of his stating that he doesn't know the nature or need for this meeting—one glance at the Time and Task Chart would make that evident.)

Larry: Well, we've had a lot of problems come up since this project was approved. Things we didn't expect. I've lost two instructors and we haven't had time to replace them. Good people are hard to find. On top of that, three new clients have come on board, and that's sort of good news and bad news right now. And on top of all that, the person who was going to draft the manuals, Alice—I think you know her—has been absent a lot. I guess it's not going so well.

Grant Leader: Excuse me for interrupting, but I see the point. All of the collaborators on the project are facing similar issues and juggling things a bit, but that was anticipated up front.

Larry *(Aside, to*
Michael and Nick): You guys can jump in here whenever you want to.

(Larry is calling for help, realizing that the problems are very clear.)

Larry *(To Grant Leader):* They can tell you what it's been like for us the past six months—even before that. But we wanted to be part of this project. It has something in it for all of us. I know it will bring us new business.

Michael: My plate's really full right now.

Nick: My vacation starts on Monday. I'll be gone two weeks.

(Larry is looking for support from his associates. He likely brought them along for that purpose. He has also revealed what may have been his true motivation for becoming a collaborator—the gain of new business. This is odd because it is contradictory to his professed "overload." He also suspects that even if he doesn't fulfill his obligations but the project is completed, new business will come his way. Obviously, no direct evidence exists of this self-serving motivation, and the grant leader can not and should not attempt to address it even in terms of there being "something for all of us.")

Grant Leader: The question that needs answering today is whether the drafts of the manuals can be prepared and available in the immediate future. Two collaborators are waiting to review them to see if they meet the sponsor's guidelines and the instructional goals and objectives of the project. They can't move ahead until they have them.

(Strategy: ask the critical question and then stop talking; place the conversational burden on Larry. Continue to ignore and not challenge the excuses being put forth because Larry, Michael, and Nick are armed with even more reasons for failure to perform. The real problem has been restated—the training manuals are incomplete—and nothing else is relevant to the discussion.

But what about the absent formative evaluation reports? These reports, while valuable, are not what's holding up the project. If Larry, Michael, and Nick were fulfilling their obligations, the reports would have been filed. It would appear that they've been sidestepping the project altogether. There's nothing to be gained by bringing up the reports because it will only reinforce the "excusing" behavior on the part of the collaborators. So now, it's up to Larry to respond.)

Larry: Exactly what do you want from us?

Grant Leader: We have a Planning Meeting of the staff actively working on the various parts of the project scheduled for next week Tuesday at 9:00 A.M. But what I must know is your intention regarding the development of the training manuals. Apparently there are some serious obstacles. As I said earlier, we can't move ahead without them.

Larry: Well, I don't know that I can promise that you'll have the manuals next week, if that's what you want. Is it?

(Larry, unwittingly, just opened the door for some firm limits and expectations to be set by the grant leader, in effect asking, "How do you want to handle this?")

Grant Leader: I'm not setting an immediate deadline. Is it reasonable that the draft manuals could be ready within, say, a month? Is that a reasonable expectation?

(Strategy: do not rise to any of the somewhat veiled challenges from Larry. Stay within the boundary of the "draft training manuals" and give Larry every opportunity to express a sincere commitment to the project. Avoid invoking the pronoun "you." Do not chastise Larry for his lack of performance nor accept his excuses. Attempt to determine Larry's intentions and judge the likelihood that there will be follow-through within a reasonable time, "within, say, a month.")

The discussion has now reached a critical decision point for both the grant leader and Larry. A double dilemma exists. The grant leader's dilemma is that Larry is the most likely collaborator who can deliver the training manuals, based on his experience and present activities. It would be difficult to replace him. Keeping him on board, however, risks more empty promises, further delays, and even failure to complete the project on schedule. Larry's dilemma involves risking the gain of new business when the project is complete and, perhaps, risking some loss of reputation and respect in the eyes of the other collaborators.

In essence, two alternatives are available: (1) the grant leader can keep Larry on board with a clear plan to catch up with the Time and Task Chart schedule and deliver the training manuals within a manageable and reasonable time for both, or (2) the grant leader can decide to end the collaborative relationship with Larry and find a replacement. Below are dialogues for each alternative.

Termination Dialogue

The grant leader has just said, "I'm not setting an immediate deadline. Is it reasonable that the draft manuals could be ready within, say, a month? Is that a reasonable expectation?" and awaits Larry's response.

Larry: Not really. I think you're being a little unrealistic. Training manuals take time, and we just don't have anyone to put on it right now or maybe anytime soon. We'd really like to stay on with the project, though. Maybe things will loosen up.

Grant Leader: I'm glad we could meet today, because I understand clearly your situation and I hope you understand mine. It's the success of the project that's the issue here, and it's my responsibility to keep it on schedule. We'll start looking for another resource at our meeting next week. I'll explain your situation, and I'm sure everyone will understand. We appreciate all of your hard work when we were in the grant proposal preparation stages. Your input was invaluable. Again, thanks for coming over.

(Strategy: invoke the pronoun "you" to personalize the discussion and to have an opportunity to express thanks to Larry for his past contributions to the project. Do not blame, express disappointment, or make empty promises for the future. Remain positive, because Larry may still be an ally and a potential future resource; he may learn from this outcome, and on another occasion his performance might be different. It would be a mistake at this point, however, to mollify Larry by explicitly suggesting that he could become involved again as the project enters its next phase.)

Second-Chance Dialogue

The grant leader has just said, "I'm not setting an immediate deadline. Is it reasonable that the draft manuals could be ready within, say, a month? Is that a reasonable expectation?" and awaits Larry's response.

Larry: Actually, I really want to be a part of this project. It's a good one and will be for all of us, as I said earlier. I know I'll get new business from it, but that's not the point. Frankly, this has just slipped up on me and I haven't been paying attention, and I apologize for that.

Larry *(Aside, to Michael and Nick):* Alice is having her problems right now, but we hope they'll get resolved. Frank, over in graphics, has written

Michael: I've seen Frank's manuals, and they're really pretty good. In fact, I've used two of them recently. I think he could do it if he has time.

Nick: I'm all for Frank, but I think his time is the big issue.

Larry: I have some input into how Frank uses his time, but I'll have talk with Dennis, his department head. I think Dennis will go along once I explain the situation. After all, we're just doing drafts right now, so we can ramp up and get them out pretty quickly and then we'll have some breathing room while they're being tested.

Larry *(To Grant Leader):* Does that work for you?

Grant Leader: The issue seems to be on the way to being resolved, and that's what we wanted to accomplish. Now you just need to make a detailed plan so we both know what's going to be happening in the coming days. This will be good news for the meeting next week. I understand your position, and I know you understand mine. Let's make that plan.

(Strategy: bring the meeting to closure. Using the pronoun "you" after the collaborators had solved the problem in their own way brings the conversation to a personal level with a show of mutual respect. The collaborators retain their involvement in the project with no loss of face and with a plain understanding of the value of a successful project outcome. It is also clear that Larry needs to make a detailed plan for the immediate future.)

Reflections

Handling nonperformers can be tricky. These individuals typically were performers at one time. They may have reputations for achieving significant outcomes. They often are personable and well-liked. And, importantly, they hold the potential to be performers again. As a result, discussions about their nonperformance should be straightforward, acknowledging past contributions and current challenges, and yet be handled delicately enough to allow both sides to preserve dignity.

In the termination dialogue, Larry was "fired" as a collaborator in the presence of two of his staff, Michael and Nick. Is this the ethical thing to do? Should it have been done in private? This is a judgment call that only the grant leader can make, given knowledge of the situation. The staff members were not invited to the meeting; it was Larry's decision to bring them, presumably as his back-up. There may be value in allowing them to witness the consequences of not living up to an agreement and thus realize the importance of being a good partner.

The alternative approach in the termination dialogue would be to allow the three of them to leave and then bring Larry back for another appointment. That's not a good use of time. It is also inappropriate to ask Michael and Nick to leave the room and then inform Larry that his services will no longer be required for this project. That would only sensitize the situation unnecessarily and put Larry in an awkward position. While attempts to redirect Larry's behavior were unsuccessful, the grant leader did effectively redirect the relationship, perhaps preserving it for the future. Larry was dismissed from the collaboration without rancor, anger, or blaming.

In the second-chance dialogue, when confronted, Larry took responsibility for his nonperformance. Rather than making excuses for past inaction, he proposed to the grant leader a way to correct the deficiencies right away. Developing a written plan with the grant leader will further show Larry's commitment to getting back on track. And during a future meeting to check progress, the grant leader will ask Larry, "How did the plan work out?" If it didn't, the next question will be "What else do you think you could do?" Very quickly it will become apparent whether Larry does or does not intend to complete the plan. Said differently, grant leaders do not punish misguided behavior, they redirect it toward the positive.

More broadly, when handling nonperformers, you should establish a friendly but businesslike atmosphere. Identify the reason for meeting, and identify specific areas of concern. Review the Time and Task Chart, noting their responsibilities and assigned tasks; avoid criticizing and blaming them for their nonperformance. Do not accept excuses or engage in finger-pointing. Instead, focus on future intentions and plans; individuals who have known they were not performing to standards and were hoping that you wouldn't notice, when called out, may develop and commit to a new plan of action. Decide to retain or dismiss them and then determine your appropriate next steps.

In sum, experienced grant leaders know that in the course of planning and implementing collaborative grants, they will encounter difficult people and situations. The five scenarios presented offer effective psychological strategies for handling common performance problems. Grant leaders seldom like the problems, but they accept that it is their responsibility to address them. What's more, they resist the tendency to "let it slide because so-and-so does good work" or think, "It's not a problem right now, but if it becomes one, then I'll be sure to act." Personnel issues rarely go away magically. Do like seasoned grant leaders do and confront performance problems early—your project and collaboration will be better off for it.

Now, with a clear understanding of the humanistic aspects of designing and leading successful collaborative projects, you can go write your best grant ever!

BIBLIOGRAPHY

Bailey, Dalene, and Kelly Koney. 2000. *Strategic Alliances among Health and Human Service Organizations: From Affiliations to Consolidations.* Thousand Oaks, CA: Sage Publishers.

Baker, G. Ross, Lisa Headrick, Marian Knapp, Linda Norman, Doris Quinn, and Duncan Neuhauser. 1998. Collaborating for Improvement in Health Professions Education. *Quality Management in Health Care* 6, no. 2: 1–11.

Barnes, Henrietta N., and Jeffrey H. Samet. 1997. Brief Interventions with Substance-Abusing Patients. *Medical Clinics of North America* 81: 867–79.

Bauer, David G. 2007. *The "How To" Grants Manual: Successful Grantseeking Techniques for Obtaining Public and Private Grants.* 6th ed. Westport, CT: Praeger Publishers.

Berger, Stu, Beth N. Whitsone, Stephanie J. Frisbee, Jeremy T. Miner, Anwer Dhala, Ronald G. Pirrallo, Loreen M. Utech, and Ramesh C. Sachdeva. 2004. Cost-Effectiveness of Project ADAM: A Project to Prevent Sudden Cardiac Death in High School Students. *Pediatric Cardiology* 25, no. 6: 660–67.

Berneman, Louis. 2003. University–Industry Collaborations: Partners in Research Promoting Productivity and Economic Growth. *Research Management Review* 13, no. 2: 28–37.

Bramson, Robert M. 1988. *Coping with Difficult People.* New York: Dell Publishing.

Browning, Beverly A. 2008. *Grant Writing for Dummies.* 3rd ed. New York: Hungry Minds.

Brunarski, David, Lynn Shaw, and Lisa Doupe. 2008. Moving toward Virtual Interdisciplinary Teams and a Multi-Stakeholder Approach in Community-Based Return-to-Work Care. *Work* 30, no. 3: 329–36.

Cabral, Rebecca J., Christine Galavotti, Paul M. Gargiullo, Kay Armstrong, Abigail Cohen, Andrea C. Gielen, and Linda Watkinson. 1996. Paraprofessional Delivery of a Theory Based HIV Prevention Counseling Intervention for Women. *Public Health Reports* 111: 75–82.

Calfas, Karen J., James F. Sallis, Brian Oldenburg, and Margot French. 1997. Mediators of Change in Physical Activity following an Intervention in Primary Care. *Preventative Medicine* 26: 297–304.

Cameron, Andrea, Sandy Rennie, Lisa Diprospero, Sylvia Langlois, Susan Wagner, Marc Potvin, Dale Dematteo, Vicki Leblanc, and Scott Reeves. 2009. An Introduction to Teamwork: Findings from an Evaluation of an Interprofessional Education Experience for 1000 First-Year Health Science Students. *Journal of Allied Health* 38, no. 4: 220–26.

Campbell, Marci K., Brenda M. DeVellis, Victor J. Strecher, Alice S. Ammerman, Robert F. DeVellis, and Robert S. Sandler. 1994. Improving Dietary Behavior: the Effectiveness of Tailored Messages in Primary Care Settings. *American Journal of Public Health* 84: 783–87.

Carelli, Francesco. 2008. Collaboration. *The British Journal of General Practice: The Journal of the Royal College of General Practitioners* 58, no. 551 (June): 438.

Carlson, Mim, Tori O'Neal-McElrath, and Alliance for Nonprofit Management. 2008. *Winning Grants: Step by Step.* 3rd ed. San Francisco: Jossey-Bass Publishers.

Center for the Advancement of Collaborative Strategies in Health. 2006. Partnership Self-Assessment Tool. http://partnershiptool.net/.

Chandler Center for Community Leadership. 1998. Community Based Collaboration: Community Wellness Multiplied. http://crs.uvm.edu/nnco/collab/wellness.html.

Coley, Soraya M., and Cynthia A. Scheinberg. 2007. *Proposal Writing: Effective Grantsmanship.* 3rd ed. Thousand Oaks, CA: Sage Publications.

Collins, Jim. 2001. *Good to Great: Why Some Companies Make the Leap . . . and Others Don't.* New York: HarperCollins.

D'Amour, Danielle, and Leticia San Martín Rodríguez. 2006. Collaboration among Health Professionals (II). Usefulness of a Model. *Revista De Enfermería (Barcelona, Spain)* 29, no. 9 (September): 47–52.

Deems, Richard S. 1986. *More than a Gut Feeling.* Des Moines, IA: American Media Inc.

Dweck, Carol. 2007. *Mindset: The New Psychology of Success.* New York: Ballantine Books.

Easter, Linda, and Eileen Shultz. 1998. Ten Heads Work Better Than One: An Innovative Model for Collaborative, College-Wide Grant Writing. *Research Management Review* 10, no. 1: 24–32.

El Ansari, Walid. 1999. A Study of the Characteristics, Participant Perceptions and Predictors of Effectiveness in Community Partnerships in Health Education Personnel Education: The Case of South Africa. http://depts.washington.edu/ccph/pdf_files/El%20 Ansari%20Partnership%20Questionnaire.pdf.

Etzioni, Amitai. 1961. *A Comparative Analysis of Complex Organizations: On Power, Involvement, and Their Correlates.* New York: The Free Press.

Frey, Bruce, Jill Lohmeier, Steve Lee, Nona Tollefson, and Mary Lea Johanning. 2004. Measuring Change in Collaboration among School Safety Partners. http://web. ku. edu/~spear/Documents/Measuring_Change_in_Collaboration_Among_School_ Safety_Partners.pdf.

Friedman, Ellen, and Jane Stafford. 2007. Networking for Community Health. Oakland, CA: Community Clinics Initiative. http://www.communityclinics.org/content/general/ detail/939.

Gajda, Rebecca. 2004. Utilizing Collaboration Theory to Evaluate Strategic Alliances. *American Journal of Evaluation* 25, no. 1: 65–77.

Gardner, Deborah B. 2005. Ten Lessons in Collaboration. *Online Journal of Issues in Nursing* 10, no. 1: 2.

Gardner, John W. 1990. *On Leadership.* New York: The Free Press, Macmillan, Inc.

Geever, Jane C. 2007. *The Foundation Center's Guide to Proposal Writing.* 5th ed. New York: Foundation Center.

Green, Paul C. 1986. *More Than a Gut Feeling: Training Leaders Guide.* Des Moines, IA: American Media Inc.

Hamilton, Patti, Valerie S. Eschiti, Karen Hernandez, and Denise Neill. 2007. Differences between Weekend and Weekday Nurse Work Environments and Patient Outcomes: a Focus Group Approach to Model Testing. *The Journal of Perinatal & Neonatal Nursing* 21, no. 4: 331–41.

Hansson, Anders, Mats Foldevi, and Bengt Mattsson. 2009. Medical Students' Attitudes toward Collaboration between Doctors and Nurses—a Comparison between Two Swedish Universities. *Journal of Interprofessional Care* 24, no. 3: 242–50. http://www.ncbi.nlm.nih.gov/pubmed/19995272.

Hogue, Teresa. 1993. Community-Based Collaboration: Community Wellness Multiplied. http://crs.uvm.edu/nnco/collab/wellness.html.

Horbar, Jeffrey D., Jeanette Rogowski, Paul E. Plsek, Paula Delmore, William H. Edwards, James Hocker, Anand Kantak, et al. 2001. Collaborative Quality Improvement for Neonatal Intensive Care. NIC/Q Project Investigators of the Vermont Oxford Network. *Pediatrics* 107, no. 1 (January): 14–22.

House, Robert J., Paul J. Hanges, S. Antonio Ruiz-Quintanilla, Peter W. Dorfman, Mansour Javidan, Marcus Dickson, V. Gupta, et al. 1999. Cultural Influences on Leadership and Organizations: Project GLOBE. In W. H. Mobley, M. J. Gessner, and V. Arnold (eds.), *Advances in Global Leadership* (Vol. 1), Stamford, CT: JAI Press, 171–233.

Hughes, John R. 1994. An Algorithm for Smoking Cessation. *Archives of Family Medicine* 3 (March): 280–85.

Kaasa, Stein. 2008. Editorial: Palliative Care Research—Time to Intensify International Collaboration. *Palliative Medicine* 22, no. 4 (June): 301–2.

Kilo, Charles M. 1999. Improving Care through Collaboration. *Pediatrics* 103, no. 1: 384–93.

Leclerc, Chantale, Julie Doyon, Debbie Gravelle, Bonnie Hall, and Josette Roussel. 2008. The Autonomous-Collaborative Care Model: Meeting the Future Head On. *Nursing Leadership (Toronto, Ont.)* 21, no. 2: 63–75.

Linsky, Martin, and Ronald A. Heifetz. 2002. *Leadership on the Line: Staying Alive through the Dangers of Leading.* Cambridge, MA: Harvard University Press.

Luntz, Frank I. 2007. *Words That Work: It's Not What You Say, It's What People Hear.* New York: Hyperion Books.

Mager, Robert. 1997. *Goal Analysis.* 3rd ed. Atlanta, GA: Center for Effective Performance.

Maurana, Cheryl. 2000. Building Effective Partnerships with Wisconsin Communities. *Wisconsin Medical Journal* 99, no. 1 (February): 31–32.

Mbarika, Victor W. A., Amrita Pal, Fay Cobb-Payton, Pratim Datta, and Scott McCoy. 2005. TeleMedicine Diffusion in a Developing Country: The Case of India. *IEEE Transactions on Information Technology in BioMedicine* 9, no. 1: 59–65.

Merkeley Keith, Kelly, and Debbie Fraser Askin. 2008. Effective Collaboration: The Key to Better Healthcare. *Nursing Leadership (Toronto, Ont.)* 21, no. 2: 51–61.

Mikelonis, Victoria M., Signe T. Betsinger, and Constance E. Kampf. 2003. *Grant Seeking in an Electronic Age.* New York: Longman.

Miner, Jeremy T. 1998. A Rhetorical Model for Proposal Writing. Master's thesis, University of Minnesota.

Miner, Jeremy T., and Lynn E. Miner. 2005. *Models of Proposal Planning & Writing.* Westport, CT: Praeger Press.

Miner, Jeremy T., and Lynn E. Miner. 2008. *Proposal Planning & Writing.* 4th ed. Westport, CT: Greenwood Press.

Miner, Lynn E. 1980. Academic Grantsmanship. *Grantsmanship Center News* (Los Angeles, CA) 35: 50–56.

Moss Kanter, Rosabeth. 2004. *Confidence: How Winning Streaks and Losing Streaks Begin and End.* New York: Crown Business.

Nagykaldi, Zsolt, Chester Fox, Steve Gallo, Joseph Stone, Patricia Fontaine, Kevin Peterson, and Theodoros Arvanitis. 2008. Improving Collaboration between Primary Care Research Networks Using Access Grid Technology. *Informatics in Primary Care* 16, no. 1: 51–58.

Nunn, Trisha, Michele L. Darby, Susan H. Kass, Connie L. Kracher, Trisha J. Nunn, Linda S. Stewart, Don R. Symington, and Cheryl Westphal. 2008. New Words to Promote Communication and Collaboration among the Oral Health Care Team. *Journal of Dental Education* 72, no. 6 (June): 641–42.

Pell, Eva. 2008. Growth in Research Funding Can Spur Innovation, Economic Development. *Penn State Live,* December 1. http://live.psu.edu/story/36326/nw1.

Peterson, Nancy. 1991. Interagency Collaborations under Part H: The Key to Comprehensive, Multidisciplinary, Coordinated Infant/Toddler Intervention Services. *Journal of Early Intervention* 15, no. 1: 89–105.

Potter, Christopher, and Richard Brough. 2004. Systemic Capacity Building: A Hierarchy of Needs. *Health Policy and Planning* 19, no. 5: 336–45.

Pratt, Julian, Diane Plamping, and Pat Gordon. 2003. *Partnership: Fit for Purpose?* London: King's Fund Publishing.

Prochaska, James O., Carlo DiClemente, and John C. Norcross. 1992. In Search of How People Change: Applications to Addictive Behaviors. *American Psychologist* 47, no. 9: 1102–4.

Ramsey, Kevin. 2009. GIS, Modeling, and Politics: On the Tensions of Collaborative Decision Support. *Journal of Environmental Management* 90, no. 6: 1972–80.

Ray, Karen. 2002. *The Nimble Collaboration: Fine-Tuning Your Collaboration for Lasting Success.* St. Paul, MN: Amherst H. Wilder Foundation.

Shaw, Lynn, Rebekah Walker, and Andrew Hogue. 2008. The Art and Science of Teamwork: Enacting a Transdisciplinary Approach in Work Rehabilitation. *Work (Reading, MA.)* 30, no. 3: 297–306.

Sidlar, Christopher L., and Claus Rinner. 2009. Utility Assessment of a Map-Based Online Geo-Collaboration Tool. *Journal of Environmental Management* 90, no. 6: 2020–26.

Smith, Sean J., Bruce B. Frey, and Nona Tollefson. 2003. A Collaborative Cohort Approach to Teacher Education: Modeling Inclusive Practices. *Action in Teacher Education* 25, no. 1: 59–62.

Sullivan, Toni J. 1998. *Collaboration: A Health Care Imperative.* New York: McGraw-Hill.

Tamura, Yumi, Peter Bontje, Yasuo Nakata, Yuichi Ishikawa, and Noriko Tsuda. 2005. Can One Eat Collaboration? Menus as Metaphors of Interprofessional Collaboration. *Journal of Interprofessional Care* 19, no. 3 (June): 215–22.

Tichy, Noel, and Warren G. Bennis. 2007. *Judgment: How Winning Leaders Make Great Calls.* New York: Portfolio Hardcover.

Tichy, Noel, and Nancy Cardwell. 2002. *The Cycle of Leadership: How Great Leaders Teach Their Companies to Win.* New York: HarperCollins.

Walsh, James, James Bridges, William Bunn, and Meir Kryger. 2006. Insomnia Management through Collaboration. *Managed Care (Langhorne, PA)* 15, no. 9 Suppl 6 (September): 18–19.

Watson, Michael S., Charles Epstein, R. Rodney Howell, Marilyn C. Jones, Bruce R. Korf, Edward R. B. McCabe, and Joe Leigh Simpson. 2008. Developing a National Collaborative Study System for Rare Genetic Diseases. *Genetics in Medicine: Official Journal of the American College of Medical Genetics* 10, no. 5 (May): 325–29.

Weinstein, Neil D., Judith E. Lyon, Peter M. Sandman, and Cara L. Cuite. 1998. Experimental Evidence for Stages of Health Behavior Change: The Precaution Adoption Process Model Applied to Home Radon Testing. *Health Psychology* 17, no. 5: 445–53.

Williams, Antony J. 2008. Internet-Based Tools for Communication and Collaboration in Chemistry. *Drug Discovery Today* 13, no. 11–12 (June): 502–6.

Wilson, Thomas, and Barbara Kimmel. Managing Collaborations among Federal Government, Academia and the Biomedical Industry. *Research Management Review* 12, no. 2: 41–50.

Young, Jeffrey. 2004. Does E-Science Work? *Chronicle of Higher Education* 51, no. 16: A25.

INDEX

ABOUT THE AUTHORS

JEREMY T. MINER, M.A., is president of Miner and Associates, Inc., a nationwide consulting firm that provides grantseeking and fundraising services to nonprofit organizations. He is also director of grants and contracts in the Office of Research and Sponsored Programs at the University of Wisconsin–Eau Claire. In addition to developing and administering proposals to public and private grantmakers, he has served as a reviewer for federal grant programs and helped private foundations streamline their grant application guidelines. Miner is a member of the National Council of University Research Administrators (NCURA) and has presented grantseeking workshops nationally and internationally to thousands of grant-getters. His successful grantwriting techniques have generated millions of grant dollars for many nonprofit education, health care, and social service agencies.

LYNN E. MINER, PH.D., is founder and principal of Miner and Associates, Inc., a leading nationwide grants consulting group that specializes in training successful grantseekers, and directs the office in Milwaukee, Wisconsin. He has been an active grantseeker in academic, health care, and other nonprofit environments for the past four decades. He has been affiliated with hospitals and public and private universities as a professor and research administrator as well as holding deanships in the Graduate School and in Engineering. Along with Jeremy Miner, he authored *Proposal Planning & Writing* (Greenwood Press) and *Models of Proposal Planning & Writing* (Praeger Publishers) and co-edits *Grantseeker Tips,* a free bi-weekly electronic newsletter on successful grantseeking, available through www.MinerAndAssociates.com.

JERRY GRIFFITH, PH.D., is a principal in Miner and Associates, Inc., who specializes in the psychological and management aspects of grantseeking. Griffith has a broad-based background in rehabilitation, health care, management, academia, and psychology, where he has served as a licensed psychologist. He is a frequent grant workshop presenter, and he consults often with nonprofit organizations and private foundations in developing strategic systems and procedures to pursue successful grantseeking. Griffith directs the Miner and Associates, Inc., office in Knoxville, Tennessee. He works with community foundations to help them strengthen their infrastructure to have a greater impact on local philanthropy. Griffith says, "Most grant problems are people problems and that's my niche—helping people solve problems through grants."